KOSHER SEX FOR ANTISEMITES

KOSHER SEX FOR ANTISEMITES

LOVE VERSUS HATE IN THE WAR FOR CIVILIZATION

RABBI SHMULEY BOTEACH

Skyhorse Publishing

Skyhorse Publishing books may be purchased in bulk at special discounts for sales promotion, corporate gifts, fund-raising, or educational purposes. Special editions can also be created to specifications. For details, contact the Special Sales Department, Skyhorse Publishing, 307 Fifth Avenue, 4th Floor, New York, NY 10016 or info@skyhorsepublishing.com.

Skyhorse® and Skyhorse Publishing® are registered trademarks of Skyhorse Publishing, Inc.®, a Delaware corporation.

Visit our website at www.skyhorsepublishing.com.

10 9 8 7 6 5 4 3 2 1

Library of Congress Cataloging-in-Publication Data is available on file.

Cover design by Brian Peterson

Print ISBN: 978-1-5107-8902-9
Ebook ISBN: 978-1-5107-8903-6

Printed in the United States of America

To my father Yoav Boteach and my mother Eleanor Esther Elka Paul of Blessed Memory

I have not been whole since my parents passed away and never will be complete again.

And still, we Jews choose life. Now and Forever!

CONTENTS

INTRODUCTION

Neither primarily a political ideology nor an economic grievance, antisemitism is a psychological and erotic pathology rooted in failed intimacy. Sexual repression, sexual distortion, compulsive indulgence, and profound loneliness reliably accompany Jew-hatred wherever it reaches its most virulent forms.

The Jew becomes the symbolic target not because of Jewish power, but because Jewish life models something the antisemite cannot integrate: disciplined desire, covenantal intimacy, continuity, and joy.

This book advances a simple but radical framework—The Intimacy–Hatred Axis:

- Intimacy: gravity—joining people to one another through trust, vulnerability, responsibility, and love.
- Hatred: antimatter—repelling, fragmenting, and exploding social bonds, converting loneliness into grievance, and grievance into ideology.

If intimacy holds the universe together, hatred rends it apart.

The ultimate, intimate act of loving—not provocation, but a theology of togetherness—*Kosher Sex* embodies total candor, mutual vulnerability, trust within covenant.

In other words—pleasure, counterbalanced by responsibility.

Antisemitism?

The photo negative: endless veils, insinuation, secrecy, conspiracy, and suspicion. Where kosher sex necessitates nakedness, both physical and moral, antisemitism craves concealment. While intimacy requires accountability, conspiratorial thinking rejects it. The very essence of conspiracy thinking is a total absence of evidence or fact.

Why Antisemitism Is Addicted to Conspiracy

Conspiracies are intimacy's counterfeit. They offer certainty without truth, belonging without love, power without responsibility. From medieval blood libels to modern fantasies of Jewish world control—conspiracies reduce life's complexity into a single hidden villain.

Jews recur as that villain because, as a moral code, Judaism refuses secrecy; it argues publicly, binds life to law, sanctifies the body, and insists on covenant rather than chaos. Conspiracy culture, however, thrives where trust collapses.

Jewish life lays that collapse bare.

Loneliness as the Recruiting Pool

The most divisive voices are rarely builders; they are isolators. They fragment—marriage, family, community, sexual meaning—digging the emotional hole antisemitism fills.

People who are deeply connected do not need enemies. But people who are lonely, shamed, and erotically fractured seek intensity in outrage and meaning in scapegoats.

Antisemitism offers both.

Joy as Resistance

Antisemitism does not fear Jewish suffering—it invites it.

What it cannot endure is Jewish joy: marriage, fertility, laughter, erotic confidence, lastingness.

It finds the joy of Jewish sex especially intolerable, however—too carnal and too physical.

Antisemites hate themselves and the world around them. They loathe all that is physical, all that is real.

And marital love is as physical as it gets.

Its joy disproves the grievance narrative insisting life is mere theft and power, only subjugation. Antisemitic envy, masquerading as ethics, reframes Jewish joy as obscene, provocative, or immoral.

The Civilizational Stakes

Sex is formative, in fact.

Cultures that cannot sanctify desire either commodify it (porn) or demonize it (repression). Both paths produce resentment and radicalization.

Judaism offers a third way: sanctified desire, within covenant.

That ethic scales—from bedroom to community to civilization—producing people resistant to conspiracies and hate.

Conclusion

Antisemitism is the civilization-level expression of failed intimacy.

Judaism is the civilization-level expression of intimacy, repaired.

The most effective response to Jew-hatred is not appeasement or abstraction, but lives that work: healed marriages, strong families, embodied communities, visible joy, and moral clarity.

Choose life publicly—and hatred starves. Fix intimacy, and you disarm hatred. Shatter intimacy, and hatred reigns.

Happy reading!

CHAPTER ONE

THE EROTIC PATHOLOGY OF HATRED

Across history, the most virulent Jew-haters—those who moved from prejudice to obsession, from resentment to extermination—share a striking psychological feature: a tortured relationship with sex, intimacy, and the body itself.

This book argues something as unfashionable as it is unavoidable: The worst antisemites are almost always erotically fractured human beings. Either brutally repressed or chaotically indulgent—often both—they do not merely hate Jews; they resent life itself.

There is a profound difference between moral discipline and sexual repression. Judaism understands that difference. Antisemitism misunderstands it.

When feared instead of integrated, desire does not disappear—it mutates, into obsession, cruelty, and voyeurism.

This is why an erotic engine has always powered antisemitism, an engine itself fueled by sexual anxiety. Because of this, sexual imagery, sexual accusation, and sexual panic always saturate Jew-hatred.

Joy—not tolerance—exists at the opposite pole from antisemitism.

Forget politics, borders, banks, or conspiracies—Jew-hatred commences earlier, deeper, nearer to the body than its perpetrators are willing to admit. It starts with erotic fear.

I'll give you a personal example.

In 2025, Tucker Carlson looked into a camera and told millions of viewers that my friend Mark Levin, the celebrated Fox News commentator, and I are the two most evil Jews in America. Instead of using my name, however—and he knows me well, since I appeared on his MSNBC show in his saner days—he sneered that I am "Rabbi Buttplug." Doing so, he believed he was delivering an insult.

Far from it; in truth, I own it.

I have no issue whatsoever with married couples using whatever sexual devices, toys, and passion-propellers that turn up the thermostat in their bedrooms and save them from the three curses of marriage: infidelity, platonic marriage, and pornography.

But for Carlson, rightly referred to by his detractors as Tucker Qatarlson for his apparent weakness for that sweet Qatari cash—having even announced he's buying a home in Qatar—sex is something dirty and degenerate.

Failing to smear me, Carlson nonetheless (inadvertently) volunteered a confession—one offered by antisemites for more than two thousand years: Jewish carnality and love of sex make us sick.

Thus, antisemites like Qatarlson can't stop talking about Jewish sex.

Megyn Kelly, once a respected journalist who has become an internet meme, actually called Mark Levin "Mr. Micropenis." Imagine a woman who once hosted the 8:00 p.m. primetime news show on Fox now reduced to openly and incessantly discussing the size of the male penis on what purports to be an issue-driven show.

Needless to say, it didn't work. Kelly became a national joke and, the next day, President Trump himself tweeted his deep respect for Levin as both commentator and friend. Neither Jewish power, nor Jewish law, nor Jewish theology, but Jewish intimacy, Jewish pleasure, Jewish sex is what most agitates the antisemites. Jewish bodies refusing shame.

This obsession is not incidental. It is diagnostic.

Throughout history, Jew-haters share a pathological fixation on what Jews do in the bedroom—how we marry, love, make love.

The medieval Church, for instance, imagined Jews as sexually deviant corrupters of Christian purity. While Nazi propaganda portrayed Jews as hypersexual predators poisoning Aryan virtue. Islamist extremists obsess over Jewish women, modesty, and family life.

Today's Western antisemites, costumed as podcasters and pundits, recycle the same sickness.

All project their own repression onto us.

Point being, while Carlson's insult might not have been clever, it was archetypal.

Because he did not call me "Rabbi Warmonger," or "Rabbi Capitalist." "Rabbi Zionist" didn't make the cut either.

No, he went straight to sex. Where antisemitism always does—in essence.

I didn't disturb him; my representation of a Judaism that rejects the choice between passion and sanctity, however, did. Those whose worldview depends on shame must reject that rejection.

I have spent my life teaching that sexual intimacy within marriage is not a concession to human weakness but a celebration of human dignity. My international best-seller and epoch-defining book, *Kosher Sex*, argued—decades before the pornified collapse of modern culture—that eros must be protected, focused, and sanctified, or it will be weaponized and degraded. The book helped define a new conversation about sexual intimacy and inspired hundreds of evangelical Christian titles about the joys of marital sex.

What I did not understand, I understand now—with brutal clarity: loathing of Jewish sexuality is no mere side effect of antisemitism. It's a primary engine.

Truth in the Tyrant's Body

History is mercilessly clear about this.

Adolf Hitler

Esteemed historians—not gossip columnists—have long documented Hitler's abnormal relationship to sex, intimacy, and the body: hypochondria, sexual dysfunction, voyeuristic fixations, sadomasochistic fantasies, and a profound terror of healthy erotic vulnerability.

His relationship with his niece Geli Raubal, widely discussed in scholarly literature, ended in her tragic suicide amid credible evidence of domination, control, and psychological coercion.

Lurid detail is unimportant.

The pattern, however, is: A man incapable of healthy intimacy, obsessed with purity, filth, and contamination ends up abusing the young woman put into his care by his own sister. The Nazis, following Hitler, obsessed over the sexual defilement of Aryan virgins by Jewish men.

This was foundational, and not incidental, to Nazism.

Hitler's genocidal antisemitism was indivisible from his horror of the living, reproducing, relishing body.

Benito Mussolini

Mussolini represents the opposite pole: compulsive sexual indulgence, narcissism, predation, and addiction. He treated women as consumables, sex as conquest, virility as spectacle, and his wife as an accessory, condemned to live in eternal humiliation.

Different pathology, same result.

Eros, reduced to domination rather than covenant, portends violence.

Mussolini boasted that he bedded thousands of women. His appetites were not merely private—they were policy. He publicized his sexual conquests, cultivating the image of the insatiable Italian Stallion and forging an entire political mythology around machismo. Fascist propaganda inundated Italy with depictions of Il Duce bare-chested, harvesting wheat, swimming, riding horses—always the virile body.

Of course, compulsion is not confidence. A man requiring thousands of women has not mastered desire. Desire, in fact, enslaves him—as much as it does the puritan who cannot glance at a woman without flinching.

The repressor and the compulsive are twins. One fears desire, caging it. The other fears desire, feeding it everything in sight. Neither can do what Judaism instills: sit with desire, sanctify it, and build something lasting.

Any pathological relationship to desire—whether starvation or gluttony—leads to the same destination. The man who cannot touch a woman and the man who cannot stop touching women are both at war with eros. And men at war with eros go to war with the world.

Unsurprisingly, intimacy for Mussolini was unsustainable. Despite being married, his infidelity was rampant. His affairs were conquests—brief, transactional, discarded. He did not repress women. He consumed them. But consumption and repression are the same contempt wearing different masks. Neither sees a woman as a partner, a subject, a soul. Both see her as a body to be used—whether by hiding it behind a veil or parading it as a trophy.

In 1938, Mussolini's Italy enacted racial laws—not because Italian fascism required them from its inception, but because the logic of domination always arrives at the same destination. The racial laws banned marriages and sexual relations between Italians and Jews—the identical sexual panic animating the Nuremberg Laws three years earlier. Different country, different dictator, same obsession.

And both, inevitably, found the Jew intolerable—because Jewish tradition insists that the body is neither prison nor plaything, but sacred ground.

Edgar Degas

In the arts, examples of sexually repressed antisemites abound—enough to fill a complete library. But one figure warrants close attention: Edgar Degas.

We remember Degas for his obsessive depictions of ballet dancers—young prepubescent bodies frozen between childhood and adulthood, watched but never met. His gaze has long unsettled critics, and rightly so: it avoids mature sexual reciprocity. The dancer becomes a body to observe without risking adult intimacy, banishing equality, vulnerability, mutual surrender. Control, not eros—voyeurism, not love—results.

Degas never married, formed no enduring intimate partnership, and lived a notoriously isolated emotional life. Contemporary accounts and his own correspondence describe a man deeply uncomfortable with adult sexual reciprocity—withdrawn, suspicious of intimacy, increasingly bitter with age. His art fixated on women's bodies, yet almost never through scenes of mutual desire, tenderness, or erotic joy. Instead, his canvases observe women exposed, bent, scrubbed, strained—objects of surveillance rather than partners in intimacy.

Although suspicions of pedophilia dogged him throughout his life, this is no accusation of criminal behavior. It is something more revealing: erotic distance without erotic integration.

As Degas aged, this unresolved pathology hardened into ideology.

During the Dreyfus Affair, he became openly and virulently antisemitic, severing friendships with Jewish colleagues and expressing conspiracy-laden hostility toward Jews. This was no sudden "political awakening"; it was the moral crystallization of a lifetime of alienation. His antisemitism followed the classic pattern: secrecy eclipsing trust, conspiracy eclipsing complexity, Jews cast as clandestine corrupters of society.

This story arc matters.

Because Degas did not move from joy to hatred. He graduated from repression to resentment, from isolation to ideology.

And this will be a pattern this book exposes again and again: eros, unintegrated into intimacy, metastasizing into suspicion. When intimacy absconds, conspiracy floods in. Conspiracy finds the Jew when it needs a face. Degas's case underscores the central thesis: Neither strength nor conviction breeds antisemitism, but lives intolerant of openness—sexual, emotional, or moral.

Hatred's presence equals intimacy's absence.

An Unchanging Pattern

As two thousand years of Christian anti-Judaism—Catholic and Protestant alike—metastasized into racial antisemitism, Nazi propagandists portrayed Jews as lechers running brothels, seducers defiling Aryan women, conspirators sterilizing the German race.

Islamist extremists today rant about Jewish immorality while legitimizing child marriage and sexual slavery.

The pattern never changes—those incapable of integrating desire seek to annihilate those who can.

Take *Kosher Sex*: its obscenity didn't scandalize polite society, its discipline did. It preached focus over indulgence, exclusivity over promiscuity. It argued erotic energy turns corrosive when diffused, redemptive when concentrated.

That message infuriates puritans and libertines alike. The former despises the insistence that pleasure could be holy. The latter hate the claim that pleasure requires boundaries. Antisemites, meanwhile, recognize something else entirely: an unapologetic Jewish argument for joy—an unforgivable offence, in their eyes.

Sex toys or book titles never sparked the outrage. Rather, the audacity of Jews to claim moral authority in an arena where others oscillate between shame and excess. A tradition refusing to outsource intimacy to pornography or suffocate it with guilt. That maintains eros—not chaos—belongs inside covenant.

The Three Erotic Lies of Antisemitism

Antisemitic cultures circulate three overlapping erotic myths about Jews. The fact that these lies contradict one another is precisely how we know they are not beliefs, but emotional discharge.

Lie #1: The Jew is sexually corrupt.

This myth portrays the Jew as the seducer, the pornographer, the corrupter of innocence, the defiler of purity. Think of the medieval church whispering about Jewish lust. Or the Nazi propaganda depicting Jews as predators of Aryan purity—semites with big noses seducing blonde German women. Or the modern conspiracy theorist claiming Jews are behind moral decline.

The same story, new outfits.

Lie #2: The Jew is sexually powerful.

Here the Jew is imagined as hyper-potent, secretly irresistible, able to hypnotize society, control women, emasculate men, bend institutions. Picture the archetypal Svengali, from George du Maurier's *Trilby*. The lie encompasses envy disguised as disgust. The fantasy of the powerless about the powerful.

Lie #3: The Jew is sexually abnormal.

This is where the antisemite projects every fear and confusion onto the Jew: perversion, deviance, "unnaturalness." It's the same urge that makes certain societies cruelly police bodies and confuse that for virtue.

What lurks beneath all three lies?

Rage at the idea that sexuality can be both joyful and moral. Because that combination demands self-control without self-hatred. Discipline without repression. Covenant without boredom. Passion without degradation.

And that—more than any argument—terrifies them.

And if you have built a life around either licentiousness (sex as consumption) or puritanism (sex as shame), the Jewish model insults your whole identity.

Judaism refuses both extremes. It says: desire is not evil. Desire is powerful. And power must be sanctified, not denied. That's what terrifies them. Not our "sex toys," or what I call "intimacy enhancers." Not our language. Not our jokes. But our refusal to be split souls.

The Tell Is Always Sex

Antisemitism loves to dress itself up as politics. It always has. It pretends to be an argument about borders, banks, media, Marxism, "globalism," Jesus, Zionism, Herzl, capitalism, communism, the Rothschilds, the Talmud, the Mossad, Hollywood, Wall Street, vaccines, pandemics, pornography, patriarchy, matriarchy, or whatever new costume the mob is wearing this week.

But antisemitism is not, at its core, a political theory. It is a spiritual panic.

And the tell—again and again, across centuries, across religions, across ideologies—is sex. Not Jewish money. Not Jewish power. Not Jewish intellect. Not Jewish influence.

Jewish sexuality.

That's why, even now, in a supposedly sophisticated age—an age drowning in pornography and yet hysterical about desire—the Jew-hater cannot stop circling the bedroom like a starving dog.

It's why the moment I open my mouth in a debate about Israel, Hamas, October 7, or the rise of modern Jew-hatred, the antisemite's mind doesn't go to geopolitics. It goes to my book *Kosher Sex,* to my daughter Chana's company Kosher.Sex, to devices for married couples, to a grotesque nickname they think is an insult but is actually a confession: Rabbi Buttplug, meaning the Rabbi who could not give a damn what husband and wife do in the bedroom, as long as they're doing it consensually and to each other.

They could have called me "Rabbi Israel."

They could have called me "Rabbi Zionist."

They could have called me "Rabbi Settler."

They could have called me "Rabbi Propaganda."

No.

They called me what they're actually thinking and marinating over constantly due to their severe sexual repression: sex.

Their sex. Your sex. My sex. Jewish sex.

Because that's the ancient obsession. It's the oldest hatred's favorite doorway into the soul.

Repression Is Not Morality. It's a Factory of Cruelty.

Here is the blunt truth nobody wants to say because it offends the self-appointed guardians of "decency": Sexual repression is one of the great engines of human cruelty.

Not desire. Not passion. But repression.

When a society teaches boys that their bodies are shameful and their desires are dirty, it does not produce saints. It produces either hypocrites or sadists. Usually both.

When a society teaches girls that their worth is in absurd standards of modesty—like the chador, where only their eyes can be seen, and even then, through a net, or even the nun's habit—rather than their dignity, it does not produce holiness. It produces fear, silence, and a marketplace of neuroses that men then exploit.

When a culture insists that "purity" means ignorance and terror, it guarantees that sexuality will erupt somewhere else—through pornography, adultery, exploitation, child sexual abuse, sexual violence, or obsessive moral panic.

And then, because humans hate admitting internal chaos, they look for a scapegoat.

Enter the Jew.

The Jew becomes the symbol of everything they can't integrate: money, intellect, influence, survival, and yes—sex.

It is far easier to scream about Jewish "degeneracy" than to confront the fact that your own culture has taught you to despise your own body.

It is far easier to mock "Kosher Sex" than to admit you've never experienced sex as tenderness, play, covenant, or joy. It is far easier to call the rabbi obscene than to confess that you are starving, or that he actually has a point.

So, the antisemite rages at Jewish erotic confidence because it reveals his internal captivity. He hates the Jew because the Jew is free.

Repression doesn't create purity. It creates pressure—and pressure always looks for a victim.

CHAPTER TWO

A HISTORY OF SEXUAL PSYCHOSIS

The Core Mechanism: Projection, Purity, and Misogyny

The structure of hatred is remarkably consistent across history.

First, desire is feared rather than integrated. The individual or society experiences it as shame. But shame is intolerable—so it gets externalized, a minority becoming the carrier of projected "filth." Women's bodies become the battleground. Violence is reframed as virtue.

Every purity cult eventually needs a scapegoat.

The cult must imagine the scapegoat as sexually corrupt because shame lives in sex. That is why antisemitism, racism, and religious extremism are so obsessed with women's bodies, bloodlines, and reproduction. And why the modern Israel-hating, Jew-libeling, virulent antisemites—inhabiting X in droves and devoting daily podcasts to desecrating Jews—have made Kosher Sex and my daughter's marriage-saving company by the same name their constant target.

Ultimately, control sex, and you control identity. Control women, and you control the future.

Psychologists and historians have long observed a link between sexual repression and extremist hatred. Their premise is that unresolved or deviant sexual urges can be "sublimated" into aggression toward scapegoated groups.

In other words, sexual psychosis—extreme anxiety, perversion, or obsession around sex—often finds an outlet: hatred of an "other."

In the following pages, we'll explore how repressive attitudes toward sex, women, and desire have fueled antisemitism and other hatreds throughout history. From medieval clergymen demonizing lust and Jews in the same breath, to modern totalitarian and fundamentalist regimes obsessively policing sexuality—a recurring pattern emerges.

Our case studies will range from Adolf Hitler's perverse relationship with his niece to the Taliban's draconian dress codes. Each example illustrates how twisted sexual psychology and misogyny contributed to history's worst outbreaks of antisemitism and bigotry.

Wilhelm Reich: The Mass Psychology of Fascism

In 1933—the year Hitler seized power—an Austrian psychoanalyst named Wilhelm Reich published a book that should have changed the world. To understate things drastically, it didn't.

But its thesis remains irrefutable.

In *The Mass Psychology of Fascism*, Reich argued something polite political science *still refuses to accept*: Fascism never descends from above.

It rises from below—boiling up from the psyches of sexually repressed individuals who, because they cannot tolerate their own desire, crave authoritarian order.

Reich prophetically wrote:

"The formation of the authoritarian structure takes place through the anchoring of sexual inhibition and sexual anxiety."

In other words—you don't create a fascist by giving him a uniform; you create a fascist by teaching him to fear his own body.

The uniform comes later—the cherry topping the cake of sexual repression and revulsion of the body.

Reich went further, arguing that the authoritarian family—patriarchal, sexually rigid, shame-driven—is a factory. Its products? Obedient subjects, primed for the totalitarian state: boys learning to suppress desire, girls learning to suppress autonomy, both conditioned to consider pleasure dangerous.

And when pleasure is perilous—when evolutionary biology—the libidinal urge toward procreation—is vilified, someone must be blamed for this peril and villainy.

Enter the Jew.

The homosexual.

The woman refusing submission.

Indeed, on this latter note, Reich furthermore predicted something history has confirmed repeatedly:

"Sexually awakened women, affirmed and recognized as such, would mean the complete collapse of the authoritarian ideology."

Read that sentence again.

Then think about the Taliban.

About Hamas.

The Iranian morality police.

Every movement chronicled in this book simultaneously hating Jews and enslaving women.

Intellectually, Reich understood what fascists, Islamists, and all Jew-haters sense instinctively: *sexual freedom and political freedom are inseparable.*

That joyful, erotically integrated human beings are ungovernable. That tyranny of the body remains the first step toward tyranny of the *demos*—the people. That the first target is always the group that most eminently, loudly, and fundamentally refuses to comply.

Reich himself was Jewish.

The Nazis burned his books. He fled to America, where he was eventually imprisoned by the FDA for unrelated controversies and died in a federal penitentiary in 1957. His work was marginalized for decades—too Freudian for the political scientists, too political for the psychoanalysts, too sexual for everyone.

But his central insight remains unassailable:

Antisemitism is not incidental to fascism. Both Jew-hatred and totalitarianism spawn from the same damaged psyche—a psyche taught to fear desire and therefore compelled to punish someone for the fact of its existence.

Theodor Adorno and the Authoritarian Personality

In 1950, the German-Jewish philosopher Theodor Adorno and his colleagues at UC Berkeley published *The Authoritarian Personality*, one of the most ambitious social psychology studies ever undertaken.

Their goal: to answer the question haunting every Jew and humanity as a whole: *Why did so many ordinary people embrace fascism?*

Their answer produced a clinical measurement tool, appropriately dubbed the F-Scale—"F" for fascist.

The scale identified nine personality traits that, taken together, constitute and delineate the authoritarian character.

Among them: rigid conventionalism, authoritarian submission, superstition, preoccupation with power, destructiveness, cynicism, and projectivity: *the tendency to project one's own unconscious impulses onto others.*

And if that wasn't plain enough, perhaps the most revealing trait for our purposes was: *exaggerated concerns over sex.*

Yes, Adorno and his colleagues discovered that what other people do in their bedrooms *obsesses* authoritarian personalities. They fixate, every time, on sexual "deviance," projecting their own repressed desires outward, punishing others for embodying everything they cannot admit in themselves.

As Adorno put it:

"The suppressed impulses of the authoritarian character tend to be projected onto other people who are then blamed out of hand."

The authoritarian does not merely disapprove of sexual freedom. Sexual autonomy *consumes* him. He monitors it, catalogues it, and fantasizes about punishing it.

His hatred of "degeneracy" leaps miles beyond indifference into obsession.

Now consider modern antisemites.

Tucker Carlson, for instance, unable to stop saying, "Rabbi Buttplug" on camera—a man whose mind, confronted with a Jewish rabbi, races immediately to anal sex, as by magnetic attraction.

Candace Owens, devoting days to raging about vibrators and intimacy enhancers sold by a rabbi's daughter in Tel Aviv—as if the thriving existence of married and passionate Jewish sexuality were a personal affront.

Nick Fuentes, *a self-proclaimed virgin*, preaching sexual "purity" while denying the Holocaust.

Andrew Tate, facing rape charges in Romania and declaring Hamas terrorists the embodiment of "masculine virtue."

On Adorno's F-Scale, every single one of them scores off the charts.

Each one, after all, demonstrates "exaggerated concerns over sex."

Each projects outward what they cannot integrate inward.

Adorno did not merely describe a psychological type. *He diagnosed a civilization.*

No aberration, the authoritarian personality is a product—one manufactured by cultures teaching shame, enforcing rigidity, and punishing desire.

And when enough of those personalities cluster together, they don't just elect authoritarians. *They become authoritarians.*

Although published in 1950, seventy-five years later, the F-Scale reads like a character study of the modern antisemite.

Consider Jake Shields, the former UFC welterweight champion who has reinvented himself as one of social media's most prolific antisemites and Holocaust deniers.

On *Piers Morgan Uncensored* in 2025, pressed by the author, Shields said he did not know how many Jews were killed in the Holocaust. As reported by *The Jewish Chronicle*, he later posted on X—albeit grammatically incorrectly—that: "It wasn't hasn't six million."

In other words: A man who built his entire public identity on masculine aggression—cage fighting, toughness, dominance—now devotes his retirement to denying Jewish suffering and increasing it.

On Adorno's F-Scale, Shields is a textbook case: a man at war with his own desires eventually, inevitably going to war with *the people representing the integration of desire into dignity.*

Hannah Arendt and the Loneliness at the Root of Jew-Hatred

If Reich diagnosed the damaged psyche and Adorno measured it, Hannah Arendt diagnosed the *damaged world that produces it.*

In 1951, a German-Jewish political theorist who had herself been detained in a French internment camp and fled the Nazis as a stateless refugee published *The Origins of Totalitarianism*—a book whose first hundred pages are devoted entirely to antisemitism. Not as prelude. Not as context. *As foundation.*

Arendt understood something most historians still treat as coincidence: Antisemitism is not a feature of totalitarianism. It is the *rehearsal.* The proving ground. The laboratory in which a society first learns to make human beings superfluous—before applying that logic to everyone.

But one of her most devastating insights was not about ideology. Instead, Arendt identified a psychological and social phenomenon that sounds tame—until you feel it in your chest:

Loneliness.

Loneliness, for Arendt, is the experience of not belonging to the world at all. It is the loss of what she called "the common world"—the shared reality that makes human connection possible. The lonely person has lost not just companionship but the very ground on which companionship could exist.

She wrote:

"What prepares men for totalitarian domination . . . is the fact that loneliness . . . has become an everyday experience."

Read that carefully.

Totalitarianism does not create loneliness. *Loneliness creates the conditions for totalitarianism.* The movement arrives afterward, offering its terrible remedy.

And what is that remedy?

Belonging through annihilation.

Purpose through persecution.

Identity through *identifying the enemy.*

Arendt described the masses drawn to totalitarian movements not as ideologues but as *atomized* individuals—people severed from class, community, family, any structure that once told them who they were and where they fit. These are people for whom, as she put it, the distinction between fact and fiction, between true and false, ceases to matter—not because they are stupid, but because *nothing in their lives gives them reason to care about the difference.*

Now consider what atomization actually destroys.

It destroys the family dinner table.

The neighborhood.

The congregation.

The friendship sustained over decades. The erotic bond between partners who know and trust each other. *The private world—that intimate domain where people are most fully themselves, most embodied, most alive.*

Totalitarianism does not merely attack public life. *It annihilates private life.* It insists that nothing—not your marriage, not your bedroom, not your body—exists beyond the reach of the movement. Arendt recognized this invasion of intimacy was not incidental to totalitarian logic. *It was totalitarian logic.* Total domination, after all, *means total.*

No spare change available. No remainder left over. *No refuge.*

The state will, and must, kick open every door.

Here is where Arendt meets Reich (though she would have resisted the introduction, and famously opposed Reich's psychologizing).

Reich said: Destroy a person's sexual freedom and you produce a fascist. Arendt said: Destroy a person's *world*—the web of relationships that make freedom meaningful—and you produce *something even worse*:

A person so desperate for any structure, any belonging, any narrative that explains their suffering, will surrender everything, including the freedom they no longer know how to use. People who have never experienced genuine connection—erotic, communal, spiritual—are thus primed to accept the grotesque counterfeit of connection that totalitarian movements provide.

And what do those movements provide?

A uniform instead of an identity. A rally instead of a relationship. An enemy instead of a self.

A conspiracy theory instead of a complicated truth.

And always—*always*—the enemy is someone who represents what the atomized person has lost. Someone who still seems to possess what has been taken from them: community, continuity, family, tradition, vitality. Whose stubborn, visible, embodied existence serves as a standing rebuke to the loneliness of the masses.

Enter the Jew. Again.

Arendt devoted so much scholarship to the history of European antisemitism because she grasped what many scholars since have tried to forget: The Jew functions in the antisemitic imagination as the figure who *has what the lonely person lacks*.

Community. Cohesion. Rootedness. A private life rich with ritual, food, family, Shabbat candles, and—let us say it plainly—a religious tradition that sanctifies and inspires sexual pleasure within marriage. All while the Christian and post-Christian West spent centuries teaching that the body is a prison and desire a sin.

The antisemite does not merely hate the Jew. *The antisemite envies the Jew*—then transmutes that envy into disgust, that disgust into conspiracy, and that conspiracy into extermination.

Arendt saw this with unbearable clarity. Superfluousness—the feeling of being *unnecessary*, of having no place in the human world—is the engine. Antisemitism is the fuel. And totalitarianism, the machine that converts both into mass murder.

She wrote that the ideal subject of totalitarian rule is not the true believer. It is the person for whom everything and nothing is believable—because the world has already stopped making sense.

Consider that in the age of social media.

A generation raised on algorithmically mediated loneliness. Young men who have never touched a woman with tenderness and take their sexual education from pornography and Andrew Tate. Young women whose bodies are simultaneously commodity and battlefield. Entire populations experiencing precisely the atomization Arendt described—*scrolling alone, in the dark, connected to everything, belonging to nothing.*

And what rises to meet them? The conspiracy, the scapegoat, and the ancient formula.

The incel forums blaming Jewish feminists for their celibacy. The far-right influencers raging about Jewish-controlled media corrupting sexual morality. The Islamists promising brotherhood and purpose to boys whose lives have offered neither—and directing their new converts, first and always, toward hatred of Jews and subjugation of women.

Arendt would not have been surprised. She had seen it before.

She had *lived* it before.

Born in Hanover in 1906 to a secular Jewish family, Arendt experienced the catastrophe from the inside. She studied under Martin Heidegger—with whom she had a now-famous affair, a relationship that itself embodies the terrible intimacy between brilliance and complicity, desire and betrayal, the private and the political. When Heidegger joined the Nazi Party, Arendt did not merely lose a lover. She watched a man she had known in the most intimate sense possible choose a movement over a person, ideology over eros, belonging-through-domination over the vulnerability of genuine human connection, and immoral racism over moral rectitude.

If that is not a parable for this entire book, nothing is.

Because the antisemite, in Arendt's framework, is the loneliest person in the room—and the most dangerous, because he has found a story that explains his loneliness and a target that promises to cure it.

If loneliness is the precondition for totalitarianism, then genuine human connection—erotic, communal, spiritual, embodied—is its negation. Not as sentimentality. *As politics.* Every Shabbat dinner is a small revolution. Every act of sexual intimacy rooted in mutuality and joy is an act of resistance against a world that prefers its subjects isolated, ashamed, and obedient.

The First Move: Turn Life into Sin

Every totalitarian ideology begins by declaring war on joy.

Joy is dangerous because it makes people hard to control. A joyful man doesn't need the mob. A joyful woman doesn't need the demagogue. A joyful couple doesn't need the cult leader, the political messiah, the grievance industry, the death cult, or the "revolution" that promises to redeem them by giving them someone to hate.

So, the first move is always the same: Turn the most life-affirming forces in human existence—desire, laughter, romance, erotic love, family warmth—into sources of guilt.

And then, once people are trained to be ashamed of their own bodies, you give them a target onto whom they can project their shame.

For two thousand years, that target has been the Jew.

The tyrant doesn't begin by banning speech. He begins by banning joy.

Ancient and Medieval Foundations: Demonizing Sex and the "Other"

Hostility toward sexuality is deeply ingrained in the Western religious tradition, and often went hand in hand with demonizing outsiders.

Early Church Fathers painted women as dangerous seductresses allied with the Devil. As one analysis notes, "the Church Fathers demonized all women as agents of the Devil"—Eve's weakness made her the devil's gateway, and thus all women were viewed as potential temptresses leading men to sin. In medieval Christendom, this paranoia about female sexuality fused with antisemitism. Church art and sermons frequently linked Jews and women as demonic figures undermining Christian society. Medieval Christians imagined both witches and Jews attending diabolical "sabbaths," committing obscene acts with Satan. Misogyny and Jew-hatred thus share a common root: fear of carnal sin and the need to blame someone for it.

One striking symbol of this overlap is the depiction of Ecclesia and Synagoga in Gothic cathedrals.

The Church (Ecclesia) is shown as a virtuous crowned woman, while the Synagogue (Synagoga, symbolizing Judaism) appears as a defeated female figure—often blindfolded, with a broken staff. The blindfold and fallen posture signified Jews' supposed spiritual blindness and moral corruption. Notably, both figures are female, reflecting how medieval Christians feminized Judaism as a lustful, fallen woman.

Such imagery sent a clear message: false religion (Judaism) and uncontrolled female sexuality were evil twins.

Portraying Jews as morally weak "daughters of Eve," medieval society justified harsh measures against them.

This climate of sexual fear fed blood libel myths—accusing Jews of ritually killing Christian children and using their blood for Passover matzah—and other paranoid fantasies, all rife with the language of impurity and defilement.

The medieval Catholic Church further institutionalized this mindset by equating piety with celibacy and bodily denial. It cast natural sexual desire as sinful, unless strictly controlled for procreation. Church authorities relentlessly warned that lust could doom one's soul—and by extension, the community's salvation. This obsession with purity found scapegoats in any group associated with carnal "impurity." Women, labeled daughters of Eve, were obvious targets. Jews, seen as the killers of Christ, were likewise cast as agents of the carnal world—or even literal partners of Satan.

It's no coincidence that demonology manuals of the Middle Ages often lumped together witches (almost always women) and Jews as servants of the Devil. In 1494, the Nuremberg Chronicle depicted a monstrous synagogue personified by a woman riding a pig—a vicious slur linking Jewish worship to filthy lust. Such grotesque images reveal how medieval anti-semites weaponized sexual disgust into religious and racial hatred.

This is how the moral imagination gets inverted. The people who will later commit violence first learn to experience the victim as a contaminant. And what contaminates more powerfully in the human imagination than sex? Indeed, many early Christian fathers adamantly supported and promoted the problematic idea that "Original Sin" was actually transmitted through sex, even in marriage, so that every child born into this world, even as a product of his parents' unconditional love for one another, was and is already born guilty.

The Blood Libel: Institutionalized Moral Pornography

The blood libel did not emerge from ignorance alone. Acting in ritualized cooperation, institutions—clergy, magistrates, monarchs, and mob—cultivated, transmitted, refined, and enforced it.

The accusation—that Jews murdered Christian children to use their blood—was a story engineered to horrify.

It fused childhood innocence, bodily violation, secrecy, religious ritual, and erotic fear.

Sexualized moral terror eclipsed theology.

The blood libel, in its modern incarnation as well as its historic one, casts Jews as mythic violators of innocence. It eroticizes fear by placing the most sacred symbol (a child) at the center of a secret, imagined crime.

The more hatred excites the imagination, the more it endures.

The Church did not merely fail to stop these accusations; in many cases, it amplified them—building shrines, canonizing legends, and sanctifying violence.

This is how repression works at scale: it renders horror fascinating by forbidding desire. The imagination turns violent fantasies into moral crusades.

Ultimately, the blood libel is antisemitism's most naked confession: *We are terrified of the body, and we need someone to blame for that terror.*

Blood, Bodies, and "Contamination"

Modern people like to imagine medieval antisemitism was purely "theological." *That is a comforting lie.* The medieval imagination was saturated with bodily panic—blood panic, purity panic, contamination panic.

The blood libel is the most grotesque example, a libel actually repeated incessantly just these last years by illiterate Jew-hater Candace Owens. You can dress it up as "religious superstition," but psychologically it is something else—a pornographic fantasy of Jewish power victimizing innocent bodies.

The obsession is not only with killing. *It is with defilement.* With the idea that Jews steal the life-force of the innocent.

And right beside blood libel in the medieval mind is another cluster of fantasies: Jews as sexually contaminating, as predators, corruptors of women—the creeping poison inside Christian society.

Why do you think antisemitic folk art and church carvings so often chose obscene sexual imagery to depict Jews? Why the relentless fixation on Jews and pigs, Jews and filth, Jews and "obscene contact"? Because the goal was never merely to disagree with Judaism. The goal was to make Jews feel physically repulsive—and to train Christian society to recoil from Jews the way one recoils from disease.

That revulsion is not incidental. *It's the point.*

When a society starts describing a people as "unclean," *it rehearses the language of extermination.*

The *Judensau*: Jew-Hate Carved in Stone

If you ever visit Wittenberg, Germany, and journey to the Stadtkirche—the very church where Martin Luther nailed his Ninety-Five Theses—you might see something surprising on the building's façade: a medieval stone carving of a Jew nursing from the teats of a pig, a sow. Behind the pig, a rabbi lifts the animal's tail to consume its excrement.

The medieval stone carving has been there for over seven hundred years. It would seem, *given the sentiments of the German government*, it will be there for many more.

The abomination fixed in stone is probably the most famous example of the *Judensau*. The "Jew-pig."

Variations of this stone emblem of Jew-hatred adorn churches, cathedrals, and public buildings across medieval Germany and beyond. Some depict Jews riding the sow. Others feature Jews in sexual congress with the animal. All share the same purpose: to depict Jews in an act as obscene as possible, physically revolting to the utmost. Doing so, the viewer's body—the nervous system itself—recoils before the mind has time to think.

The *Judensau* is not theology. Nor, despite the rulings of the German judicial system we'll detail below, is it a powerless, if not offensive, historical relic.

It is pornography.

It is moral pornography, specifically, designed to bypass reason and operate directly on the unconscious, on the limbic brain. It conditions the viewer to associate Jews with filth, with bestiality, and the most degraded imaginable physical acts. It's a dehumanizing technology of pornographic hatred addressed not to the intellect—but to the gut.

Even stripped of its antisemitic connotations, the degree of overt, pornographic sexuality adorning a *church*, of all places, is striking.

The pig is an animal associated in Jewish law with impurity. Jews don't eat pork; it's not kosher—everybody knows that. So, on the most superficial level, depicting a sow in intimate, carnal contact with Jews insults them. Yet the insult runs deeper and reveals the insulter's own perversion. The imagery shocks for its deliberate, grotesque eroticism: suckling, penetration, close contact between genitalia and excrement. The message implied is that Jews are more than merely wrong about God: They are quite physically depraved.

Their law of *halacha* no more than pretext for particularly perverse bestiality.

It really must be emphasized: *These carvings were not hidden.*

Some of the most sacred buildings in Christendom flaunt them. They protrude prominently from the exterior walls of churches where, every

Sunday, parishioners gathered, seeing them over and over again. Consider the *Judensau* medieval public education; indeed, that was a role the Church fulfilled. These churches and their antisemitic gargoyles taught generations of illiterate Christians what a Jew was: a creature of bodily horror relishing the vilest sexual crimes.

Many of these carvings survive today. For example, The Wittenberg *Judensau* remains on the church wall despite decades of controversy and a lawsuit that reached Germany's highest court. In 2022, the Federal Court of Justice ruled the sculpture could stay, provided an informational plaque remained nearby. The court said the plaque gave the carving "context."

Context.

After seven centuries of teaching Christians to associate Jews with bestiality, excrement, and sexual filth—and a plaque is supposed to undo it.

At any rate, the *Judensau* represents this book's thesis carved into stone. Further and perhaps most impactful proof that antisemitism has been and continues to be a carnal force. Yes, it encompasses the theological, political, racial—you name it. But its source and its target remain the body. Sexual disgust saturates it. A motivation to make the Jew seem physically subhuman powers and animates it.

Looking at the *Judensau,* it's impossible to pretend Jew-hatred is an intellectual disagreement, an objection to Jewish religion, or even Jewish influence.

The *Judensau* makes patently obvious that Jew-hatred functions as a visceral and erotic revulsion. This libidinal, obsessive hatred chiseled itself into the walls of European civilization and remains there still.

It still watches and it still teaches, however silently—however moderated by a plaque—to hate and fear the Jew.

And to do so as much as one hates and fears their own body.

Repression and Rage in the Inquisition Era

By the late medieval and early modern period, anxieties about "impurity" reached fever pitch in institutions like the Spanish Inquisition. The Inquisition enforced rigid Catholic orthodoxy, including sexual morality, through terror. Its leaders, notably Tomás de Torquemada (Grand Inquisitor from 1483–1498), were *celibate clerics living in extreme sexual repression*. Torquemada himself was rumored to have *converso* (Jewish-convert) ancestry, and some historians suggest this fueled his zeal to prove his "purity" by persecuting Jews.

Father of the Spanish Inquisition and confessor to Queen Isabella, Torquemada did not merely enforce doctrine. He enforced lineage.

Under his influence—and with the blessing of Isabella and Ferdinand, who expelled all Jews from Spain in 1492—ancestry became destiny. Conversion could not cleanse blood. Identity became hereditary sin and reproductive paranoia replaced theology.

The Inquisition treated Jewishness as a transmissible stain, passed through bodies and generations—converting marriage, childbirth, and ancestry into sites of surveillance.

Spain's *limpieza de sangre* ("purity of blood") statutes barred anyone of Jewish descent from many positions. In essence, the Inquisition treated Jewish lineage like a sexual contamination of Christian society.

Spanish churchmen often framed Jewish practices in lurid sexual terms. For example, they accused secret Jews (crypto-Jews) of indulging in lecherous orgies during Sabbath. In reality, most conversos of course lived ordinary family lives—but the inquisitors projected their own morbid fantasies onto these communities.

Moreover, a perverse sexual tinge even pervaded the torture chambers of the Inquisition: prisoners were stripped and physically violated under the guise of extracting confessions. This state-sanctioned sadism targeted heretics, witches, and Jews alike. The same era that saw mass trials of Jews also saw witch-hunts in which thousands of women were burned at the stake. Both phenomena sprang from the same source—a pathological fear of sexuality, an urge to purge society of imagined "pollution."

Torquemada's system weaponized fear of contamination to justify torture, exile, and execution. It taught Europe a devastating lesson: *If you convince people impurity exists, they will beg you to destroy it.*

Martin Luther: Certainty, Rage, and the Pleasure of Annihilation

Martin Luther is often remembered as a religious revolutionary, a man who challenged corruption. But revolutionaries can curdle into fanatics—and

Luther's later writings against the Jews represent one of the most toxic transformations in religious history.

While Luther's early texts concerning Jews were not uniformly hostile—he was hoping they would convert to Christianity and embrace his Protestantism—his later writings were something else entirely: furious, annihilatory, obsessed. In the greatest tragedy to his legacy, Luther became one of the most reviled antisemites in all human history. By the end of his life, Luther no longer argued theology. He demanded eradication: burning synagogues, destroying Jewish homes, confiscating sacred texts, banishing Jews from German lands.

In effect, the language of extermination banished the language of polemic.

What changed in Luther was not his intellect but his tolerance for ambiguity. Like all early reformers, he coexisted with tension. Like all late fanatics, though, he eventually demanded resolution: annihilation.

The critical psychosexual point: Luther's theology was deeply anxious about the body. Desire was suspect; pleasure, dangerous; women, morally perilous; and the flesh, a battlefield between God and sin. Biographically, as a young monk, Luther struggled with intense guilt over sexual thoughts—by his own account, he engaged in self-flagellation and prayer to suppress "carnal lusts." Such inner turmoil may have predisposed him to harsh judgment of others' faith and morals. Like most of the world's most notorious antisemites, he was an obsessed sexual deviant.

He also equated the "carnality" of the Catholic Church (which he saw in its lavish rituals and corruption) with Jews—an age-old Christian trope. Fascinatingly, Luther at times conflated Jewish women with witches in his imagination. A recent analysis notes Luther's "overlapping fears" of women and Jews, especially embodied in the figure of the "Jewish witch."

In other words, Luther's mind linked the two great bogeymen of medieval lore: the seductive woman and the blasphemous Jew. He reframed desire as threat, the awakening of which required someone to blame.

The Jew became that figure: stubborn, embodied, resistant to spiritual abstraction. Jewish life—rooted in law, family, continuity, and physical ritual—stood as a rebuke to Luther's increasingly brittle spirituality. His was a religiosity intolerant of the body, and so it turned on those living comfortably with it.

Rather than a mere accident of temperament, Luther's antisemitism is the predictable endpoint of a worldview *mandating absolute purity and incapable of enduring contradiction.*

The Nineteenth Century: Pseudoscience and the Sexualization of Race

Modern racial "science" dressed ancient hatred in a lab coat. It rendered Jews biologically suspect, Black men, sexually monstrous, and turned White womanhood into sacred territory.

The Ku Klux Klan and white supremacists regularly portrayed Black men as possessing outrageously outsized genitalia, seeking to desecrate the flower of white female purity with their depraved desire. The Confederacy raised these fears to new heights, arguing Lincoln's Emancipation Proclamation unleashed predations of the monstrous Black male libido, endangering every Southern white woman. Race theory obsessed over skulls, bloodlines, reproduction, and degeneration. No accident, this was racism dressed as science—a fantasy of sexual control.

Because once hatred equals hygiene, genocide equals public health.

American racism, like European antisemitism, based its hatred on a sexual lie.

The "Black brute" myth—Black men as hypersexual predators lusting after white women—was preached from pulpits, printed in newspapers, codified in law, and enforced by lynch mobs.

This myth accomplished three simultaneous things:

It justified terror against Black men.

It rationalized control over white women.

It disguised male supremacy as moral protection.

White women became property whose purity symbolized racial order instead of autonomous moral agents. Any suggestion that a white woman might desire a Black man was unthinkable; it shattered the fantasy of white male dominance.

It was a myth reversing reality, its structure identical to Nazi racial paranoia: different targets, same pathology.

In American history this reached its most infamous and abominable apogee when fourteen-year-old Emmett Till was brutalized and lynched in Mississippi for allegedly whistling at a white woman. The horrors against him allegedly included having his genitals cut from his body and stuffed into this mouth. Today, his coffin is exhibited at the Smithsonian National Museum of African American History and Culture.

Édouard Drumont: The Godfather of Sexual Antisemitism

Before the Nazis, before the *Protocols of the Elders of Zion*, before Henry Ford—there was Édouard Drumont.

Drumont was a nineteenth-century French journalist and polemicist whose 1886 book *La France Juive* ("Jewish France") became the bestselling work of antisemitism in French history.

It ran to over a thousand pages and went through two hundred editions. It was, in its time, what *Mein Kampf* would become a generation later: the bible of Jew-hatred.

And sexual obsession drenched it.

Drumont depicted Jews as physically repulsive, morally corrupt, and sexually predatory. He described Jewish men as effeminate yet simultaneously sexually dangerous—weak-bodied parasites who nonetheless possessed a sinister erotic power over Christian women.

He accused Jews of running prostitution networks, of seducing and "defiling" French women, of spreading disease through sexual contact, and of using their erotic influence to undermine French civilization from the inside.

His writing reads like a fever dream of sexual panic: everywhere he looked, he saw Jewish bodies penetrating, corrupting, contaminating the pure body of France.

Drumont also founded the newspaper *La Libre Parole*, which would become one of the primary engines of antisemitism during the Dreyfus Affair. His influence shaped an entire generation of French antisemites and, through them, the broader European movement that would culminate in the Holocaust.

He was, in short, the man who industrialized the sexual accusation against Jews—who took the scattered medieval fantasies about Jewish carnality and turned them into a systematic, publishable, saleable ideology.

Every modern antisemite who sneers about Jewish sexuality is, whether he knows it or not, reciting Drumont.

The Dreyfus Affair and Its Sexual Undertones

The facts of the Dreyfus Affair are well known:

In 1894, Captain Alfred Dreyfus, a French Jewish artillery officer, was falsely convicted of passing military secrets to Germany.

He was publicly degraded—his insignia torn from his uniform, his sword snapped in two—before a howling mob screaming "Death to the Jew!"

He then endured nearly five years on Devil's Island on fabricated charges of treason before the conspiracy against him unraveled, leading to his eventual exoneration.

However, what is considerably less well known and discussed is how antisemitic press *depicted Dreyfus.*

Indeed, caricatures in *La Libre Parole* and other antisemitic newspapers portrayed Dreyfus as hook-nosed, bug-eyed, hunched, and physically grotesque. They feminized him, projecting their own latent misogyny onto the scapegoated Captain, degrading Dreyfus as weak, unmanly, cowardly, incapable of real French virility.

French press—and thereby culture, at least in part—presented his very physique as evidence of guilt. For Dreyfus, and Jews as a whole, suspicion was *bodily.* A real Frenchman, the implication goes—a proper officer, ethnically our own—would never betray his country. But a Jew?

Look at him. *His body tells the tale.*

The public degradation ceremony itself evidenced unmistakable sexual overtones—a ritual *stripping,* a breaking, a humiliation performed before a crowd jeering, spitting. It was not merely military justice. It was a public shaming designed to expose the Jew's body as *fundamentally wrong.*

Because the accusation was never merely espionage. It did not stop at treason, or crime. It ventured further.

The deeper accusation was penetration.

So, for the entire bulk of antisemitic Western Europe, Dreyfus represented the *Jew as infiltrator*—a foreign body, a viral pathogen, crawling within the sacred organism of the French army, the French nation, the French race.

Much of the French press and public cast his treason as a kind of violation—the Jew, slipping past defenses, worms his way within, contaminating and corrupting. Thus the language of the anti-Dreyfusard press frothed and oozed with biological metaphor—infection, poison, defilement.

Indeed, even when it came to the most "rational" accusation—that of espionage, treason; of military intelligence—the antisemitic imagination, unable to help itself, reached for the body, reveling.

Because every antisemitic road ultimately reaches the same destination: libeling the Jew as physically repulsive, racially contaminating, and bodily wrong.

The Dreyfus Affair severed France into two bleeding halves. Moreover, it radicalized a brilliant Austrian journalist named Theodor Herzl, who witnessed screaming Paris mobs clamor for Jewish blood. Their craving, Herzl sensed—like any perceptive witness to Jew-hate's true pathos—was for more than the destruction of idea, culture, or religion: It was for a body, its blood, their hatred of which doubtlessly reflecting a hatred of their own. Herzl's front row seat to the societal scapegoating and bloodlust for the Jewish body convinced him that assimilation would never protect the Jewish people.

That the Jews—*Am Yisrael*—required sovereignty and self-determination.

So yes, the degradation of Dreyfus, perhaps ironically, helped birth modern Zionism. But the affair also revealed even more about the nature of antisemitism itself: bodily disgust fueled the flames of the "treason" accusation—of "espionage."

A disgust, as always, aimed at the Jewish body.

Houston Stewart Chamberlain: The Blood Theorist

Houston Stewart Chamberlain was a British-born, German-naturalized racial theorist whose 1899 book *The Foundations of the Nineteenth Century* became one of the most influential works of scientific racism in European history.

Kaiser Wilhelm II adored it. German schools mandated it as required reading. Hitler called Chamberlain a prophet.

Chamberlain was obsessed with blood.

Not blood as metaphor—*as substance.* Blood as the carrier of racial destiny. As the medium through which civilizations rise and fall.

His entire intellectual project, in fact, was built on the premise that racial mixing—particularly the mixing of "Aryan" blood with Jewish blood—was the engine of civilizational collapse.

This is, at its core, a sexual theory. Blood "mixes" through one act: sex.

So, stripped of its pseudoscientific veneer, Chamberlain's horribly influential racial science was a sustained panic about who was sleeping with whom. His feared "contamination" was not political or economic. *It was biological and was reproductive.*

It was—crime of crime, sin of sins, fear of fears—what happened when an Aryan woman lay down with a Jewish man, or tried to. Because Chamberlain described Jews as a biologically distinct "counter-race" whose very DNA corroded Aryan civilization from within. No mere outsider, the Jew was a contaminant.

A biological agent whose reproductive contact with gentiles eventuated racial decay.

The Nazis would eagerly, directly adopt this language of contamination, defilement, pollution, and biological corruption.

The Nuremberg Laws, criminalizing sexual relations between Jews and non-Jews, constituted Chamberlain's thesis turned into legislation.

Every German woman shamed in the streets for loving a Jewish man—every Jewish man tortured for "race defilement"—all of it descends from Chamberlain's terror of mixed blood.

Which is to say: *his terror of sex.*

Like so many chronicled in this book, Chamberlain was a man frightened of desire. It terrified him to such an extent that *he built an entire racial cosmology to justify banning it.*

The Lynching of Leo Frank

On August 17, 1915, a mob of twenty-five men drove to the Georgia State Penitentiary in Milledgeville, cut the telephone and power lines, overpowered the warden and guards, and dragged Leo Frank from his cell.

They then drove him 175 miles, all night long, to Marietta, Georgia—the hometown of Mary Phagan, the thirteen-year-old girl he had been fraudulently convicted of murdering—and hanged him from an oak tree.

For the prosecution, though, it was not enough to accuse Frank of murder. That alone would not have summoned the crowd. *The prosecution had to make it sexual.*

Prosecutor Hugh Dorsey—who would ride the conviction to the governor's mansion—painted Frank to the grand jury as "a sexual pervert who was both homosexual and who preyed on young girls." The charges were never merely that Frank killed Mary Phagan. The charge was that he was a degenerate, a predator, a corrupter of innocence. *A Jew whose sexuality was itself an indictment.*

The trial was a carnival. Witnesses described Frank's alleged "perversions" in lurid, pornographic detail. The press gorged itself. The public salivated. And the mob—waiting outside the courthouse—didn't merely want justice. It wanted cleansing.

Because a murderer is a criminal. But a sexually deviant Jew is a *contaminant.*

And you don't jail contaminants. You eradicate them.

The men who lynched Leo Frank were not drifters or drunks. They were the aristocracy of Georgia: a former governor, a former mayor, a sitting judge, a state senator's son, prominent lawyers, and businessmen. They called themselves the "Knights of Mary Phagan." Within a month of the lynching, several of these same men gathered at the summit of Stone Mountain, Georgia, and announced the rebirth of the Ku Klux Klan.

Let's linger on that.

The Klan's resurrection—the single most destructive white supremacist movement in American history—was born directly from the sexual rage manufactured by a Jewish man's trial.

Half of Georgia's three thousand Jews fled the state in the aftermath. Not because of the murder conviction. Because of what the conviction revealed: that in America, as in Europe, as in the medieval courts and the Inquisition chambers, antisemitism reaches for the body. It cannot simply accuse the Jew of a crime. It must accuse the Jew of a *sexual* crime. It must paint the Jew as physically revolting, erotically dangerous, carnally depraved.

The Frank case was America's blood libel—dressed in courtroom procedure but powered by the same engine: a Christian girl's innocence violated by a Jewish man's alleged perversion. The fact that Frank was almost certainly innocent only deepens the diagnosis. The mob didn't need evidence. It needed a story. And the story that works—the story that *always* works—is the one about the Jew and the body.

Murder is a legal problem. But a Jew defiling a Christian child? That is a spiritual emergency. And spiritual emergencies justify anything.

Henry Ford and *The Dearborn Independent*

Henry Ford was the most admired industrialist in America—perhaps the most admired in the world. He democratized the automobile, revolutionized manufacturing, and remains a symbol of American ingenuity.

He was also one of the most prolific antisemites of the twentieth century.

From 1919 to 1927, Ford published *The Dearborn Independent*, a weekly newspaper distributed through Ford dealerships across the country that reached seven hundred thousand subscribers. Its centerpiece: a ninety-one-issue series titled "The International Jew: The World's Foremost Problem"—later compiled into four volumes, translated into sixteen languages, and disseminated worldwide.

It's for this reason, and no surprise, really, that Adolf Hitler kept a portrait of Henry Ford on the wall of his office in Munich.

Ford was also the only American mentioned favorably in *Mein Kampf.*

But here is what matters for our purposes:

Ford could not attack Jews without making it sexual.

For example, his newspaper accused Jews of corrupting American morals through the entertainment industry. Specifically, *The Dearborn Independent* claimed Jews promoted jazz—which Ford described as "moron music" engineered to stimulate base physical desires and destroy the self-discipline of Christian youth. His paper also alleged that Jews ran the "white slave trade," thereby deliberately ensnaring and degrading Christian women. It moreover charged that Hollywood was a Jewish weapon—a propaganda psy-op, of sorts—designed to spread sexual degeneracy into American homes.

"The International Jew" thereby surpassed the confines otherwise normally associated with antisemitic filth; Jews as economic puppet-masters, and the like. Rather, it depicted Jews as erotic saboteurs. Its drivel insisted more than that Jews had too much money or influence—it propounded that Jews *used that influence* to corrupt the American body.

To loosen morals.

To destroy the sexual discipline that held Christian civilization together.

It was a formula that, by now, is unmistakable.

Ford—a man who enforced puritanical social standards in his own factories, sending inspectors to workers' homes to check on their moral habits, drinking, and marriages—could not conceive of Jewish power *without* conceiving of Jewish sexual corruption.

His hatred went well beyond the economic or political. *It was erotic.*

It conceived of Jews as contaminators, a charge the most respected industrialist in America, over and over again, taught millions of readers to believe.

The Third Reich: Hitler's Perversion and Purity Obsession

Nazi antisemitism was not merely political. It was eroticized.

Hitler and the Nazi regime exemplify sexual repression twisted into genocidal antisemitism.

On the surface, Nazi ideology championed "family values" and condemned the decadence of Weimar-era liberalism. The Nazi regime outlawed pornography, persecuted homosexuals, and promoted a cult of "wholesome Aryan motherhood." But beneath this puritanical facade churned currents of fetishism, hypocrisy, and personal perversion—beginning with Hitler himself.

Hitler's own sexual psychology was deeply problematic.

Esteemed historians—not gossip columnists—have long documented his abnormal relationship to sex, intimacy, and the body: hypochondria, sexual dysfunction, voyeuristic fixations, sadomasochistic fantasies, a profound terror of healthy erotic vulnerability.

He famously carried on a secret relationship with his half-niece, Geli Raubal, which combined avuncular control, jealousy, and—quite possibly—incestuous obsession. For over two years in the late 1920s, Hitler kept the much younger Geli as a close companion, living together under the same roof and controlling her every move. Contemporary accounts and later testimonies suggest a volatile and unhealthy relationship. Geli grew restive under Hitler's tyrannical protectiveness; he dictated whom she could befriend or date, even while he himself flirted with other young women. According to friends, their fights were intense, and Geli feared Hitler's rages.

Most disturbingly, multiple sources (including Hitler's close associates and the testimony of Otto Strasser to U.S. intelligence) indicated Hitler forced Geli into degrading sexual acts to satisfy his peculiar fetishes. Strasser recounted that Geli described "disgusting" acts demanded by Hitler—things she "had never dreamed could happen."

Geli Raubal's tragic fate—a gunshot wound in Hitler's apartment in 1931, widely deemed suicide under duress—only underscored the pathology. Lurid details matter less than the pattern: a man incapable of healthy intimacy, obsessed with purity, filth, and contamination.

Hitler's sexual impotence and paraphilias dovetailed eerily with his antisemitic fanaticism. In his manifesto *Mein Kampf*, he repeatedly casts the Jew as a sexual menace. He fulminated that syphilis—the era's most feared sexually transmitted disease—was a "Jewish" plot to corrupt Aryans. He wrote "the prostitution of love" and the spread of venereal disease were the result of "Judaization of our life," the "mammonizing of our mating instinct," poisoning the blood of German youth.

In Hitler's mind, through sex, Jews literally embodied pollution of the pure German body. He railed that even noble families had allowed "any department store Jewess" to bear their children—a "sin against blood and race," one he dubbed "the original sin of the world."

Hitler's fixation on racial purity was at heart an extreme sexual anxiety projected onto an entire people. His genocidal antisemitism was indivisible from his horror of the living, reproducing body.

Julius Streicher and *Der Stürmer*

It is telling that Hitler's trusted propaganda chief in Nuremberg, Julius Streicher, was himself a sexually deranged personality and one of the most lurid perverts in recorded history.

Streicher's newspaper *Der Stürmer* specialized in pornographic antisemitism—it printed lurid cartoons of Jewish men molesting blonde German maidens and grotesque tales of Jewish sexual crimes. Streicher seemed obsessed with sexual depravity, to the point that even fellow Nazis found him repulsive. By 1940, his reputation as a "corrupt, sadistic sexual pervert" had become an embarrassment.

After the war, at the Nuremberg Trials prison, Streicher would make lewd comments to female staff and even washed his face in the toilet bowl—earning him the moniker "the dirty old man" of the Nazi prisoners. A prison doctor wondered whether Streicher's "lewd sexual perversions and rabid anti-Semitic writings" sprang from the same diseased mind. At Nuremberg, all the senior Nazis being put on trial told their American captors they refused to share a cell with Streicher because of his demented homo-erotic obsessions. Just imagine—even mass murderers who engineered the Holocaust saw Streicher as a sick sexual pervert and feared him.

The pattern recurred throughout Nazi ranks.

Joseph Goebbels: Propagandist in Heat

The Reich Minister of Propaganda, Joseph Goebbels, controlled what every German read, saw, heard, and believed. His was the voice of Nazism. Its most gifted communicator, the architect of the regime's most devastating lies, Goebbels was also a relentless, compulsive sexual predator.

He wielded the power of his office to coerce women into his bed, especially screen starlets whose careers he could make or break.

Goebbels's diaries—kept meticulously throughout the war—reveal a man consumed by sexual conquest, carnal desire, and impulsive lust.

He pursued actresses, singers, and young women in the German film industry with the single-minded determination of an addict. His method was simple: By controlling the careers of every performer in the Reich, he ensured unrivaled despotic leverage over their very bodies. A favorable word from Goebbels could make a career. An unfavorable one could end it—*or worse.*

The coercion was structural, total, and inescapable. A predatory lust powered it.

So, Goebbels used the German film industry as a personal harem.

Actresses who wished to work understood, implicitly or explicitly, that Goebbels expected access. Those who complied advanced. Those who refused disappeared from the screen or suffered worse fates. The Czech actress Lída Baarová, for example, became his most famous mistress, a relationship so publicly brazen and scandalous that even Hitler eventually intervened to end it, fearing it would embarrass the regime.

The irony and hypocrisy suffocates: The man who produced the most virulently antisemitic propaganda in history—depicting Jews as sexual predators corrupting German womanhood—was himself an apex sexual predator. Goebbels exploited German women on an industrial scale.

Accusing Jews of running Hollywood to degrade Christian morals, he ran the German film industry to satisfy his own sexual appetites. Accusing Jews of using cultural influence for sexual exploitation, he used his cultural influence for exactly that.

Across the entire scope of German media, Goebbels painted the Jew as the seducer, the defiler, the corrupter of innocence.

Yet he was the seducer, the defiler, the corrupter—and much more, much worse.

Every accusation, indeed, comprises a confession.

In Goebbels's case, the erotic engine churned at the heights of state power: a man whose private life was a catalogue of sexual coercion producing propaganda accusing Jews of the very crimes he committed nightly. Projection, on a civilizational scale.

Hermann Göring: Hedonist of Hate

If Hitler was the ascetic face of Nazism—gaunt, vegetarian, supposedly celibate—then Hermann Göring was its bloated id.

The founder of the Gestapo—Nazi Germany's secret police—and the Luftwaffe, its air force—Göring was a man of monstrous appetites. He craved food, drugs, art, luxury, and power over human bodies—all of which was reflected in his own corpus. A morphine addict for much of his adult life, Göring began abusing opiates shortly after he was shot during the Beer Hall Putsch of 1923. Increasingly heavy doses translated to an increasingly debilitating addiction. His addiction even survived World War II; at the Nuremberg Trials, doctors had to wean him off the drug before he could stand trial.

Göring's relationship to sexuality was as chaotic, disordered, and compulsive as the rest of his appetites. He was famously, extravagantly vain—parading in elaborate uniforms, donning jewels, and even wearing makeup. He hosted lavish parties at his hunting estate, Carinhall, where the décor consisted of looted art, all drenched in an atmosphere of boozy, decadent excess. He surrounded himself with beautiful objects and beautiful people, in equal measure, not as a lover but as a collector—someone who "took" beauty the way he "took" morphine: compulsively, desperately, addictively.

The architect of the Luftwaffe's terror bombing campaigns and a primary organizer of the Holocaust's logistics, Göring signed the order authorizing Reinhard Heydrich to prepare the "Final Solution of the Jewish Question." Allied interrogators and psychologists who examined him at Nuremberg noted his narcissism, grandiosity, and peculiar combination of charm and cruelty. Göring could be jovial and generous one moment, murderous the next.

Unable to sublimate pleasure into intimacy, he therefore converted it into domination. Like other sociopathic, sadistic, and narcissistic antisemites, Göring did not love people.

He acquired them.

He did not experience joy.

He consumed it.

As it does for every addict, Göring's dependency failed to fill his void. No amount of morphine, stolen art, or theatrical splendor could make him whole. But he also relished a drug that never disappoints the addict—at least the especially diseased, depraved kind: power over the helpless.

As if yet another symptom of his ailment, the dependent hedonist indulged himself in antisemitism—this vice more than anything else. Its ultimate expression was his attempt to annihilate the Jews, a people whose tradition teaches that pleasure must be earned through covenant. That acquisition without gratitude is emptiness. That true joy cannot be stolen.

It must be grown, nursed, cultivated, fostered, guarded, sanctified.

Göring could not build. He could only take—could only consume. And destroy.

The Nuremberg Laws: Sexual Panic as State Policy

The Nuremberg Laws of 1935 criminalized intimacy between Jews and non-Jews, crystallizing the Nazi obsession with racial defilement. Sexual relations became treason. Love, pollution.

If an "Aryan" German woman had sexual relations with a Jew—or worse, married him—her hair was shorn, she was dressed in filthy rags, and paraded through the streets with a sign announcing her desecration of sacred Aryan womanhood.

For the Jewish man, the penalties were far worse. Well before the genocide officially began, he was tortured and lynched.

Because genocide begins not with gas chambers, but with fantasies of contamination.

Lavrentiy Beria: Stalin's Rapist

Lavrentiy Beria was the head of Stalin's secret police—the NKVD—from 1938 until Stalin's death in 1953.

He was one of the most powerful men in the Soviet Union and among the most feared human beings on earth. For good reason.

Because, in addition to a mass murderer—whose killings, to put it mildly, fell under the auspices of political repression—Beria was also a serial rapist and, by multiple credible accounts, a serial killer of women and girls.

Beria prowled the streets of Moscow in his government limousine, pointing out young women—sometimes teenage girls—and having his bodyguards force them to his home. Those who resisted were threatened. If they continued to resist his advances, Beria strangled them to death. Those who submitted were given flowers the next morning—a grotesque parody of courtship.

Those who "disappeared" were, according to testimony that emerged after his execution, buried in his garden.

When his home was later excavated, human remains were found in the grounds.

This was the man who, in addition to arresting, torturing, and murdering untold masses of innocent people as the head of Stalin's secret police, and who likewise stalked Moscow's streets as a serial killer and serial rapist, also orchestrated Stalin's antisemitic purges.

Indeed, in the last years of Stalin's rule, Beria oversaw the Doctors' Plot—a fabricated conspiracy alleging Jewish physicians were plotting to poison Soviet leaders. The campaign unleashed a wave of antisemitic terror across the Soviet Union: Jewish doctors were arrested, tortured, and forced to confess. Thousands of Jews were fired from their jobs. Many were murdered.

Moreover, plans were reportedly drawn up for the mass deportation of Soviet Jews to Siberia. Only Stalin's death in March 1953 prevented the plot from reaching its genocidal conclusion.

No surprises here: A man who kidnapped, raped, and murdered women and girls for his own pleasure led the campaign to destroy Soviet Jewry.

Beria's pathology was total: He could not relate to other human beings except through domination, violence, and sexual conquest. Guided by sociopathic—even psychopathic—impulses only sharpened, heightened, and augmented by his own homicidal and sexually sadistic experience, Beria was remote from intimacy and tenderness, foreign qualities to the NKVD tzar.

Like Stalin and other totalitarian mass killers, Beria's dearest currency was power—power over bodies, over populations, over life and death.

As if by hidden mechanics, the clockwork of perversion, such a person always chooses for his target of state-sponsored terror a people whose civilization is built on everything he cannot comprehend or countenance.

Covenant, family, mutual obligation, the sanctification of desire rather than its weaponization.

Beria was executed in December 1953, shortly after Stalin's death. But the pattern he embodied—the sexual predator who becomes the antisemitic persecutor—did not die with him. It lives, sweats, and breathes wherever power is exercised without accountability and desire is expressed without empathy.

Sayyid Qutb: The Virgin Who Declared War on Joy

If you want to understand the intellectual engine of modern Islamist terrorism—its theology of death, its obsession with sexual purity, its virulent antisemitism—you must understand one man: Sayyid Qutb.

Qutb was the chief theorist of the Muslim Brotherhood and the intellectual godfather of virtually every Islamist extremist movement of the last seventy years. Osama bin Laden studied his works. His teachings shaped Ayman al-Zawahiri, the arch-terrorist who assumed command of Al-Qaeda following bin Laden's death. Despite Qutb being Sunni, the Shia cleric Ayatollah Khamene'i personally translated Qutb's writings into Farsi. A 2015 conference in Tehran celebrated his legacy. His influence on global Islamism and terrorism is incalculable.

And he was, by all credible accounts, a lifelong virgin—a man who never married, never experienced intimacy, and spent his entire adult life in a state of acute sexual terror.

The Man Who Could Not Touch

Born in 1906 in the Egyptian village of Musha, Qutb was by all accounts brilliant, introverted, and chronically unwell. Memorizing the Quran by the age of ten, he suffered from respiratory ailments throughout his life. Biographers consistently describe him as pale, withdrawn, depressive—a man known for being introverted, isolated, and depressed.

He was also, in contemporary parlance, catastrophically unlucky in love. Or rather—he was catastrophically afraid of it.

In 1947, Qutb published a semi-autobiographical novel called *Ashwak*—"Thorns." The book tells the story of a young clerk named Sami who learns about women exclusively from books and finds himself paralyzed by an engagement to a girl named Samira, a woman with—as Qutb took pains to note—a tempting bosom. The entire novel constitutes a grueling portrait of romantic paralysis: Sami cannot commit, cannot trust, cannot surrender to desire.

He oscillates daily between longing and revulsion, between wanting Samira and suspecting her of betrayal. Eventually, exhausted, she leaves him.

Qutb later explained his lifelong bachelorhood by claiming he could never find a woman of sufficient "moral purity and discretion" (Nick Fuentes come to mind for anyone?). Read that excuse through the lens of his own novel and it becomes something else entirely: The rationalization of a man so terrified of intimacy, so incapable of the vulnerability that erotic love demands, he wrapped his paralysis in the language of piety and called his prison an ethic.

He would spend the rest of his life building an ideology to match.

The Eugenicist in the Foundations

Before Qutb ever set foot in America, he had already absorbed the intellectual framework that would structure his hatred of the modern world. And the source was not the Quran, but a French eugenicist named Alexis Carrel.

In the early 1940s, Qutb encountered Carrel's bestselling book *Man, the Unknown*, published in 1935. Carrel, a Nobel Prize–winning surgeon, had devolved from medical genius into fascist ideologue.

In *Man, the Unknown*, he argued that Western civilization had degenerated into "barbarism"—that modern society, with its materialism, its sexual permissiveness, its abandonment of spiritual discipline, bred weakness. His proposed solution: eugenics—the sterilization of the "unfit," euthanasia for criminals and the insane, and the establishment of an intellectual aristocracy to guide the human race.

Carrel was no fringe crank.

His book was an international bestseller, serialized in *Reader's Digest* and translated into dozens of languages. Carrel was a close friend of Charles Lindbergh—the aviation hero who was also, not incidentally, an ardent antisemite. Just as modern antisemites like Tucker Carlson and Candace Owens falsely accused Israel of pushing American into war against Iran in 2026, Lindbergh and his "America First" movement lied rabidly about how American Jewry (Israel did not yet exist as a state) were pushing America into war against Hitler. In 1941, Carrel returned to occupied

France and accepted a position from the Vichy government to head the French Foundation for the Study of Human Problems, an institution that implemented eugenic policies including mandatory premarital physical and psychological screening.

Carrel was a man Sayyid Qutb regarded as a visionary.

Qutb devoured Carrel's work, quoting him extensively and at length. He saw in Carrel a rare Western thinker—one honest enough to admit that his own civilization rotted from within. Scholars documented that Carrel's concept of modern "barbarism" became, in Qutb's hands, the Islamic concept of *jahiliyyah*—the state of pre-Islamic ignorance Qutb applied not merely to pagan Arabia, but to the entire modern world.

The intellectual pipeline is eye-watering in its perversity and infamy.

A Vichy eugenicist, a man who advocated gassing criminals and breeding a master race under Nazi occupation, provided the conceptual architecture for the most influential Islamist ideology of the twentieth century. Carrel's disgust at Western sexual permissiveness became Qutb's theological war on the body. Carrel's dream of an elite vanguard purifying civilization became Qutb's vision of an Islamist avant-garde waging jihad against the modern world.

Fascism did not merely *influence* Islamism. In this case, it provided the blueprints. Qutb simply translated them into Arabic and added Quranic citations.

The Church Dance That Launched a Thousand Jihads

In 1948, the Egyptian Ministry of Education sent Qutb to the United States on a scholarship to study the American educational system. He arrived in Washington, D.C., then transferred to Colorado State College of Education in Greeley, Colorado, where he would spend the bulk of his stay.

Greeley, in 1949, was about as morally dissolute as a glass of warm milk. A planned community founded by Utopian idealists on the dry plains north of Denver, the town had criminalized alcohol. Churches lined the streets. Residents crowded the campus tennis courts on weekends for square dancing. The local newspaper ran front-page stories about a turtle named Tootsie trying to cross a busy road.

But Qutb looked at Greeley, Colorado, and saw Gomorrah.

The green lawns repelled him. The way Americans salted their watermelon, too. The quality of the haircuts. The football players and jazz music.

Everything, in short, that constituted the texture of ordinary American life in the middle of the twentieth century.

But nothing horrified him more than the bodies.

Specifically, women's bodies. He wrote, barely concealing his own arousal beneath the costume of moral outrage:

> "The American girl is well acquainted with her body's seductive capacity. She knows it lies in the face, in expressive eyes, and in thirsty lips. She knows seductiveness lies in the round breasts, the full buttocks, and in the shapely thighs, sleek legs—and she shows all this and does not hide it."

That passage is not the dispassionate observation of a social critic. *It is the catalog of a man drowning in desire he cannot acknowledge.* Every curve, every feature—every inch of the female body—is described with the agonized, but also the salivating, precision of someone who cannot stop looking. Who cannot forgive himself for looking. For wanting to look.

Then came the church dance.

One evening at a Congregationalist church in Greeley, the pastor organized a social dance after services. The lights were dimmed—not to simulate a brothel, but because the minister wanted his self-conscious parishioners to feel comfortable enough to get up and move. The song playing on the gramophone was "Baby, It's Cold Outside"—the Frank Loesser standard, written two years earlier. It had just won the Academy Award.

Frank Loesser, it should be noted for the purposes of this book, was Jewish.

Qutb's account of the evening reads like dispatches from the innermost circle of hell:

The dance hall, he wrote, convulsed with tapping feet, seductive legs. Arms circled waists. Lips met lips. Chests pressed against chests. Desire fattened the atmosphere. And the pastor—the *pastor*—encouraged those who had not yet participated to join in.

In a dry town. In a church basement. To a pop song written by a Jew.

It was, for Sayyid Qutb, the apocalypse in miniature. Everything he feared about desire, about the body, about freedom—crystallized in a single evening of small-town Americans shuffling awkwardly to a gramophone in a dimly lit church hall.

He would never recover.

A War on Joy

Qutb returned to Egypt and declared war.

Not on American foreign policy—*on American joy*. On music, dancing, mixed-gender socializing; *on the freedom of women to move through the world unashamed.*

He joined the Muslim Brotherhood and quickly became its most influential intellectual, transforming the organization from a political movement into an ideological vanguard. He developed the concept of *jahiliyyah* mentioned above and applied it to the entire modern world.

Everything Western was corrupt.

Everything joyful, satanic.

Everything bound up with the human body—especially the female body—was a temptation sent to destroy the faithful.

In his 1964 manifesto *Milestones*, Qutb laid out a vision of global Islamic revolution. Existing Muslim societies, he wrote, were no better than pagan Arabia before the Prophet. All contemporary governments—Muslim ones included—were illegitimate. The faithful must form a revolutionary vanguard, separate themselves entirely from the corrupted world, and wage jihad. Only through holy war could this global Muslim offensive—including, in due time, the Shia of Iran (the Islamic Republic), Lebanon (Hezbollah), and Yemen (the Houthis)—establish a society governed solely by divine law.

In this society, as Qutb made clear in his broader writings, *women's roles would be strictly defined: subordinate to men, removed from public life, their bodies hidden, their autonomy extinguished.*

Thus, there is a direct line from Qutb's inability to touch a woman in Cairo to the Taliban forcing girls out of school in Kabul.

From his terror at a church dance in Greeley to the morality police beating women in Tehran for showing their hair.

A trajectory begun by a man who could not manage his own desire and so decided the entire world must be reorganized to ensure he never had to.

The Jews as Cosmic Pornographers

And the Jews?

Qutb blamed them for all of it.

He was a staunch antisemite, influenced by earlier Islamist thinkers like Rashid Rida who had embraced anti-Jewish conspiracy theories wholesale. In 1950, Qutb published *Our Struggle Against the Jews*, a book that forms a central pillar of contemporary Islamist antisemitism.

In it, he accused Jews of deliberately engineering the collapse of the Ottoman Caliphate, of infiltrating and corrupting Muslim societies, and of waging a cosmic war against Islam itself.

He wrote that behind every revolution, every secularizing reform, every erosion of Islamic authority—stood the Jews.

But Qutb went further than political conspiracy.

He accused Jews of spreading what he called "animalistic sexuality" throughout the world. He described Jewish influence as a deliberate campaign to dissolve Muslim morality through sexual corruption. In his framework, Jewishness itself was a cosmic source of sexual degradation—the hidden hand turning the world into the Greeley church.

Consider the psychic architecture.

A lifelong virgin, incapable of intimacy, saturated in desire he could neither express nor extinguish, absorbed a framework of civilizational disgust from a French fascist eugenicist.

He then traveled to America and was overwhelmed—not by poverty, violence, or injustice, but by the sight of women's bodies, the sound of a pop song.

He returned home and constructed a totalizing ideology, one in which all human desire is a weapon, all joy, corruption.

The ultimate source of that corruption is the Jew.

Martyr, Monster

In 1954, following a failed assassination attempt on President Gamal Abdel Nasser by the Muslim Brotherhood, Qutb was arrested and imprisoned. The conditions were brutal. He was tortured. Already a sickly man plagued by respiratory problems, depression, and chronic fragility, prison nearly killed him.

But it also radicalized him beyond anything he had written before.

It was in prison that Qutb composed the bulk of his most influential works, including his thirty-volume Quranic commentary *In the Shade of the Quran*, as well as the incendiary *Milestones*.

Briefly released in 1964 through the intervention of the Iraqi president, Qutb was rearrested almost immediately when *Milestones* was linked to an alleged Brotherhood plot against the government. On August 29, 1966, likely based on charges that were at least partly fabricated, Sayyid Qutb was executed by hanging.

He thus became a *shahid,* a martyr.

Not merely a martyr for the Muslim Brotherhood—a martyr for Islamism as a whole.

A symbol of purity pitted against the corrupt, feckless failure of Pan-Arabism and secular nationalism.

His writings became scripture. His execution lit what Ayman al-Zawahiri later called "the jihadist fire." His brother Muhammad fled to Saudi Arabia, became a professor of Islamic studies, and spent decades editing, publishing, and promoting Sayyid's works. One of Muhammad's most devoted students was a young Egyptian, that very same Ayman al-Zawahiri, who had been introduced to Qutb's legacy by his uncle—a man who had been one of the last people to see Sayyid Qutb alive.

Indeed, the pipeline from one sexually terrified man's writings to the deadliest terrorist attack in American history runs through a single family connection. A single set of books. A single, sex-obsessed pathology dressed in theological robes.

Children of Qutb

So, every suicide bomber strapping on a vest while declaring the purity of his intentions, every morality police officer beating a woman for showing her hair, every Hamas militant who murders, rapes, and oppresses while calling his victims "infidels"—all of them are, in some sense, Qutb's children.

Heirs to a theology born not from revelation—*but from one man's unbearable encounter with his own desire.*

And the ideology they inherited carries, embedded in its DNA, the double helix of sexual terror and Jew-hatred that has defined authoritarian pathology since Reich first diagnosed it. Qutb feared the body. *He could not possess a woman, so he built a theology that imprisoned all women.* He could not account for his own lust, *so he blamed the Jews for the existence of lust itself.* He absorbed the civilizational disgust of a Vichy eugenicist and baptized it in Quranic Arabic.

The church dance in Greeley, Colorado, has been over for seventy-five years. The gramophone is silent. The pastor, long dead. Probably, too, the couples who shuffled bashfully to "Baby, It's Cold Outside"—a song written by a Jewish composer, played in a Christian church, in a town where you couldn't even buy a beer.

But the man who watched them from the margins, burning with a desire he mistook for righteousness, still shapes the world.

His books are still read. His concepts still deployed. His pathology still transmitted, generation after generation, from imam to recruit, from prison cell to battlefield, from one lonely, sexually terrified young man to the next.

Sayyid Qutb never touched a woman. *The world is still paying for it.*

Iran Under Khomeini: Purity and Persecution

The same dynamics appear in modern religious fundamentalism—particularly Islamist extremism. Groups like Iran's Islamic Republic, Hamas, and the Taliban combine virulent hatred (including antisemitism) with obsessive control of sexuality and women's bodies. Their ideologies make female modesty and sexual morality a pillar of identity—as important as, if not inseparable from, their enmity toward Jews or "infidels."

After the 1979 Iranian Revolution, Ayatollah Ruhollah Khomeini established a theocracy that harshly policed personal behavior. Khomeini and his clerics developed an almost surreal focus on sexual "sin." In his writings and sermons, Khomeini issued detailed pronouncements on sexual matters ranging from marital relations to bizarre hypotheticals about bestiality and incest.

For example, in a 1961 legal manual, he calmly ruled on scenarios like: "If a man sodomizes the son, brother, or father of his wife after their marriage, the marriage remains valid." He even addressed intercourse with animals. Such fixation on sexual minutiae earned the post-revolutionary regime a reputation for hypocrisy and prudish absurdity. As one commentator put it, "in the Islamic Republic of Iran all politics may not be sexual, but all sex is political."

This extreme sexual puritanism went hand in hand with fierce antisemitism and anti-Westernism in Iran's official ideology. The hijab (veil) was made compulsory for all women—not just as a religious rule, but as a revolutionary symbol. In fact, Iranian officials often cite the hijab as one of the regime's three core ideological pillars, alongside opposition to the United States and Israel. The message is stark: If the veil were removed, the entire Islamic Revolution's integrity (including its stance against Israel) would collapse.

The most famous example in modern tyranny is that of the arch religious fraud Ayatollah Ruhollah Khomeini, the bloodthirsty dictator of Iran whose reign began in 1979 and lasted ten years. The first thing he did, after slaughtering all his political opponents and Shah loyalists following his return from a thirteen-year exile in Najaf, Iraq and then, oddly, in Paris, France, was close all the cinemas, all the movie theaters, and turn state television—I kid you not—into scintillating shows about things like sewing, something he thought women eminently qualified for—and little else.

Khomeini regularly referred to America as the "Great Satan" and Israel as the "Little Satan," casting the political struggle in religious terms loaded with moral disgust. The regime's propaganda frequently depicts Israel (and Jews by extension) as a corrupter of Islamic values—spreading immorality, drink, and uncovered women.

Iran's theocracy has enforced its sexual code with brutality reminiscent of the Inquisition. Morality police patrols have beaten or arrested women for showing a wisp of hair, and courts have ordered floggings and even stoning for adultery. The regime murdered twenty-two-year-old Kurdish-Iranian Mahsa Amini on September 16, 2022—in a hospital, no less—for improperly wearing a hijab.

In other words, the regime governs by terror when it cannot govern desire.

Relatedly, antisemitism in the Iranian system functions as a pressure valve: it externalizes moral failure and redirects rage away from domestic repression.

Hamas: Demonizing Sex and the Jew

Hamas's antisemitism is not merely political opposition to Israel. It is theological, conspiratorial, and sexualized. Their propaganda portrays Jews as more than enemies—corrupters of the moral order, manipulators of culture, media, sexuality, and power. Classic purity-panic antisemitism.

Explicitly antisemitic, Hamas's 1988 founding charter quotes the *Protocols of the Elders of Zion* and describes an eternal struggle against the Jews.

In the same document, Hamas delineates a strictly traditional role for women: They are to be the homemakers and child-rearers of the Islamic nation. The charter extols Muslim women primarily because they "manufacture men"—i.e., sons—and guide the next generation. Obviously, this language reduces women to vessels of reproduction for the cause, stripping them of individual agency.

After seizing power in Gaza in 2007, Hamas incrementally imposed its moral code on the population. By 2009, it launched a self-described "virtue" campaign to curb "immoral" behavior in Gaza. Armed Hamas police would stop couples in public to verify they were married or related and even beat young men for swimming shirtless on the beach. Human rights monitors reported that school administrators, under Hamas orders, turned away female students not wearing hijab and full-length robe. In one case, an administrator slapped a schoolgirl for not wearing the jilbab.

Hamas ideology frames the conflict as one between chastity and defilement, faith and corruption. And like all movements obsessed with honor, Hamas's is equally obsessed with shame.

When Hamas terrorists perpetrated the October 7, 2023 massacre in Israel, not only did they murder some 1,200 Jewish men, women, and children—they also carried out acts of rape, sexual torture, and grotesque mutilation. They cut off Israeli women's breasts and threw them to each other like bloody baseballs. They repeatedly shot women in their vaginas. Investigations by human-rights organizations and forensic experts found evidence of systematic gang rapes and sexual violence on that dark day. Hamas terrorists sexually brutalized Israeli women (and even men), in scenes so horrific that many details are unfit to print. *The Guardian* reported that at least seven women who were killed were also raped during the onslaught, and dozens of female corpses showed signs of genital mutilation and abuse.

This is a stark reminder that for the most extreme antisemites—those who literally commit genocide—sexual violence is not an afterthought; it is synonymous with their hatred.

Their rage at Jews blends with their rage at women.

Osama bin Laden: Pornography of Purity

In May 2011, U.S. Navy SEALs raided a compound in Abbottabad, Pakistan. There, Osama bin Laden had been hiding for years. The SEALs killed him, recovered his body, and catalogued the contents of his home.

They recovered among these items a massive—truly, staggeringly large—collection of pornography.

Let's marinate in that.

The man who declared war on Western civilization in the name of Islamic purity—the man who orchestrated the murder of nearly three thousand Americans on September 11, 2001—the man who blamed Jews for spreading sexual corruption throughout the Muslim world—was himself a compulsive, top-tier consumer of pornography.

Taking his Islamist cues from Sayyid Qutb, bin Laden railed against Jewish control of the media, thundering that Western culture—infected by Jewish influence, of course—was degrading Muslim morals.

He called for holy war to purify the world of sexual degeneracy.

But in the privacy of his compound, surrounded by concrete walls and barbed wire, he watched it to a degree that would seem addictive.

The hypocrisy is almost overwhelming. But it is not surprising. It is, in fact, this book's thesis in miniature.

Simply put, Bin Laden could not integrate his desire.

He could not admit it, could not sanctify it, could not bring it into the light of honest intimacy. *So, he did what every sexual authoritarian does: he split himself in two.*

One half preached purity and waged war. The other half consumed in secret what the first half condemned in public. And the gap between the two—the unbridgeable chasm between his public theology and his private appetite—filled with rage. Till it overflowed.

Rage at the West.

Rage at women.

Rage at Jews.

Because if the Jews were truly responsible for pornography, then it wasn't his fault. If the West was truly corrupted by Jewish influence, then his secret consumption was a symptom of *their* evil, not *his* weakness.

The conspiracy theory absolved him. It converted private shame into cosmic warfare. *The classic alchemy of tyrants, antisemites, and perverts—who are all, by the way, the same.*

The Taliban: Gender Terror as Governance

Surpassing even the Iranian mullahs and Hamas, the Taliban represent the most explicit fusion of sexual repression and political domination in the modern world.

Over a quarter of a century into the new millennium, today's Taliban:

Erases women from public life.

Forbids their education.

Restricts their movement.

Enforces their dress code.

Criminalizes their very voice—singing is banned.

Calling this cultural conservatism is a sick joke; this is gender incarceration. Women's autonomy, not immodesty, petrifies the Taliban.

During their rule—1996 to 2001, and again since 2021—the Taliban imposed a gender apartheid system without modern parallel. They forced women to wear the burqa, a head-to-toe shroud with mesh over the eyes, banned girls from attending school past puberty, and forbade women from working or even leaving home without a male guardian. Any deviation was met with public floggings or executions—stadium spectacles were held where "adulteresses" were shot in the head or whipped.

The Taliban frame their war as defense of women's honor against infidel corruption. It's notable that whenever Taliban conquered territory, one of the first things they did was destroy anything deemed "immoral"—smashing televisions, banning both music and dancing, and beating men who didn't grow beards.

Like all purity cults, the Taliban need an enemy to embody corruption. Jews scarcely exist in Afghan society. But ideologically, they function as symbols of global decadence, Western immorality, and sexual chaos.

Antisemitism doesn't require Jews. It was never about Jews.

It's about the bigot's fear—of freedom particularly.

Female Genital Mutilation: The War on Women's Pleasure

If there is a single practice that embodies the thesis of this book in its most brutal, literal form, it is female genital mutilation.

FGM involves the partial or total removal of external female genitalia—most commonly the clitoris. Though it predates Islam and is not prescribed by the Quran, this savagery is practiced predominantly in Muslim-majority regions of Africa and the Middle East. The World Health Organization estimates that 200 million girls and women alive today have undergone FGM—with three million more at risk every year.

The abomination has one purpose: to eliminate female sexual pleasure.

It is not about hygiene. Nor is it about health or religion. It's about control.

Specifically, about controlling female sexuality—which terrifies male authority, male honor, and an entire, femicidal social order built upon both. Left intact, remaining capable of pleasure, female sexuality endangers the misogynist hegemony.

After all, a woman who can experience pleasure is a woman who might *choose.*

She could choose her partner. *She could choose her life.* She could choose joy.

And a woman choosing joy is ungoverned by shame.

So, they cut the joy out of her body.

FGM is the erotic engine made surgical.

It is the belief that desire is so dangerous, so destabilizing—so threatening to authority—that it must be *physically excised* from the body of every girl before she is old enough to know what was taken from her.

And it is no coincidence that the cultures most likely to practice FGM are also cultures rife with antisemitism.

The connection is structural and not incidental. A society that mutilates its daughters' genitals to prevent them from experiencing pleasure is a society that has declared war on the body.

A society at war with the body will inevitably wage a war with the Jews—because Judaism refuses that war; in fact, it joins ranks with the opposing army.

Indeed, rather than cut away pleasure, Judaism consecrates it. The Torah insists on a woman's right to sexual satisfaction within marriage. The tradition of *onah*—conjugal obligation—is not a suggestion. *It is a legal requirement.*

A husband who neglects his wife's pleasure violates Jewish law. In Jewish law, a husband is obligated to have his wife climax first, so that she is not merely used as his masturbatory material. Likewise, a husband is forbidden from thinking erotically about another woman while making love to his wife. There is no intimacy in being physically present while being mentally absent.

The contrast could not be starker: One tradition mutilates girls to destroy desire; another commands husbands to fulfill it.

And the tradition that sanctifies desire is the one the world calls dangerous.

Why Sex Works So Well as Hatred-Fuel

Sex sits at the intersection of two forces that human beings struggle to integrate: power and vulnerability.

In healthy love, sex is mutuality—two people offering themselves without fear. In a diseased psyche, sex becomes domination—someone must be conquered, someone must be humiliated, someone must be owned.

Antisemitic movements are almost always movements of domination. They cannot tolerate mutuality. They cannot tolerate dignity. They cannot tolerate the idea that love can be holy.

So they do two things simultaneously: They degrade sex into filth and control. They accuse Jews of embodying that filth.

That way, they can persecute Jews and call it "purification."

This is why antisemitic ideologies so often come paired with oppressive sexual ethics—not a morality of love, but a morality of fear: segregation, shame, control, harshness, obsession with female "purity," and a constant atmosphere of sexual accusation.

The more sexually repressed the culture, the more it needs scapegoats. And the Jew is the perfect scapegoat because Judaism refuses the core bargain of repression: It refuses to declare the body the enemy of God.

The Straight Line from Sexual Shame to Social Violence

Here is the progression you can watch in real time: A culture teaches people to fear their bodies. They seek relief in secret. Secret relief breeds shame. Shame breeds rage. Rage demands a target. The movement supplies one: the Jew.

This is why antisemitism is so often accompanied by misogyny, by sexual paranoia, by obsessive regulation of women, by a hunger to humiliate. It isn't "random overlap." It's the same engine.

CHAPTER THREE

MODERN ANTISEMITES AND THEIR SEXUAL PERVERSIONS

Andrew Tate: Misogyny, Rape Charges, and Antisemitic Conspiracy

Andrew Tate, one of the most notorious figures blending misogyny and antisemitism, is a British-American social media influencer who openly and proudly calls himself a "misogynist." Tate first gained infamy boasting a "steady diet of hateful content about women" to millions of followers. In recent years, however, he has "added considerable antisemitism and intensely anti-Israel statements to his streaming content." This shift became evident after Tate's highly publicized arrest in Romania on charges of rape and sex trafficking; while facing prosecution, he was barred from leaving that country from 2022 until early 2025. Tate's history of alleged sexual violence—he and his brother are accused of luring and abusing women—dovetails grotesquely with his antisemitic rants.

Freed from travel bans in 2025, Tate returned to the United States and immediately began blending his conspiracy theories about Jews with his trademark machismo. He accused Romanian authorities of being part of "the Soros network," invoking the longtime antisemitic trope that

Jewish billionaire George Soros secretly controls governments. *Mother Jones* reported that Tate's content would "promptly segue into antisemitic claims clearly rooted in the blood libel," as he increasingly painted Israel and Jews as demonic.

After Hamas's attack on Israel on October 7, 2023, Tate erupted with vicious anti-Israel invective. Declaring (falsely) that Israel was committing genocide, he celebrated Hamas terrorists as embodiments of "masculine" virtue—even praising slain Hamas leader Yahya Sinwar as "defiant in the face of evil." When asked if he would condemn Hamas's atrocities, Tate defiantly replied, "No, I'm not going to condemn the masculine spirit of resistance." In Tate's warped worldview, violent misogyny and violent antisemitism are two sides of the same coin: he glorifies brute male dominance (even in the form of terrorists and rapists) and demonizes Jews as the opposite—an alleged source of societal "weakness" or "degeneracy."

Tate's antisemitism also led him to mingle with fellow far-right figures who share his toxic mix of hatreds. He forged links with the execrable Candace Owens, hosting interviews with her even as Owens drifted into Holocaust denial territory. He also flirted with Holocaust revisionism himself, asking his followers if it was possible history "lied about World War II"—an unmistakable nod to Holocaust denial.

In short, Tate emerged as a globe-trotting avatar of "misogynistic antisemitism," someone who in the same breath belittles women as objects and blames Jews for the world's evils. The case of Andrew Tate starkly illustrates how sexual predation and antisemitic conspiracy-thinking reinforce one another: his hatred of women and his hatred of Jews spring from the same twisted craving for dominance, a paranoid need to violently target perceived "weakness."

Nick Fuentes: The Incel White Nationalist and Repressed Desires

If Tate represents the abusive playboy side of this phenomenon, Nick Fuentes embodies its flip side: the bitterly repressed and ideologically puritanical misogynist simultaneously spewing anti-Jewish vitriol. A twenty-seven-year-old American white nationalist and leader of the alt-right "Groyper" movement, Fuentes has openly and proudly embraced antisemitism, earning notoriety as a Holocaust denier and Hitler admirer.

As the Center for American Progress summarized, Fuentes "has made numerous antisemitic statements, including saying "I love Hitler"; attacking "organized Jewry" as a "transnational gang"; and lifting up the so-called "Great Replacement theory," which posits that shadowy Jewish elites are orchestrating the replacement of white Christians with immigrants. The Anti-Defamation League documented him telling a white-supremacist audience, "I love you, and I love Hitler." He routinely blames Jews for everything from undermining American "sovereignty" to promoting "degeneracy," and has a "history of denying or questioning the Holocaust." In November 2025, Fuentes was even infamously given a high-profile platform on Tucker Carlson's show, where his toxic views reached millions—a fact we'll revisit in the Tucker section.

What makes Nick Fuentes particularly relevant here is the profound sexual pathology underlying his ideology. Fuentes despises women and modern sexuality to such an extreme degree that he boasts about being an "incel" (involuntary celibate) who has never once been intimate with a woman. In a 2025 interview with Piers Morgan, Fuentes admitted he's a virgin.

Morgan pressed him on his misogynistic remarks—Fuentes, Morgan pointed out, has said "a lot of women want to be raped" and crudely insisted that "women suck . . . they're talking too much, they're not hot anymore." When asked point-blank if he is even attracted to women or if he's secretly gay, Fuentes bristled and insisted, "I am attracted to women . . . I'm not gay," but then immediately added that "women are very difficult to be around." Morgan retorted that Fuentes is a "misogynist old dinosaur" despite being only in his twenties. Indeed, Fuentes declared in the same interview that women should not have the right to vote, cementing his belief that female agency itself is a mistake.

What makes this more interesting is that his booster, antisemite Tucker Carlson, actually referred to him as "some gay kid" not long before their interview, directly referencing his alleged homosexuality.

Of course, it goes without saying that I couldn't care less if he's gay or straight. I have an openly gay orthodox Jewish brother who came out when he was seventeen years old. In this regard, I'm like most Americans—indifferent to his sexual preference.

Not so Fuentes's extremely homophobic, gay-hating followers, who would reject him in an instant—or perhaps do even worse, God forbid—if he came out as gay.

Remember what Hitler did to his partner who created Nazism alongside him, SA head Ernst Röhm, on The Night of the Long Knives from June 30 to July 2, 1934? He was assassinated by the SS on July 1, in no small part because of Hitler's disgust with his open homosexuality, in addition to Hitler perceiving him as a threat.

Indeed, Fuentes's sexual repression is not merely a personal quirk: it's a core feature of his politics. He preaches an ultra-traditional, puritanical view that sex should only occur within marriage (something he tells his followers constantly), which sounds like wholesome traditional values—but in reality masks his own depraved sexual repression. It is a stance not couched in respect for women, but contempt for them. He tells his fans that marriage is necessary "in spite of the fact that women are annoying . . . they talk too much . . . we can't get them to lose weight."

Women, in Fuentes's mind, are a necessary evil—objects to be tolerated for procreation, not individuals with equal dignity. This extremely repressed and hostile attitude toward female sexuality correlates with his vicious antisemitism. Just as he wants to erase women's social and political power, he also rails against Jews as an alien force destroying "traditional" (white Christian male-dominated) civilization. It is telling that Fuentes and his followers often fixate on conspiracy theories involving Jews and sexual "degeneracy." (For example, alt-right networks frequently claim Jews are behind feminism, pornography, and LGBTQ rights, portraying Jewish influence as the root of modern sexual liberation—evils in their eyes.) Fuentes himself lifts talking points from this playbook: he attacks "pornography, the sexual revolution, and all forms of 'deviance'" as part of what he calls a Jewish-orchestrated plot against Christian America (sentiments he's expressed on his podcast and streams).

Ironically, Fuentes's own personal life betrays the fragility beneath his hateful puritanism. The fact that a healthy romantic or sex life utterly eludes him seems to fuel his rage. Piers Morgan mockingly observed, when Fuentes lectured about women's flaws, "Wow, says the guy who's never got laid." Online, Fuentes is often ridiculed for closet-like behavior, such as a widely-discussed episode where he appeared with an effeminate "catboy" companion—raising questions about his own suppressed desires. While Fuentes denies being homosexual, his public persona of hyper-conservative celibacy invites speculation that he may be projecting his internal conflict outward as misogyny and antisemitism.

Whether or not his sexuality is secretly queer, what's clear is that Fuentes's hatred of Jews intertwines with his hatred of sexual freedom.

He cannot stand that Jews (and the modern liberal world he imagines they control) encourage people to enjoy life, love whom they choose, and pursue pleasure. Like many fanatics before him, Fuentes responds by preaching a doctrine of repression and scapegoating: Women must be silenced; Jews must be banished.

Only then, he imagines, will the pure patriarchal order be restored.

The Incel-to-Antisemite Pipeline

There is a corner of the internet where the erotic engine of antisemitism operates in its purest, most undisguised form.

It is the world of the incels.

"Incel" stands for "involuntarily celibate"—i.e., men who believe they are unable to find sexual or romantic partners (despite, of course, desiring them). What began as a fringe online community has metastasized into a global subculture, one responsible for multiple mass murders, including the 2014 Isla Vista killings and the 2018 Toronto van attack.

Research has established that the movement's primary online gathering places, 4chan's /pol/ board and incels.is, rank among the highest-volume sources of antisemitic content anywhere on the internet. Together, these two dark pools of the internet account for roughly half of all online antisemitism.

Half.

This demands explanation.

Why, after all, would men for whom sexual failure is such a grievance they let it define their whole identity become the most prolific Jew-haters on the internet? Wouldn't Neo Nazi, Islamist, or radical leftist forums supply more antisemitism?

No, it turns out, they wouldn't—because sexual problems are always nearly synonymous with the world's oldest bigotry.

The sexual darkness of the incel world is hard to fathom.

Their forums seethe with hatred of women—whom they call "femoids"—alongside elaborate hierarchies of physical attractiveness that determine a man's worth. But the rage raced beyond women and extended, inevitably, to Jews. Claims that Jews control the media and direct it to promote feminism saturate the forums. They are flanked by similar claims that Jews invented feminism to destroy Western men, or that Jews run dating apps designed to humiliate white men. Likewise, that Jews benefit from—indeed engineer—male sexual frustration.

The logic is uncomplicated. It is, in fact, achingly simple:

I cannot get a woman to love me. Someone must be responsible.

The Jews.

The last thing you can expect these types to do is look inward. Introspection would demand they confront their own failures of empathy, their contempt for women, and inability to treat another human being as a partner rather than a conquest.

So they project outward, constructing a *conspiracy theory transforming personal misery into cosmic injustice.*

The Jew is the architect of said injustice.

Thus, the incel embodies the erotic engine stripped of all pretense. It's actually refreshing—or would be if it weren't so sick. Because the incel does not even bother to dress his hatred in politics or theology. No, he loathes Jews because he cannot get laid. He admits this—he types into forums, unashamed.

And while most people might not listen—other incels do, nodding along, in addition to the recruiters from white nationalist movements, who harvest the rage.

Nick Fuentes is their prophet.

A "proud" virgin. A vocal antisemite. A proud misogynist.

The perfect synthesis.

No mere metaphor, the incel-to-antisemite pipeline is a documented, measurable phenomenon. And it confirms vividly that *when men cannot form intimate relationships, they seek meaning in hatred.*

Dan Bilzerian: Playboy Objectification and Violent Jew-Hatred

In contrast to Fuentes's involuntary celibacy, Dan Bilzerian, with whom I have sparred openly on social media, epitomizes hypersexual excess—yet he too combines it with virulent antisemitism.

Bilzerian, an American social media celebrity dubbed the "King of Instagram," built his fame on an ostentatious playboy lifestyle: guns, luxury cars, and hordes of scantily clad women at his beck and call. He boasts of sleeping with scores of models and presents himself as the ultimate male hedonist. But behind the flashy harem imagery lies a pattern of real-life violence and abuse towards women, alongside a descent into unhinged conspiracy theories about Jews.

Bilzerian famously agreed to debate me, only to renege, knowing I would eviscerate him, then changed the rules by challenging me to an MMA fight. I'm nearly sixty years old and he is in his early forties and is a trained MMA fighter. So, when I suggested instead that he could choose from a list of some 100 ex-IDF MMA fighters, all of whom were eager to enter the ring with him, he ran for the hills and never responded. Ever since then, I have called him "No Balls Zerian." Needless to say, the invitation remains outstanding.

Bilzerian's misogyny has manifested in alleged assaults. In one 2014 incident at a Miami nightclub, Bilzerian was involved in an altercation with model Vanessa Castano, who, as reported by *TMZ* and *Courthouse News*, sued him for assault and battery, alleging he shoved her off a platform and kicked her in the face while she was down. Bilzerian denied the allegation, said he had been breaking up a fight, and Miami Beach police closed their investigation without charges.

That same year, as reported by *Miami New Times*, Bilzerian was sued by adult-film actress Janice Griffith, then eighteen, who said he threw her off a rooftop toward a pool during a Hustler photoshoot and she broke her foot on the pool's edge. Rather than show remorse, Bilzerian shrugged off responsibility and fought her lawsuit. These episodes illustrate how little regard he has for women's safety or dignity. To Bilzerian, women seem to be props in his narcissistic performance of masculinity, easily discarded or abused if they get in his way.

Astoundingly, this man who has been sued for kicking a woman in the face also proclaims himself a moral critic of others' behavior—particularly Jews. Bilzerian has, for over a decade, propagated a laundry list of antisemitic conspiracy theories. As early as 2010, he blamed Jews for a litany of world evils, from claiming "the Jewish people perpetrated the Holodomor" famine in Ukraine, to saying Jews "assassinated JFK," "orchestrated 9/11 and the Iraq War," and even "created the transgender nonsense." He approvingly remarked that Nazi Germany "flourished" once Hitler removed Jews from banking—he conveniently forgot that not only did Hitler lose the war but also left Germany a desolate ruin—and that Spain's golden age began after "it expelled the Jews" in 1492.

In a 2024 interview with Piers Morgan, Bilzerian escalated his rhetoric further into outright grotesquery. He declared that Judaism "promotes supremacy and rape" and teaches Jews to steal from non-Jews—an outrageous inversion, given Bilzerian's own record of abusing women. He went on to claim that "most of the problems today are caused by Jewish supremacy," parroting classic neo-Nazi ideology. Bilzerian has also dabbled in Holocaust denial, saying he'd bet his fortune that the Nazi death toll of Jews was exaggerated and implying the Holocaust was a Jewish invention. In short, he portrays Jews as the ultimate cause of societal ills and even sexual crimes—even as he himself has faced repeated lawsuits over violence against women.

The hypocrisy and evil of Bilzerian is staggering.

He embodies the very "degraded" sexual ethos that antisemites often decry—a world of promiscuity, pornography, and male domination. Yet he absurdly accuses the Jewish religion of promoting rape, and claims Jews lie behind modern sexual freedoms he considers degenerate. This again is projection: he projects onto Jews the sins that he and his own milieu are guilty of.

It is hard to miss the irony that Bilzerian's description of Nazi Germany "flourishing" without Jews merges with his praise of those regimes' tightly controlled, repressive approach to sexuality. Like many antisemites, Bilzerian seems to yearn for a world of strict hierarchies—racial and gender hierarchies—where men are unchallenged. He does not promote patriarchy so much as unbridled violence against (and male domination of) women. Jews, in his mind, represent a threat to that order, perhaps because Jewish ethics celebrate the dignity of every person and the sanctity of marital intimacy, rather than the brutality of male conquest.

Whatever the twisted psychological root, Bilzerian's case reinforces a pattern: Those who hate Jews often also glorify sexual aggression, or conversely, they rail against "sexual degeneracy," but indulge in it privately.

The playboy posting orgies on Instagram somehow convinces himself the Jews are the immoral ones—a delusion as big as his ego.

Kanye West (Ye): Hate-Fueled Outbursts and Harassing Behavior

No discussion of modern antisemitism would be complete without Kanye West—now known as Ye—who in 2022–2023 went from world-famous rapper to one of the most vocal antisemites on the planet. Ye's anti-Jewish tirades were shocking in their brazenness: he tweeted that he was going to go "death con 3 on Jewish people" and proceeded to embark on a media tour spouting Holocaust denial and praise for Hitler. These hate-filled outbursts cost Kanye dearly in professional terms—he was swiftly dropped by Adidas, Gap, Balenciaga, and other partners after his antisemitic comments, effectively imploding his business empire.

Yet what garnered fewer headlines (amid the chaos of his anti-Jewish screeds) was Kanye's increasingly disturbing sexual conduct in the workplace, which was documented by former employees. As it turns out, Ye not only hates Jews; for those around him, he has also created a "toxic and chaotic environment," replete with sexual harassment and bullying.

Multiple Yeezy and Adidas staffers came forward to describe Kanye's abusive behavior toward women and boundary-crossing sexual antics. Ye would frequently show pornography—including his own sex tapes—to colleagues during meetings. In one meeting, he even showed a pornographic video to two high-level Adidas executives, ostensibly to make some bizarre point about creative inspiration.

Former employees wrote an open letter stating that Kanye's habit of showing explicit material was "a tactic to break a person down . . . testing and destroying people's boundaries," and noted "a very sick pattern of predatory behavior toward women" under his leadership. Female employees in particular felt targeted by his tirades and sexually charged comments. One young woman recounted that Kanye showed her an explicit photo of his ex-wife Kim Kardashian during a job interview—an intimidation move under the guise of "it's from my wife."

On other occasions, he would hurl "offensive sexual remarks" at women who worked for him, explosively berating them in ways completely unrelated to work. By late 2022, a group of staff had seen enough and urged Adidas to address what they called "the toxic and chaotic environment that Kanye West created," alongside his pattern of "verbal abuse, vulgar tirades, and bullying attacks." In essence, Kanye's unchecked power led him to treat his creative team as captive recipients of his most perverse impulses—a scenario that one might call sexual tyranny.

Kanye West also infamously embarrassed and utterly degraded his current wife, Australian architect and performance artist Bianca Censori. The incident at the 2025 Grammy Awards that generated significant controversy involved Censori wearing a completely see-through dress on the red carpet and being, at Kanye's demand, totally naked.

Censori initially arrived wearing a large black fur coat but removed it to reveal a completely transparent dress with no undergarments, exposing her body, her breasts, and her genitalia, to photographers. Eyewitness accounts and lip-reading experts suggested that West completely orchestrated the display, with a body language expert noting signs of "suppressed fear" and discomfort from Censori during the photo session.

West later defended the controversial look on social media, declaring that his wife was the "most Googled person on the planet" following the stunt and claiming, "We beat the Grammys."

It is no coincidence that someone who acted with such entitlement and cruelty also gravitated to antisemitic conspiracy theories. Kanye himself drew a direct link: As his partnership with Adidas crumbled, he ranted that the company's Jewish executives had betrayed or controlled him. He infamously railed about Jewish people "having too much influence," fell in with white nationalist Nick Fuentes and far-right provocateur Milo Yiannopoulos, and even appeared on Alex Jones's show to declare: "I like Hitler."

This antisemitic meltdown was accompanied by increasingly erratic personal behavior, including Kanye's admission that pornography had "destroyed his family." In late 2022, he announced a self-imposed thirty-day cleanse: "No alcohol. No adult films. No intercourse," seemingly recognizing his own porn addiction and hypersexuality as problems. But rather than seek genuine help, Ye had lashed out, externalizing blame onto Jews. In his conspiratorial worldview, the pornography industry and/or sexual liberation became equated with Jewish influence, echoing classic antisemitic tropes.

The tragedy of Kanye West is that a once-influential Black artist fell prey to the very worst impulses—both personal and ideological.

He leveraged his fame to spread Jew-hatred just as he was inflicting sexual trauma on those around him. One former colleague described Ye's behavior as intended to "establish . . . unwavering allegiance"—he would humiliate and intimidate underlings (for example, by forcing them to watch porn) as a means of control. This mindset of domination and humiliation is the common thread between Kanye's treatment of women and his targeting of Jews. In both cases, he sought to degrade and vilify, perhaps as a way to cope with his own inner turmoil.

But the damage he caused—to individuals he bullied, and to the Jewish community he vilified—is very real. Kanye's story stands as a stark reminder that antisemitism often festers in environments of unchecked abuse. When someone believes they can do anything without consequence, hate finds fertile soil. And when that hate goes public from a celebrity megaphone, it spreads like wildfire, legitimizing the darkest of sentiments others may hold.

Candace Owens: Blood Libels and the War on Kosher Sex

Candace Owens presents yet another facet of the modern antisemitic landscape: the self-styled conservative "moralist" whose obsession with sexual purity masks a deep-seated bigotry.

Owens, a hate-filled right-wing commentator and conspiracy theorist, has a history of not just flirtation with antisemitic rhetoric but outright blood libels—often under the cover of "just asking questions," as she puts it, or pushing back against what she sees as liberal moral decay.

Notably, in 2019, she infamously remarked that Adolf Hitler's only mistake was "going global"—implying that his aims were not objectionable until he tried to conquer Europe. Hitler, to Candace Owens, was righteous so long as he kept his ambitions limited to Germany and nationalism. Remember, this includes justification of Kristallnacht on the night of November 9th, 1938, during which thousands of Jews were murdered and over a thousand synagogues burned to the ground—all while the police and fire brigades were ordered to stand down. This statement, directly downplaying Hitler's evil, drew widespread condemnation and forced Owens to clarify her words.

In late 2022, Owens also repeatedly defended the antisemitic tirades of her friend Kanye West. Rather than denounce Ye's hate, she attacked Jews for criticizing him, accusing Jewish commentators like Ben Shapiro (her then-colleague and boss at *The Daily Wire*) of overreacting. By 2023, Owens had drifted further: She began dabbling in outright Holocaust trivialization, even engaging with Holocaust deniers.

The *Times of Israel* notes that Owens's "journey of punditry" pushed her into Holocaust denial territory. For instance, she amplified social media content that questioned the veracity of well-documented Holocaust accounts and invoked Biblical verses about the "synagogue of Satan" when sparring with Jews online. All this earned Candace Owens a reputation as a rising figure in antisemitic circles, despite her protestations that she simply opposes "globalism" or "censorship." Watchdog organization StopAntisemitism named her 2022's "Antisemite of the Year," citing her growing list of anti-Jewish dog-whistles.

In 2023, I debated Owens on *Piers Morgan Uncensored*. She accused me of being evil and called me the father of the Synagogue of Satan. She humiliated herself when, after I challenged her fraudulent and libelous assertions that the IDF had committed genocide in Gaza, she actually turned to her laptop and started using ChatGPT to debate me on live air. Yes, in her abysmal and conspiratorial, historical ignorance, she humiliated herself irreversibly. Against the cascade of historical facts I threw at her, she had no response, reduced to using the internet on live television. After that humiliation, she has steadfastly refused to debate me again, despite constant invitations from third-party media.

Candace, if you're reading this, the invitation to debate me at any reasonable time or place remains. And you can come with your laptop and ChatGPT and I will arrive with nothing but the internalized Jewish values and knowledge that sustains me.

What truly distinguishes Owens, however, is how fixated she became on Jewish sexuality as a target of ridicule—specifically, my work on "Kosher Sex." This gets personal for me, as I and my family were on the receiving end of Owens's attacks.

By way of background: As a child of divorce who has dedicated his life to strengthening marriage, I have written extensively about healthy, holy sexuality within marriage, including my international bestseller *Kosher Sex* and subsequent works like *Kosher Lust*, *Kosher Adultery*, and *The Kosher Sutra*. My daughter Chana runs a Kosher Sex boutique in Tel Aviv, of which I could not be more proud, that provides intimate counseling as well as lingerie and intimacy enhancement products for married couples seeking to rejuvenate moribund sexuality in marriage—all in keeping with Jewish teachings and Jewish law (*halacha*) that celebrate conjugal intimacy.

To Candace Owens, this was apparently anathema.

In early 2024, she fixated on me and Chana with increasingly unhinged, sexually tinged smears. On March 7, 2024, for example, Owens, who became fixated on attacking me almost daily, suddenly inverted her attacks with the furious tweet: "Rabbi Shmuley and his hag daughter have spent TWO YEARS harassing me . . . I've had enough"—while escalating her public attacks on me to her followers on social media and her podcast. She accused us of "routinely attacking Christians" (I am one of the world's foremost architects of modern bridge-building between Christians and Jews and authored the international best-seller *Kosher Jesus*) and ranted about my "deep hatred" for various groups—a breathtaking example of projection, given her record of vilifying minorities.

Days later, Owens escalated to a blatantly antisemitic and prurient line of attack. She labeled me "the unholy rabbi" and claimed I was "promoting a website that sells vibrators and butt plugs on behalf of his daughter."

This comment is worth unpacking.

Her tone drips with puritanical disgust. She specifically chose lurid words—"vibrators and butt plugs"—to paint the picture of a depraved, perverted rabbi, corrupting others. In reality, the products my daughter's store sells are standard marital and intimacy aids intended for committed couples who long to reignite desire in their marriages. Our message is one of joyful, monogamous intimacy weaning married couples off pornography and infidelity and steering them away from even emotional attachments to outsiders.

But Owens deliberately framed it as something seedy and sacrilegious. Her phrasing "on behalf of his daughter," and previously calling my younger daughter, the world-renowned influencer Rochel Leah Taktuk, a "hag" betray a particular venom toward the idea of a Jewish father and daughter working together on both defending Israel and a sex-positive project that empowers women to respect their bodies and never allow themselves to become a man's plaything. It is as if Candace cannot fathom—or cannot tolerate—the notion that Jewish culture might embrace sexuality within marriage as healthy and sacred. To her, the very term "Kosher Sex" was an oxymoron and a ripe target for scorn.

Owens even stooped to one of the oldest antisemitic tropes in the book: the blood libel.

She "liked" a tweet on X that sneeringly asked if I, Rabbi Shmuley, was "drunk on Christian blood again"—a direct reference to the medieval accusation that Jews ritually murdered Christian children and drank their blood. That Owens would countenance such a vile myth speaks volumes about her degeneracy, idiocy, and indeed lunacy. It shows that, beneath her polished media persona, she harbors or at least encourages the most deranged and damaging anti-Jewish fantasies and is an unhinged and demented Jew-hater.

My response to Owens's onslaught was to call her out as an inveterate antisemite. And indeed, observers across the political spectrum noted that her attacks on me and Chana were steeped in undisguised Jew-hatred.

Piers Morgan, on his show, actually defended my daughter and the Kosher Sex shop, chiding Owens by saying: "Why shouldn't Jewish people be allowed to have sex if they want to use stuff from a sex shop? . . . Sex is wholesome, people. You should try it."

His tone was half-joking, but the point was clear: Owens's insinuation that Jews shouldn't be doing this (or that it's somehow especially dirty because Jews are doing it) is absurd and prejudiced.

Why does Candace Owens obsess over Jewish sexuality? The answer likely lies in her own repressed Victorian and medieval Catholic sensibilities. It speaks volumes about her own intimate relationship with her husband, or lack thereof. Owens peddles an ideology that sex should be purely procreative and that any focus on erotic pleasure—even within marriage—is sinful or shameful.

In fact, I wrote at the time that Owens holds "outdated views that sex is only for procreation and not for marital intimacy," which is why the very concept of Kosher Sex drives her mad. She cannot stand that Judaism, unlike the strain of medieval fundamentalist, Crusade-era Christianity she gravitates toward, affirms passionate intimacy between husband and wife as a mitzvah, a blessing. When she sees a rabbi teaching that "moral, passionate, joyful sex between husband and wife . . . is a celebration of human dignity," as I wrote in *Kosher Sex*, it clashes with her austere and sexually repressed worldview. Rather than reconsider her stance, she opts to attack the messenger—with antisemitic vitriol. In her mind, I became not just a rabbi with whom she disagreed, but "Rabbi Buttplug"; a caricature to be mocked on the basis of my religion's presumed depravity. As for the butt plugs, they're one of thousands of items sold on the Kosher Sex website, amid Owens's obsessions with the product, and I state emphatically, yet again, that I have no issue whatsoever with a husband and wife experimenting with whatever intimate "toy" they wish to, so long as it is done with mutual consent. To all the married couples reading this who have sadly joined the statistics of being the one out of three couples who are now sexually platonic, my advice is this: Try new positions, locations, and yes, even devices, that get you sexually connected without resorting to the degradation of pornography or the sin of infidelity.

Candace Owens's saga illustrates a broader phenomenon: Antisemites are often obsessed with the sexual mores of Jews. They paint Jews as either hyper-debauched corrupters (in the far-right imagination) or, paradoxically, as repressed prudes (in some far-left or Islamist imaginations)—whichever stereotype suits their needs.

In Owens's case, she clearly leaned into the former: the "demented" idea that Jews are out to corrupt Christian sexual ethics. This is why she conflated my critique of her politics with an attack on "Christians" writ large, and why she fixated on the fact that my daughter and I openly speak of sex. It is textbook erotic anti-Judaism: an irrational fixation on Jews and sex. Owens's online fanbase eagerly lapped it up, bombarding my family with sick messages echoing her insults. And Owens, seeing the response, only doubled down. When addressing me, she quoted a New Testament verse (Revelation 3:9) about the "synagogue of Satan"—essentially casting me as a diabolical Jew who only pretends to be godly.

It doesn't get more hateful and anti-Jewish than that.

In the end, Candace Owens was fired by her employer, *The Daily Wire,* after I put immense public pressure on my orthodox Jewish colleague to stop humiliating himself by employing an American Nazi who leverages the platform he gives her to assail and defame his people. I urged Ben to donate the millions of dollars he allegedly accrued from Candace's antisemitism to the widows of IDF soldiers and the victims of October 7. I told him publicly and repeatedly that there would be no blessing in any money *The Daily Wire* made off of Candace's Holocaust denial. True to form, they have since become inveterate enemies, attacking each other relentlessly on social media daily. Yet Candace continues to enjoy a large following, and her brand of sanctimonious, sexually repressed antisemitism is sadly, today, far from an anomaly. What Candace learned from her heroes like Adolf Hitler is that the most surefire way to instant celebrity and success is to become a loudmouth antisemite.

On the contrary, Candace's Jew-hatred sadly resonates with many on the fraudulent Christian far-right who nurse similar anxieties about modern sexual liberation and see Jews as symbolic of everything they fear.

The Tradwife Movement and Antisemitic Undercurrents

Scroll through social media long enough and you will encounter her:

The "tradwife."

The "traditional wife," she dons a linen apron and bakes sourdough bread. She homeschools in a farmhouse kitchen. She submits cheerfully to her husband's authority. She is—she'll insist to you, and millions of others on TikTok—living the life women were *meant* to live; that is, before feminism destroyed everything.

Thus, the tradwife movement offers itself as wholesome rebellion against modern excess.

And some of it, let's be fair, genuinely is—women creating meaning in domesticity, rejecting corporate careerism, choosing family. As is their right to do.

Of course, Judaism too has always honored the home as sacred ground.

But scratch the surface of the movement's ideological infrastructure—its influencers, its podcasts, its recommended reading lists—and you will find, with disturbing regularity, a familiar villain lurking beneath the sourdough, the aprons: the Jew.

In fact, many tradwife influencers and their audiences believe that *feminism was invented by Jews*—Betty Friedan, Gloria Steinem, they'll point to, frothing—to destroy the family.

Many likewise maintain that Jewish media promotes career women *to lower white birth rates.*

The sexual revolution, too, in their eyes, was a Jewish plot to dismantle Christian civilization.

Indeed, not unlike the incels, scores of tradwives consider everything wrong with modern womanhood traceable to a Jewish conspiracy against the home.

Part of this pathology stems from the movement fetishizing a 1950s domestic ideal that never actually existed—an America of spotless kitchens and submissive wives that owes more to television fantasy than to historical reality.

Here lies a deep irony: Orthodox Jewish communities *actually practice* many of the values these influencers claim to champion.

Think about it.

Large families. (My wife Debbie and I are blessed, thank God, with nine children.)

A celebration—not a condemnation—of gender roles.

Marrying young and being fruitful and multiplying.

Deep investment in children's education. Marriages built on covenant rather than convenience. The list goes on and on.

Yet the very communities that embody the tradwife ideal are often the targets of tradwife-adjacent antisemitism. Because the tradwife movement is not really about traditional values, after all. It is a cult of nostalgia—a reminiscence of paradise lost.

But if paradise was lost, then someone, surely, is to blame for that loss.

The tradwife phenomenon demonstrates how sexual politics and antisemitism merge in unexpected places but merge all the same. No, it's not the overt hatred of the street marcher or the podcast extremist. Rather, it constitutes a quiet suspicion—whispered in comments on social media posts, coded in hashtags: *They took something from us.*

They made women want independence.

They destroyed the natural order.

Tucker Carlson: Platforming Hate

If Candace Owens waged a crusade against "the Butt Plug Rabbi" on social media, Tucker Carlson took that crusade to an even larger audience. The former Fox News prime-time host—arguably and sadly one of the most influential conservative voices in America—gave oxygen to Owens's claims and helped legitimize them to millions. In 2025, as part of the Candace vs. Shmuley saga, Tucker devoted a segment of his show to attacking me. By his own description, he cast me as "the evil Jew in America" and gleefully repeated the slur "Rabbi Buttplug" on-air.

The moment was surreal: An anchor who once helmed a major news network was now stooping to childish playground name-calling—in explicitly antisemitic terms—because a Jewish rabbi had dared to challenge a fellow antisemitic right-wing pundit. I could only conclude, as I wrote later, that "this was not an insult. It was a confession." Tucker's on-air taunt revealed more about him (and the movement he represents) than it did about me.

By calling me "Rabbi Buttplug," he signaled to his audience that Jews and sexuality are something to snicker at, that a rabbi who wrote an epoch-defining book on marital sexuality, that saved countless marriages and positively influenced tens of millions of Christians promoting lost marital passion, must be a figure of derision, even hatred. It was a dog whistle for the ages: Look at this Jew with his sex talk—isn't he just the embodiment of evil? Sex is dirty. While my hair may be perfect, the rest of the body is unclean.

It is important to place this in context.

Carlson has long danced around the edges of antisemitic tropes. While he insists he's only against "global elites" or "George Soros" (a frequent target on his show), the narratives he pushes often parallel white nationalist and antisemitic conspiracy theories.

Most notoriously, Carlson became a chief mainstream proponent of the "Great Replacement" theory, warning viewers that "demographic replacement" by Third World immigrants is underway and threatening Western civilization. He rarely said "Jews" explicitly but he didn't need to, and he knew it. The theory's origin (and its champions like Fuentes) center on an alleged Jewish plot to undermine white majorities by importing other ethnic groups.

Carlson gave this theory airtime in over four hundred episodes, according to an analysis, making it a household concept for the American right. White supremacists praised him for it, understanding the subtext exactly.

In November 2025, Carlson brazenly hosted psychotic antisemite and Hitler cheerleader Nick Fuentes for a lengthy interview on his new platform, after being fired like a dog by Fox. This sparked condemnation and split the conservative movement—after all, Fuentes is an open Holocaust denier and proud, if illiterate, antisemite, as documented by the ADL and his widely reported "cookies in the oven" remarks questioning the six-million figure.

But Carlson defended it as free discourse.

The upshot: Carlson has shown a willingness to mainstream antisemitism, whether through coded rhetoric or explicit platforming of bigots.

Equally notable is Carlson's own record on gender and sexuality—a record that provides a clear through-line to his antipathy toward "kosher sex." Years earlier, leaked audio from Carlson's appearances on a shock-jock radio show (circa 2006–2010) revealed his deep-seated misogyny and even apologia for sexual abuse. In those recordings, Carlson says "women are extremely primitive, they're like dogs" who can smell weakness. He opines that underage marriage is not as serious as violent rape, suggesting a sixteen-year-old girl can be married off without it being a big deal.

He calls rape-shield laws "totally unfair" and belittles women who report sexual assault, implying women should just "get up and say what happened" instead of needing anonymity or support. He muses that Hillary Clinton "would castrate you if she could"—a strangely sexualized smear against a powerful woman. He even advises that if you debate a feminist, you should tell her "to be quiet and kind of do what you're told," because "that's what men do." In short, Tucker exhibited textbook sexist contempt and a tolerance for sexual exploitation long before he turned his sights on me or Israel.

This background sheds light on why he eagerly amplified Owens's sexually depraved attacks on me and *Kosher Sex*. Here is a man who clearly has issues with women who speak up, who sees strong women as threats to be metaphorically neutered. Who even defended a polygamous cult leader (Warren Jeffs) that married underage girls. As released by Media Matters, in 2006–2011 call-ins to the Bubba the Love Sponge radio show, Tucker said arranging a marriage between a sixteen-year-old and an older man was not the same as rape.

The idea of a Jewish rabbi—one whom *Newsweek* called "America's Rabbi" and the *Washington Post* dubbed "the most famous Rabbi in America"—teaching people to have mutually satisfying, egalitarian sex would naturally rankle someone like Tucker. In his worldview, sex is about power (notice his focus on castration and dominance in those quotes), and he likely views my perspective that sex can be "holy, disciplined, and joyful" as laughable, subversive, or both.

By labeling me "Rabbi Buttplug," he was not just mocking the use of intimacy aids; he was trying to reduce the entirety of Jewish sexual ethics to something crude and obscene. He also revealed where is mind is often at.

It's an old antisemitic trick: Shrink what you fear or don't understand to a dirty joke. Tucker likely felt that by making *Kosher Sex* a punchline, he was avenging his friend Candace and reasserting his own macho, puritanical bona fides.

Tucker's sneer was, as I said, a confession. It admitted his fear—fear that the Jewish approach to life (which celebrates living fully, loving deeply, and finding sanctity in pleasure) stands opposed to the dour, repressive ideology he favors.

It also perhaps revealed a personal discomfort.

One cannot help but notice an anal fixation in Tucker's insult. My riposte did not miss this: I quipped that no one needs our intimacy aids more than Tucker himself, to help with his "deeply anal sexual repression." Come on. Of thousands of products Chana sells on Kosher.Sex online, he fixates on butt plugs?

Crass as that exchange was, it underscored the point: Those who scream the loudest about others' sexual morals often have deeply unresolved issues of their own.

Indeed, Carlson's infamous unhinged laughter—which he could not even control at his "eulogy" for Charlie Kirk—invites comment. At Kirk's memorial, in front of some eighty thousand people in Arizona, Carlson compared Kirk's Christian evangelism to the story of Jesus arriving in Jerusalem to denounce people in power, and how "hummus eaters"—read, Jews—murdered him.

In his own words:

> "Jesus starts doing the worst thing that you can do, which is telling the truth about people, and they hate it, and they just go bonkers. They hate it, and they become obsessed with making him stop. And I can just sort of picture the scene in a lamp-lit room with a bunch of guys sitting around eating hummus, thinking about what to do about this guy telling the truth about us. We must make him stop talking. And there's always one guy with the bright idea, and I could just hear him say, 'I've got an idea. Why don't we just kill him? That'll shut him up.'"

But Carlson's repetition of the most ancient of blood libels—accusing Jews of deicide—does not even constitute the lowest point of his career.

In September 2024, he hosted Darryl Cooper, an antisemitic joke of a "historian" whom critics have compared to the disgraced Holocaust denier David Irving. During the interview, Cooper claimed that it was not Hitler but, get this, Winston Churchill who was the "chief villain of World War II" and promoted Nazi apologist views and Holocaust denial.

You heard that right. Not Hitler, who shot, gassed, and murdered six million Jews and plunged the world into its most deadly conflict in history—but Churchill, who saved Western civilization, was the true villain.

Whether driven by an urge to control others or insecurity about himself, Carlson projects his vitriol outward as moral crusading. He built a brand as a champion of "family values" even as his off-air words revealed a rather perverse set of values.

So, when he lambastes a rabbi for promoting passionate monogamy, it's worth asking: who is truly on the side of wholesome sexuality here?

In sum, Tucker Carlson used his megaphone to bolster antisemitic narratives under the guise of defending tradition. By hosting extremists like Nick Fuentes, by winking at Great Replacement theory, and by ridiculing Jewish voices like mine advocating joy over repression, Carlson firmly planted himself in the camp of modern antisemites—just with a preppy bow tie on top.

His influence helped meld these ideas into a coherent package for many viewers: Don't trust Jews; they're trying to corrupt your women and weaken your men. It's the same age-old hate, repackaged for prime time. And it perfectly encapsulates how sexual panic and antisemitism go hand in hand among today's far-right leaders.

Matt Gaetz: The Man Who Blamed the Jews for His Own Desire

In December 2025, Matt Gaetz—the utterly depraved and disgraced former Florida congressman who was the subject of a years-long federal investigation into sex trafficking, whose close associate pled guilty to trafficking a child, and about whom the House Ethics Committee found substantial evidence of statutory rape, prostitution, and illicit drug use—went on Tucker Carlson's show and explained who was really responsible for his downfall.

It was the Jews.

Specifically, Gaetz claimed that the allegations against him—paying for sex with a seventeen-year-old girl, the drugs, the Venmo payments to young women—were all part of an Israeli intelligence operation. Its goal? To silence him because of his foreign policy positions.

"It was an op to silence me," Gaetz told Carlson, "and Israel was involved, and I hate to say that."

He did not, in fact, seem to hate saying it at all.

Take that in.

A man accused of the sexual exploitation of a minor—a man whose own associate went to prison for trafficking a child—looked into a camera and declared that the real villains were not his own appetites but a Jewish conspiracy to expose them.

If Wilhelm Reich had invented a case study to illustrate his thesis, he could not have improved on Matt Gaetz.

The Record

It's worth being precise about what Gaetz was accused of and what he did, because precision matters. Especially when the subject himself has made a career of blurring the line between grievance and reality.

In 2021, the *New York Times* reported that Gaetz was under federal investigation for possible sex trafficking violations. His close friend and political ally Joel Greenberg—the former Seminole County Tax Collector—pled guilty to sex trafficking of a child, identity theft, wire fraud, and stalking. The Department of Justice ultimately declined to charge Gaetz himself, citing concerns about witness credibility. Gaetz trumpeted this as exoneration.

It was not.

The House Ethics Committee, in its 2024 report, concluded that there was substantial evidence Gaetz had engaged in prostitution, statutory rape, and illicit drug use. Gaetz resigned from Congress shortly before the Ethics Committee was set to vote on releasing its findings—a move that, whatever its legal rationale, carried the unmistakable scent of a man fleeing the room before the lights came on.

He denied everything. He always has.

And then he found someone to blame.

The Catalog

To understand Gaetz's trajectory toward lecherous antisemitism, it helps to see it as a progression—each step a little further from the mainstream, each incident a little harder to explain away.

In 2018, Gaetz invited Charles C. Johnson as his guest to the State of the Union address. Johnson is a right-wing figure who has publicly denied the Holocaust, having written that he agreed with denier David Cole "about Auschwitz and the gas chambers not being real" and that he never believed the six-million figure, as documented in the Anti-Defamation League's 2018 letter to Gaetz. The ADL condemned the invitation. Gaetz expressed regret for insufficient vetting but denied Johnson was a Holocaust denier. He *then* hosted Johnson again at a fundraiser months later. Repugnant.

In 2018, Gaetz accused George Soros—the Jewish Holocaust survivor who has become the right's preferred avatar of sinister Jewish influence—of personally funding the migrant caravan approaching the southern border. Three days after Soros's foundation publicly rebuked Gaetz for the accusation, a man obsessed with the caravan conspiracy murdered eleven Jews in their synagogue in Pittsburgh—the Tree of Life massacre. This is not to say Gaetz caused the massacre. It is to say he helped contribute to the atmosphere in which it occurred.

In 2024, Gaetz voted against the bipartisan Antisemitism Awareness Act. His reason? The bill classified the claim that Jews killed Jesus as antisemitic—and Gaetz considered this an attack on the Gospel. "The Gospel itself would meet the definition of antisemitism under the terms of this bill!" he wrote. "The Bible is clear. There is no myth or controversy on this." The congressman from the Florida Panhandle planted his flag alongside two thousand years of the oldest antisemitic libel in Western civilization.

As an aside, I should mention that should the former Congressman prove himself literate enough to actually read a factually historical work like this, I am happy to debate him at any reasonable time or place as to whether it was the Romans who murdered Jesus, as the New Testament makes absolutely clear, or the Jews. Gaetz can even prepare by simply watching some of the world-renowned Christian scholars whom I eviscerated on this issue, in front of live audiences of thousands, after the publication of my book *Kosher Jesus*, which deals extensively with the question of who killed Jesus.

And then came 2025 and 2026, when Gaetz—now out of Congress, hosting a show on One America News, competing in the increasingly crowded marketplace for right-wing outrage—abandoned any remaining pretense.

In December 2025, the interview with Carlson: The sex trafficking allegations were an Israeli intelligence operation. Antisemitism, Gaetz explained, "used to mean somebody who didn't like Jews. Now it just means somebody Jews don't like."

Then, in January 2026, Gaetz devoted a segment of his show to promoting a conspiracy theory about wildfires raging in Argentina's Patagonia region. The claim—already debunked by Argentine fact-checkers, disavowed by the radio host who originally spread it, and condemned by Argentina's own president—held that Israeli agents were deliberately setting fires to cheapen the land and establish a "new Jewish ethnostate in the Americas." The conspiracy was a modern revival of the Andinia Plan, a fabrication rooted in Tsarist-era antisemitic propaganda, recycled by Argentine neo-Nazis in the 1970s. Argentina's military dictatorship used the conspiracy theory as a pretext to arrest and torture Jewish prisoners for information about nonexistent Israeli invasion plans.

Gaetz, teasing the segment on social media, framed it as a question: "Are these intentional fires in Argentina part of a globalist master plan to create a new Jewish ethnostate in the Americas?"

He knew what he was doing.

The Pattern

Now step back.

A man accused of paying for sex with a minor child. A man whose political ally is in prison for trafficking a child. Whose own Congress found substantial evidence of statutory rape, prostitution, and drug use.

Who cannot—by the institutional verdict of his own colleagues—govern his sexual appetites.

And this man, confronted with the wreckage of his own conduct, reaches for the oldest script in the Western world: it was the Jews.

The Jews orchestrated his downfall, of course. The Jews silence critics. They burn forests to steal land. They murdered Christ.

The Jews, the Jews, the Jews.

Gaetz is not Sayyid Qutb. He is not an ideologue tortured by desire he cannot name. Nor does he have even a thousandth of Qutb's intelligence, however diabolical. He is something both simpler and, in its way, more revealing: an opportunist whose opportunities keep leading him to the same destination. Every time he needs someone to blame—for the caravan, for the culture, for the investigation into his own behavior with a teenage girl—he finds the Jew.

This is not sophisticated antisemitism. Nor is it the product of deep reading or wounded ideology. It is something more instinctive, more pathological.

It is the reflex identified by Adorno and documented in this book: the authoritarian personality projecting outward what it cannot integrate inward. But then, no one ever accused Gaetz of being the brightest bulb on the Christmas tree.

A man who cannot account for his own appetites aligns himself, again and again, with movements that blame Jews for *the existence of appetite itself.* A man under investigation for the sexual exploitation of a minor declares—on camera, to millions—that the real crime was committed by Israel.

The projection is so transparent that, if it weren't dangerous, it would be comical.

And this is arguably the most important point: Gaetz is no aberration. He is a specimen. He represents the intersection of sexual scandal and antisemitic conspiracy in twenty-first-century America. Not in the grand, operatic mode of a Qutb or a Reich case study, but in the grubby, Venmo-and-hotel-rooms register of a man whose reach exceeds his depth—but whose instincts are ancient all the same.

He may not have read the *Protocols of the Elders of Zion.*

But he doesn't need to.

The pattern is encoded in the culture, anyway—and available to anyone who craves an explanation for his own failures. *Any explanation, that is, that doesn't require looking in the mirror.*

Ilhan Omar: Antisemitism by Insinuation

The worst antisemitism, of course, emanated not from the emerging alt-right MAGA extremists, but from the Islamists, who have desecrated Islam, a great world religion, and focused their ire on Jews for generations. Nearly every Islamist I ever debated, and nearly all of whom are wretchedly antisemitic, are not even aware that the Prophet Muhammad had a Jewish wife, Safiyya bint Huyayy.

It lies beyond the scope of this book to fully detail the utterly disgusting tropes—especially sexual—that the Islamists inveigh against Jews, whom they call "monkeys" and "beasts." But let us suffice with just a single example, as she is, remarkably, an actual member of the United States Congress.

Ilhan Omar represents a different but equally dangerous strain of modern antisemitism: the antisemitism of insinuation. It does not shout slurs or wave flags. It suggests. It frames Jews not as inferior but as controlling—and it does so through the most timeworn trope of all: money.

Antisemitism doesn't always shout "Jews." Sometimes it whispers "money"—and expects you to fill in the rest.

Thankfully, when Omar tweeted, "It's all about the Benjamins baby," referring to hundred-dollar bills as the foundation for support for Israel and suggesting AIPAC owns Congress, the backlash was swift and bipartisan. Democratic leadership publicly rebuked her. Jewish organizations across the political spectrum called it out for what it was: the resurrection of a classic antisemitic stereotype straight from the Protocols of the Elders of Zion—that Jewish political participation is fundamentally purchased and is geared toward world domination.

When Jewish political engagement is reduced to "the Benjamins," it isn't policy critique. It's a stereotype with a beat.

Omar later apologized, acknowledging the harm. But apologies do not erase the damage, because the damage surpassed mere intent—it was activation. That single phrase activated centuries of suspicion portraying Jews as hidden financiers pulling the strings of power, buying rather than earning influence.

This is how antisemitism survives in polite society. It cloaks itself in the language of justice, activism, and critique, while smuggling in ethnic suspicion. It is antisemitism with plausible deniability.

Modern antisemitism rarely arrives with torches. It arrives with talking points—and a wink.

Omar's rhetoric matters precisely because it normalized this framing within progressive discourse. You can debate lobbying. You can debate Israeli policy. But when the conversation slides from policy to Benjamins, from advocacy to cash control, the line has been crossed.

At the same time, Omar's personal life became a recurring feature of political controversy—illustrating how sexual scandal and moral posturing often coexist with antisemitic rhetoric. In August 2019, a divorce filing by Beth Mynett alleged that her husband, political consultant Tim Mynett, was having a romantic relationship with Omar; she later married him. While the Federal Election Commission found no wrongdoing in related campaign payments, the episode became part of her public narrative.

In modern politics, scandal is often treated as proof of victimhood—not a call for accountability.

This matters not because private lives should be policed, but because moral absolutism is often selectively applied. Movements that speak endlessly about justice and ethics can become strangely forgiving when the behavior belongs to one of their own—while remaining quick to demonize ideological opponents, especially Jews.

Tribal politics forgives anything on "our side"—while demanding purity from everyone else.

The responsible lesson here is not to repeat unproven claims, but to observe how innuendo and insinuation function as tools of power. Antisemitism thrives on exactly this terrain—half-said accusations, coded language, and the insistence that nothing offensive was really meant.

So let us remember: Devoutly "religious" Ilhan Omar, who weaponizes her Islamist observance as a political virtue against enemies she perennially derides as immoral, was having an affair with a married man!

It's a perfect mirror to the patterns you see with figures like Fuentes and Carlson: One side cloaks antisemitism in moral posturing while turning a blind eye to personal hypocrisy, and the other side exploits every scandal for tribal point-scoring. This is the same antisemitism fueled by sexual scandal deriving from a different ideological flank: moral posturing on the surface, tribal hypocrisy beneath, and the ever-present use of antisemitic tropes to fuel outrage.

In other words, Omar's story plugs right into the same architecture: on the far right, you get pornographic sneers and sexual humiliation of Jews; on the progressive left, you get coded insinuations and moral hypocrisy.

Same old poison, different label.

It requires only a microphone, a slogan, and an audience willing to pretend they're hearing a new tune. It's an old song—the same song—whether it's pretending to be "activism" on the left or "just asking questions" on the right.

Mohammed Hijab: The Sex-Obsessed Islamist

Some antisemites cloak their hatred in the language of geopolitics. Others dress it in theology—or in economics. Often, lately, they costume it in the rhetoric of "decolonization."

And then there is Mohammed Hijab.

Hijab—born Mohammed Hegab in London in 1991 to Egyptian immigrant parents—is, by any objective measure, the most influential Islamist antisemite in Britain today.

He broadcasts to over 1.28 million subscribers on YouTube, sports over eight hundred thousand followers on Instagram, and nearly half a million more on X. Hijab also holds multiple degrees.

Having debated the likes of Noam Chomsky and Jordan Peterson, Hijab befriended Andrew Tate following Tate's conversion to Islam. And he debated me on Piers Morgan's show in November 2023—one of the ugliest hours of my public life, and I do not say that lightly.

That debate illuminated something this book argues from its first pages: the erotic engine does not merely run beneath antisemitism like a hidden current; it is often the engine itself, roaring in plain sight—even when the man operating it insists he's making some geopolitical argument.

Hijab's biography, on an extremely superficial read, appears precisely the kind of story Western liberals celebrate: the son of immigrants earning his way into elite institutions, engaging with ideas across religious lines, debating rather than dismissing.

The Campaign Against Antisemitism, however, has compiled a comprehensive dossier on what rots beneath that surface. Harvard Islamic studies scholar Javed Hashmi has identified Hijab as part of a cohort he calls the "akh right bros"—Muslim male influencers positioning themselves as defenders of Islamic tradition while adopting the aggression, dominance-posturing, and contempt for women characterizing the Western "manosphere."

It's a combination as combustible as it sounds.

The Debate on Piers Morgan

Morgan had brought us together to discuss the Israel–Hamas war in the aftermath of October 7—the largest massacre of Jews since the Holocaust.

Within minutes, any pretense of geopolitical discourse collapsed.

Hijab refused to shake my hand. He also refused to call Hamas a terrorist organization—suggesting, when pressed, that labeling Hamas terrorists would require labeling the IDF terrorists, too. He called Winston Churchill a war criminal for the bombing of Dresden, but, when Morgan challenged him, could not cite a single figure for German civilian casualties.

So, Morgan told him flatly: "You don't actually know what you're talking about."

And then—and this is what I want to emphasize, because it is the most diagnostically revealing moment of the encounter—when the pressure intensified, when he was cornered with Hamas's documented rape and murder of Jewish women, the beheading of Jewish children, Hijab changed the subject.

Not to international law. Not to Palestinian casualty statistics. Not to theology.

To sex.

Hijab declared on live television, before millions of viewers, that I was "more slippery than the lubricants that he sells in his daughter's sex shop."

Then he taunted, repeatedly: "You sell dildos, don't you? You sell dildos, don't you?" Followed by—and I am not embellishing—announcing to the international audience that he believed I had "one of his daughter's vibrators" in my pocket.

This was his argument, faced with the fact of Hamas's brutality. This was his contribution to a discussion about mass murder.

I laughed. I told him to get his head out of the Jewish bedroom. I called him a bully and a coward—both accurate.

What I want to add now, benefiting from the analytical distance a shouting match on live television does not permit, is this:

What Hijab did in that moment was the oldest move in the antisemitic playbook. And it was performed in real time, in front of millions, by a man with enough academic credentials to know exactly what he was doing.

The argument had beaten him. So he went for the Jewish body.

After the Debate: Threatening My Son

If the debate itself was ugly, the aftermath made it look pretty in comparison.

During the broadcast, Hijab turned to face me and said—of my son Mendy, who serves as a soldier in the Israel Defense Forces—that he could be "returned in a black bag."

I told him what he and antisemites should know: *Jews do not cower*. I meant it.

After the debate concluded, Hijab went on X and posted a message about Mendy that Breitbart and other outlets reported as wishing for his death.

I reported the matter to U.S. authorities and consulted an attorney about bringing it to the Metropolitan Police's hate task force.

Do not mistake this for the behavior of an intellectual engaging in robust debate. It's a grown man threatening the life of a soldier who is also somebody's son—my son—because he could not win an argument on television.

And yet this man was described, in a BBC antisemitism documentary the same year, as a potential voice for coexistence.

The Campaign Against Antisemitism responded to that with appropriate outrage:

"It is astonishing that the BBC has tried to portray this man as some kind of champion of coexistence."

The Jewish Chronicle, meanwhile, accused the BBC of choosing to "lie and pick a fight with Jews."

Hijab's own response to being labeled antisemitic? To post on X: "Being labelled anti-semitic by a Zionist is a badge of honour."

So, when a Zionist calls him a Jew-hater, that's a badge of honor. His words, not mine. This is the measure of his contempt for Jewish life.

Golders Green, Shabbat, and the Art of Incitement

In May 2021, Hijab and two fellow YouTubers descended on Golders Green—one of the most densely Jewish neighborhoods in London, an area synonymous with Jewish life—on a Saturday.

On Shabbat.

They brought a van with an LED billboard displaying Holocaust images alongside images from the Gaza War, bearing the question: "Did we not learn from the Holocaust?"

They then filmed themselves approaching observant Jews on the street—Jews in Shabbat clothing, walking to synagogue—and demanding that each one condemn Israeli military operations. When Jewish members of the public refused to engage, Hijab and his companions grew more aggressive.

Upon the arrival of police, one of the YouTubers approached an officer and asked: "What's the reason you came so fast—has there been kids blown up by bombs by Israel?"

The Community Security Trust described the stunt as "a disgusting and seemingly deliberate act of incitement." The incident was understandably reported to a hate crime unit.

The CST noted:

"It's the equivalent of Britain First going to Newham or Tower Hamlets and confronting Muslims on the streets there."

Later, at a separate rally, Hijab was captured on video at an event where chants of "We'll find some Jews" and "We want their blood" were heard from the crowd. Video of the scene was shared by Henry Jackson Society writer Wasiq Wasiq. Hijab's presence at and leadership of such events is documented. His relationship to those particular chants remains his to account for.

Hijab went to court over a related incident—his defamation suit against journalist Douglas Murray and *The Spectator*, which Hijab brought and lost in August 2025. The defense asked him whether "turning up on a Jewish Sabbath with those images was very confrontational."

His reply: "Yes."

The judge found that Hijab had lied on significant issues—his evidence, the court ruled, was "overall worthless"—and dismissed the case, finding Murray's characterization of him substantially true.

But a court verdict, however damning, did not slow him. He puts his agenda in the open, for all to see.

For example, at an earlier rally outside the Israeli embassy in Kensington, Hijab was filmed declaring to a crowd:

"We believe that life begins at death. We don't care about death. We love death."

We love death.

Classic jihadi rhetoric—as redolent of terrorism as any statement can be.

And it's no philosophical proposition. It's no theology. It is the precise negation of everything Judaism has ever taught about the sanctity of life—about choosing life and sanctifying the body. About the proper understanding of desire as sacred when bounded by covenant.

And yet this same man—the one who publicly loves death—cannot stop bringing up sex the moment Jews confront him on television.

The connection is not a mere correlation. *The connection is everything.*

"Pedophilia Is Relative"

There is a dimension of Hijab's record that mainstream coverage consistently underreports, and which this book cannot in good conscience leave unexamined, because it is directly relevant to the book's central argument.

B'nai Brith Canada, in its January 2025 formal call for the Burlington Convention Centre to cancel Hijab's appearance, documented that he had stated—in his own words—that "pedophilia is very relative," and had argued that being intimate with a thirteen- or fourteen-year-old girl with, and I am quoting the documented language, "huge hips and huge breasts" would not cause harm.

Critics have documented how, in a livestream with the social media figure Sneako—himself an associate of neo-Nazi Nick Fuentes—Hijab stated that a strict reading of Surah 65:4 of the Quran, without contextual interpretation, would lead one to what he termed "a severe type of pedophilia." Meaning, the position that a girl can be contracted in marriage at any age, including infancy. His phrasing was explicit.

He was not condemning the position; he was describing it with an equanimity that rings of endorsement.

What does this have to do with antisemitism?

Everything.

The man who cannot protect children from sexual exploitation is the same man who told a television audience that October 7—when Hamas men raped Jewish women and beheaded Jewish children—was morally equivalent to Israeli military policy. The moral framework that relativizes the violation of children relativizes the violation of Jewish women.

These are not two separate pathologies.

The Misyar Marriage Scandal: Sex Without Covenant

In April 2025, a woman identifying herself as "Sister Aisha" published a detailed account—with WhatsApp screenshots—on the website Behind Veils (behindveils.com), alleging that Mohammed Hijab had manipulated her into a Nikah Misyar—an Islamic marriage contract in which the woman waives her rights to cohabitation and financial support from her husband.

The allegations, which Hijab denies, are worth examining in detail, because they constitute—if true—a precise illustration of this book's thesis.

According to Sister Aisha's documented testimony: Hijab refused to show his face to her father during the ceremony, which was conducted via Zoom with anonymous witnesses. He would not permit her father to see who he was marrying his daughter to. After the marriage was consummated, Hijab announced that the union would be, in his words, "strictly confined to hotel rooms." He declared he had no intention of providing financially for her or her daughter. He told her, explicitly, that he only wanted a "sex marriage"—not a traditional marriage with its attendant duties and rights. When she requested the full marital rights that Islamic law entitles a wife to, he divorced her.

She later alleged she was ignored when she raised her grievances to people in Hijab's orbit.

Hijab's response on X was: "A sister recently made a false allegation against me. It has been addressed."

It was, notably, not addressed with any specificity.

The judge in the Murray defamation case—the case Hijab brought and lost—noted in his findings that Hijab "has also come under online scrutiny after accusations surfaced that he manipulated and tricked a woman into a Nikah Misyar."

What makes this more than merely a personal scandal—what makes it a case study for this book—is what was already on the public record before Sister Aisha came forward.

Hijab had advocated publicly for Misyar marriages. He had argued in YouTube videos for what he called "one-minute nikkahs on Zoom." He had discussed, on camera with fellow YouTuber Ali Dawah, whether a man could take a secret second wife and lie to his first wife about it—and cited hadith to suggest this was permissible.

So: a man who preaches Islamic purity and modesty. Who positions himself as a guardian of sexual ethics against Western degeneracy. Who went on Piers Morgan to sneer at a rabbi's support for marital intimacy.

This same man allegedly used an Islamic legal mechanism—specifically employed to give men sex without commitment—to enter a marriage conducted in secret, consummated in a hotel room, terminated the moment his "wife" asked for her rights.

Calling a Jewish Lawyer a Deviant on Live Television

In October 2024, Hijab appeared again on Piers Morgan's show, this time alongside Alan Dershowitz, the celebrated Harvard Law professor and one of the great civil liberties attorneys of the twentieth century. Dershowitz also happens, as Hijab well knew, to be Jewish. Both were there to discuss Israel and the war in Gaza.

Hijab's contribution to that discussion?

To call Dershowitz, on live international television, "an old pervert."

Hijab's unacceptable rationale, of course, stemmed from the fact that Dershowitz had once legally represented convicted sex trafficker Jeffrey Epstein. Accusing a defense attorney of a crime their client was convicted of is low and predictable—but not too low or predictable for Hijab.

Dershowitz subsequently announced he would pursue defamation claims in both U.S. and U.K. courts.

"Pervert."

Let's consider Hijab once again, from a bird's eye view.

This is a man documented defending child marriage, allegedly using Islamic legal mechanism to obtain sex from a woman while hiding his identity.

This is a man who made comments critics described as threatening toward the wives of Jewish public figures, including Ben Shapiro's wife. A man who even discussed golden showers and sexual gimping on live streams.

This was the person libeling another as a pervert.

Psychologists term this "projection."

Another term for it is antisemitism.

Nearly always—and especially in Hijab's case—they're one and the same.

After all, Wilhelm Reich, whose work haunts this volume, identified the authoritarian personality as one that suppresses desire publicly while indulging it privately. The would-be authoritarian then projects their own sexuality outward—onto the designated enemy. This way, the enemy's supposed sexual depravity becomes a screen onto which the authoritarian broadcasts his own unresolved desires.

So the inquisitor, the fascist, the Islamist, accuse, expose, and shame. All while, in private, doing exactly what they condemn.

Mohammed Hijab is not a subtle case. *He is the case.*

Judith Butler, Queers for Palestine, and the Betrayal of the Body

It's one of the strangest phenomena of the modern era: the spectacle of queer activists marching in solidarity with movements that would literally execute them.

"Queers for Palestine" has become a fixture at anti-Israel demonstrations on college campuses—and in city streets across the West. The irony is unsubtle: Hamas criminalizes homosexuality and exposes gay men to unspeakable brutality. The Palestinian Authority persecutes gay men. Iran hangs them from cranes in town squares. LGBTQ Palestinians who can escape often flee to Israel—the only country in the Middle East where they can live openly and safely.

Yet on campuses across the West, on Manhattan avenues and down London thoroughfares, the signs wave. The chants drone on.

And the intellectual godmother of this movement—Judith Butler, the celebrated gender theorist at UC Berkeley—supplies the academic scaffolding, the veneer of legitimacy.

While it might be difficult to believe, Butler has defended Hamas as a "social movement"—one "part of a global left." And in the wake of October 7, Butler minimized, qualified, and contextualized Hamas's atrocities—including the documented rape and sexual mutilation of Israeli women. Doing so effectively denied the victims their suffering.

Perversely, when confronted with evidence of systematic sexual violence—evidence gathered by the *New York Times*, by lawyers, doctors, NGOs, and journalists, all of whom testified to genital mutilation, to women paraded naked through streets, to bodies violated beyond recognition—the response from Butler and like-minded academics was not outrage but theory:

They deigned to opine from their ivory tower: *Let us consider the context. Let us interrogate the narrative. Let us question the framing.*

Whether or not there is documentation, Butler mused. Whether or not. As if the broken bodies of Jewish women constituted a proposition to be debated at a seminar rather than an atrocity to be mourned and condemned.

This is especially appalling because Judith Butler built her entire career on the politics of the body.

She is, to put it plainly, the most influential gender theorist alive. Her 1990 book *Gender Trouble: Feminism and the Subversion of Identity* did not merely contribute to feminist and queer scholarship—it rewrote the field's operating system.

The book's thesis—stripped of its famously impenetrable prose—was fundamentally an argument about *the body as the central battleground of political power.*

Butler claimed that gender is not an interior essence but something inscribed onto the body through culturally enforced repetition: the way you walk, speak, dress, carry yourself through the world. Society doesn't merely describe bodies as male or female—it disciplines them into those categories, policing the boundaries with shame, violence, and exclusion.

The body, in Butler's framework, is not incidental to politics. *The body is where politics happens.* It is the surface on which power writes its demands—and the site, she insists, from which the oppressed can resist.

This was the revolutionary core of her work: that the regulation of bodies is not a side effect of political power but its primary mechanism.

Her follow-up, *Bodies That Matter* (1993)—note the title—made the stakes even more explicit. Butler argued that the very question of which bodies *count*, which bodies are recognized as fully real and human, is itself a political act. To render a body abject—unreal, ungrievable, beneath consideration—is to lay the groundwork for its violation.

First you define certain bodies as outside the circle of the fully human. Then the violence follows, because it is no longer violence against *a person*. It is merely something that happened to a body that didn't matter.

This is the intellectual tradition that gave rise to queer theory. This is the framework that taught an entire generation of scholars to pay attention to *which bodies are disciplined, which are celebrated, and which are erased.* Butler's entire career has been a sustained argument that *the body is sacrosanct as a political category*—that to ignore the suffering of a body, to look away from its violation, to refuse it recognition, is to participate in the system of power that made that violation possible.

She even wrote a book called *Precarious Life* (2004), in which she asked the question that should haunt her now: *Whose lives are grievable?*

Which deaths does a society recognize as losses, and which does it treat as non-events? Butler argued that the failure to grieve certain lives—to acknowledge certain bodies as fully human—is not merely callous. *It is the precondition for the violence that destroys them.* First you make a people ungrievable.

Then you make them dead.

Whose lives are grievable, Professor Butler?

Apparently not Jewish ones.

Because when Jewish women's bodies were raped, mutilated, and paraded through the streets of Gaza—when the evidence arrived, documented and undeniable, of precisely the kind of gendered, sexualized political violence that Butler has spent thirty-five years theorizing—she could not bring herself to simply say:

This is evil. This is wrong. I object.

Instead: context. Framing. The passive voice. The academic hedge. The quiet suggestion that perhaps the documentation requires further scrutiny—a scrutiny she has never once applied to any other claim of sexual violence against any other population on earth.

The broader campus phenomenon disturbs equally. A generation of students steeped in gender theory, trauma-informed pedagogy, and the sacredness of "lived experience" suddenly discovered that none of these principles applied to Jews.

"Believe all women"—*unless the women are Israeli.*

"Center the marginalized"—*unless the marginalized are Jewish.*

"The body is politically sacrosanct"—unless the body is a Jewish woman's, in which case: *contest the narrative.*

Here lies the left-wing variant of the erotic engine. Unlike the right, which shrieks unendingly about so-called Jewish sexual depravity, the left-wing branch simply erases Jewish sexual suffering altogether.

By rendering Jewish pain inadmissible and invisible, the leftist erotic engine performs a different but equally savage dehumanization. It treats the rape of Jewish women as a meaningless footnote to a larger political and historical arc—the implication being, of course, that the rape of Jewish women is deserved, or at least insufficiently interesting to merit condemnation. It subordinates the bodies, lives, dignity, and freedom of Jewish victims to the ideological slaughterhouse of the "right side of history."

And here is the perversity that Reich, Adorno, and Arendt would have recognized instantly: The very framework designed to protect vulnerable bodies—Butler's framework, the framework of performativity and precarious life and the political significance of flesh—becomes the instrument of their erasure. The theory built to make invisible bodies visible is deployed to make Jewish bodies invisible again.

Nonetheless, it should be said that the students marching under "Queers for Palestine" banners are not, most of them, consciously antisemitic. They are products of an education. They learned their principles from syllabi and seminars. They were taught by academics like Butler that certain bodies matter and certain forms of violence demand attention—and they absorbed, through the structuring silences of that same education, that *Jewish bodies do not qualify.*

Butler herself is Jewish. Born to a family of Hungarian-Jewish and Russian-Jewish descent, she grew up in a practicing household. Most of her maternal grandmother's family was murdered in the Holocaust. She holds the Hannah Arendt Chair at the European Graduate School—named for the very thinker who warned that rendering people "superfluous" is the first step toward destroying them.

The irony does not require commentary. It requires only acknowledgment—and perhaps, for those who still believe that intellectual honesty matters, grief.

Because the framework Butler and her disciples have constructed, however sophisticated its academic packaging, eventuates the same result as the medieval blood libel*: the dehumanized Jew.*

The Jew whose pain is unreal. The Jew whose suffering is an inconvenience to the narrative. The Jew whose body, violated and desecrated, does not register on the instruments designed—by Butler's own hand—to detect precisely this kind of violation.

Different vocabulary. *Same perverted outcome.*

A Global Pattern of Repression and Projection

The examples above might seem like a rogues' gallery of disparate figures: an online hustler, a neo-fascist youth, a playboy, a rapper, a pundit, a TV host, a congresswoman, among others.

But an underlying psychology unifies them.

Each in their own way demonstrates how extremist hatred of Jews deeply intertwines with twisted sexual attitudes. Nor is this pattern limited to one country or subculture; it is global, cutting across different ideological causes.

Whether it's the far-right Christian nationalist or the radical Islamist militant, a common denominator emerges: obsession with controlling sexuality, especially women's sexuality, and a parallel obsession with vilifying Jews.

The pattern couldn't be clearer: Antisemitism and sexual pathology feed off each other. Those who hate Jews often do so in part because they cannot deal with some aspect of human sexuality or gender relations, and so they demonize Jews as the symbol of whatever it is they fear—be it women's liberation, sexual expression, or simply joy.

Conversely, those who abuse or fear women often find antisemitic tropes readily available as a grand theory to explain why the world isn't the orderly patriarchal paradise they wish it to be. It's "the Jews' fault," they tell themselves, that women demand equality or that sexual temptation exists. This toxic mentality has real-world consequences, from broken relationships and personal misery to harassment, violence, and even mass murder.

In confronting modern antisemitism, therefore, we must recognize this insidious erotic undercurrent. It is not just a battle of ideas about Israel or banking or history—it is also, on a fundamental level, a battle about life and love. The antisemite despises the vibrancy and intimacy that Jewish culture (at its best) exemplifies. They prefer a world of stark hierarchies, whether it's male over female, or one race over another, or one religion over others.

By shining a light on their sexual perversions and misconduct, as we have in this chapter, we expose their hypocrisy and insecurity. We see that the "butt-plug" rabbi was never the problem; the problem lies with those so devoid of joy and empathy that their heads languish in devices like butt plugs, or whoever may be more sexually adventurous than they are, lashing out at a Rabbi whose religion teaches him that sex in in marriage is the highest form of knowledge, as in "and Abraham came to know his wife Sara." Antisemitic sexual deviants—and as we're discovering the terms are interchangeable—live in constant envy of those who find human dignity through healthy sex.

The ultimate irony is that while these antisemites claim Jews are degenerating society, it is often they themselves who inflict degradation—through rape, harassment, abuse, and the spread of hateful lies. In unmasking them, we do more than defend Jews; we defend the very idea that love, equality, and pleasure can coexist with faith, morality, and order. That idea is at the heart of the Jewish view of humanity. And it is an idea that terrifies the modern antisemite to his core—for if people cease to fear joy, they will certainly cease to heed the apostles of hate.

The Sexual Signature of the Bigot

Here's a rule: When someone becomes obsessed with controlling other people's sex lives, you are not dealing with a stable moral mind. You are dealing with an insecure and repressed one.

Everywhere you find organized hatred, you find sexual pathology nearby.

Not always in the same form. Sometimes it's puritanism—panic at desire, fear of women, terror of lust, repression masquerading as righteousness. Sometimes it's pornographic excess—using bodies as disposable entertainment, stripping sex of tenderness, reducing intimacy to domination. But both extremes share the same spiritual sickness: the inability to integrate desire into dignity.

Healthy sexuality says:

"I desire; therefore, I must be responsible."

"I long; therefore, I must be loyal."

"I want; therefore, I must be honorable."

Pathological sexuality says:

"I desire; therefore, someone must be punished."

"I long; therefore, someone must be controlled."

"I want; therefore, someone must be shamed."

Antisemites almost always live in the second category. That's why they can't stop talking about Jews as sexual corrupters, sexual predators, sexual deviants, sexual manipulators. That's why so much of their mind is focused on butt plugs. That's why they invent fantasies about Jewish men "stealing" women. That's why they accuse Jewish culture of poisoning the purity of their society.

Here are just a few examples:

- Adolf Hitler wrote in *Mein Kampf*: "With satanic joy in his face, the black-haired Jewish youth lurks in wait for the unsuspecting girl whom he defiles with his blood, thus stealing her from her people. With every means he tries to destroy the racial foundations of the people he has set out to subjugate."

- Julius Streicher, publisher of the virulently antisemitic newspaper *Der Stürmer*, is quoted as proclaiming: "Every German girl who even once gives herself to a Jew is lost forever to the German people." Propaganda materials from his publication used caricatures and inflammatory language to constantly warn against this perceived danger.
- Nazi Propaganda materials for teachers reinforced this message, stating that: "A woman defiled by the Jew can never rid her body of the foreign poison she has absorbed. She is lost to her people." The material emphasized that "Racial defilement is racial death. Racial defilement is bloodless murder."
- The Nuremberg Laws (1935): These laws officially criminalized sexual relations and marriage between Jews and "Aryans" to prevent what the Nazis termed "race defilement."
- Visual Propaganda: Magazines like *Der Stürmer* routinely published cartoons showing Jewish men as grotesque figures preying on blonde "Aryan" maidens to provoke "cultural anxiety" and emasculate German men by suggesting they could not protect their women.

Their hatred is not rational. It is eroticized. *It is a kind of arousal—dark, resentful, humiliating—directed into violence.* And that is exactly why it is so dangerous.

CHAPTER FOUR

THE JEWISH BODY IS NOT THE ENEMY

Judaism's Revolt Against Repression

Most people believe that Judaism's most important contribution to world civilization was monotheism, with Abraham as its father. That is true. But I would argue that an even more enduring contribution was Judaism's emphasis on the holiness of the body and the sanctity of life.

Before Judaism humankind's highest aspiration was the afterlife. The Pharaohs spent their lives building huge pyramids that would serve as their tomb for an eternal afterlife. They stuffed it with gold and jewels, the most famous example being that of King Tut, discovered by British explorers in 1922.

Christianity embraced that *weltanschauung* (worldview) and still does this very day. Live a virtuous, yet ephemeral life in this world so that you can inherit Paradise in the next.

The soul is eternal. The body is a festive meal for worms.

And the Islamists? Blow yourself to smithereens and you get a bordello in heaven with seventy virgins, which is kind of sick when you think about it. Sex for death and death that leads to sex.

Hamas, Israel's most sworn enemy, is nothing if not a bloodthirsty culture of death.

In 2014, at the height of Israel's third war in Gaza, Operation Protective Edge, I took out a full-page ad in the *New York Times* with my hero and mentor, Elie Wiesel, the Nobel Peace Laureate and most famous survivor of the Holocaust.

In a massive advertising campaign organized by our World Values Network, Wiesel condemned the terrorists of Hamas for using children as human shields—a perverse art they would develop in the later and far more serious war following the October 7 massacre.

In stirring advertisements also appearing in other national publications, Wiesel invoked the story of Abraham and the sacrifice of Isaac to frame the modern conflict between Israel and Hamas.

Elie stated that, though Abraham lifted his knife to sacrifice his own son Isaac, God's own command stayed Abraham's hand, thereby rejecting child sacrifice forever. Death is not a virtue, in other words, but a sin. The body—not an abomination, but a sacrament.

Wiesel added that, "Jews rejected child sacrifice 3500 years ago. Now it's Hamas' turn." He further argued that while the suffering of those in Gaza is immense and a true tragedy, the blame lies squarely and solely with Hamas, who use children as human shields and store rockets and ammunition in nurseries, schools, hospitals, and family homes.

For Hamas and the Islamists, life is expendable because martyrdom and the desecration of the body for a higher, more spiritual end is life's primary goal.

I told the media:

> "Our purpose is to bring one of the greatest moral voices of our time and one of the most respected human beings alive, who bore witness to the atrocities of genocide and the Holocaust, to respond to the ugly and fraudulent criticisms of Israel and call for an end to the genocidal aspirations of Hamas."

I added,

> "Hamas' charter is clear—they seek the annihilation of the State of Israel and the murder of Jews wherever they may be found. Not

> only is it unreasonable to ask Israel not to defend itself against rockets launched and tunnels dug by Hamas with the intent to destroy, it is also deeply immoral. If Israel did not resist the terrorists of Hamas, it would be guilty of contempt for the lives of its own citizens. We all lament the loss of Palestinian life brought about by the murderous Hamas regime. This is especially true of the children. That is why we have produced this advertising campaign with Elie Wiesel, to stop the terrorist cowards of Hamas from hiding behind innocent children and pregnant women."

The ad campaign included full page ads in leading American publications including: *The Washington Post*, *The New York Times*, *The Wall Street Journal*, *The Chicago Tribune*, *The Los Angeles Times*, *The Miami Herald*, as well as an extensive social media campaign.

I concluded:

> "Our organization seeks to promote universal Jewish values and the light of the Jewish people. Israel is the supreme embodiment of these Jewish values, in which we all take such immense pride. Israel is a culture of life which promotes the infinite value of life while Hamas is a gay-murdering, women honor killing, deeply misogynistic, stone-age, barbaric terrorist death cult, dedicated to genocide. Hamas is an affront to peace-loving Muslims everywhere who should join us in its condemnation. And we Jews will join the fight with our brothers in Israel against Hamas until peace prevails."

By contrast, in Judaism we desecrate the Sabbath—God's holiest day—for medical purposes to save the body. The body is holier than the soul. Can you think of a more revolutionary idea than that?

Especially for a religion?

Judaism is not naïve about sex. It does not worship desire and it does not extol unsanctified material life. It disciplines it.

But it disciplines desire the way a musician disciplines talent—not to kill it, but to make it beautiful.

Religious Sexual Repression: A Contrast

Even as Christian Europe descended into rape, concubinage, and clerical abuse, the Church Fathers accused Jews of sexual corruption. No need to mention that clerical abuse has only intensified and worsened in our time.

And why?

Because celibacy simply fails.

It is not simply unnatural. It does not work.

The nine-hundred-pound gorilla staring down the Catholic Church, namely the constant sexual abuse scandals, saddens me. As a Jew, I want to see the Catholic Church—with its global network of hospitals, orphanages, soup kitchens, and schools—flourish and grow. I count myself fortunate to have met Pope Benedict prior to his resignation and Pope Francis after his ascension to the pontificate. I have visited the Vatican and met with the Cardinals and leaders of the Church countless times. Traveling the world, I'm awed by the global network of Catholic humanitarian institutions. No other organization comes close.

But the seemingly endless sexual scandals plaguing the Church eclipse much of that, even as I find that grossly unfair. Even in the brief interregnum between the announcement of Benedict's resignation and its taking effect, Britain's most senior Catholic cleric abruptly resigned, confessing to decades of sexual misconduct.

The Jewish community is of course not immune to sexual scandal or abuse of children. But the numbers, even adjusted per capita, aren't in the same universe as the Church's, which I state not to attack a beautiful and glorious world religion but to focus on the need to address an urgent issue.

Just before the millennium, when I published *Kosher Sex*, I never intended to address sexual repression in religion. Quite the opposite: I was offering sexually liberated, secular society a philosophy of how sex could recapture emotional, psychological, and spiritual intimacy.

My purpose was to demonstrate how sex generates even deeper emotion—how specific sexual techniques, like eyes-open sex, can bond husband and wife rather than condemn them to the empty, passionless intercourse common today.

But within a few weeks of publishing the book I began receiving a steady stream of emails, nearly always with pseudonyms, from very religious couples around the world—both Jewish and Christian. All asked specific advice about curing sexual dysfunction in their relationships. They wrote to me because the answers they were getting from their clerics often lacked a human dimension.

Many Christians were told sex is mostly for procreation. Additionally, some Jews wrote to me about how Rabbinical misguidance forbade nearly everything in the Orthodox Jewish bedroom—except the missionary position, in the dark. Both groups were misled.

The Bible makes clear in Genesis that sex is primarily for *intimacy*, not procreation: "Therefore shall a man leave his father and leave his mother. He shall cleave to his wife"—(a clear sexual euphemism)—"and they shall become one flesh." (2:24) The Bible having no word for sex other than "knowledge" echoes this idea.

So why were religious authorities misleading couples?

Indeed, fraudulent sexual teachings in religion have destroyed countless lives, extinguished countless marriages. Worse, false and repressive piety may also cause some of the aberrant sexual behavior observed in otherwise Godly men and women. Is clerical celibacy in the Catholic Church one of the prime drivers of abuse? No one knows.

Similarly, could sexual suppression in some religious Jewish circles—suppression Jewish law would never countenance—explain why more stories of abuse are emerging? Perhaps. Though there may be other, stronger forces at work.

But this much is certain: sexuality strikes at the very heart of the human condition. A healthy, fulfilling married sex life is not a luxury but a necessity—one the Bible recognizes innumerably. It forms the basic narrative of so many Biblical marriages, like the famous story in Genesis of Isaac being "sexually playful" with his wife Rebecca.

Examining the many historical and theological reasons the Catholic Church made clerical celibacy obligatory a millennium ago lies beyond the scope of this book. Nor is my purpose to preach to another faith what their basic tenets ought to be. However, it is my purpose to clarify that any religion basing itself on the Hebrew Bible cannot escape its healthy encouragement of carnal intimacy.

Such intimacy remains the cornerstone of connectedness between a husband and wife.

Upon publication, *Kosher Sex* drew severe attacks from clerical colleagues who found the subject unseemly and, strangely enough, the attacks helped propel the book to becoming an international bestseller. But, I asked on my TV interviews as I addressed my critics, where were married couples supposed to learn about sex? From a Rabbi—or Hugh Hefner? Torah or porn? Genesis or *Playboy*?

Yet, a quarter of a century later, even though the religious market was never its intended readership, the book remains standard issue for countless religious, marrying Jewish and Christian couples.

But it's essential that more priests and pastors start teaching their congregants the glories of sex in marriage. Equally important: the need for physical desires to achieve their fullest satiation within the confines of a loving, committed relationship. A man in love with his wife, concentrating his fullest erotic attention on her, lives a holy life.

The Tenth Commandment clarifies this by commanding us not to covet our *neighbor's* wife which, by direct implication, means we should sure as heck covet our own. We don't need more horror stories of porn-addicted husbands or abuse by religiously committed teachers and counselors.

Judaism's Scandal: Holiness Has a Body

The modern world is confused about sex because it inherited two terrible teachers: The pornographers, who say sex is meaningless consumption. The puritans, who say sex is shameful and dangerous.

Porn drains sex of meaning. Puritanism drains sex of joy.

Both produce misery.

But Judaism advances a scandalous third option: sex made sacred by covenant.

In this third option, bodies are holy, not dirty. Desire is powerful, not evil. Pleasure is a divine gift—grounded in loyalty—and not suspicious.

Judaism does not treat the body as the enemy of the soul. The body is the instrument through which the soul expresses love.

The Hebrew Bible does not give us a theology of disgust. It gives us a theology of embodied blessing. And the most subversive proof is this:

among our sacred texts is an erotic poem—"Shir HaShirim," the *Song of Songs*—filled with longing, praise, kisses, fragrances, celebration of the beloved's body.

I wrote an entire book, *Kosher Lust*, as a commentary on this incredible Biblical tome, which the Talmud, unbelievably, says is the holiest of all twenty-four books of the TaNach, the Hebrew Bible. It is a sacred erotic love poem in which a man glories and revels in the erotic attraction of the woman he loves, which she heartily reciprocates. The idea of Christianity or Islam ever extolling a book of this nature is an absolute impossibility.

You don't put that in Scripture if you believe desire is inherently shameful.

You put that in Scripture if you believe desire can be elevated. Judaism does not worship sex. *But it refuses to demonize it.*

That balance is exactly what antisemitic ideologies cannot tolerate.

Because extremists need one of two things to control people: permission to indulge without consequence (so they can exploit), or permission to repress without mercy (so they can dominate).

Judaism offers neither.

It offers sanctification.

It says: "Commit, then rejoice. Covenant, then delight. Loyalty, then ecstasy."

The antisemite hears that and thinks: "If I accept this, I will have to become a better man."

And he would rather remain a hater. Indeed, Tucker Carlson, Nick Fuentes, and especially Candace Owens have not only seen their clicks, following, and monetization go through the stratosphere when they turned to full-time antisemitism and Israel-hatred, but, in doing so, they were forced to up the ante.

So, after Candace Owens started with her claptrap that the Jews killed JFK, she had to graduate to the Jews killed Charlie Kirk. From there, it was a hop, skip, and a jump to—the Jews actually drink Christian blood and use it in their matzos.

Conjugal Obligation: Sex as Justice

That is why the Torah speaks bluntly about conjugal obligation.

A husband is commanded not to deprive his wife of intimacy. Indeed, in Jewish law—*halacha*—a husband refusing to have sex with his wife for more than a month at a time is grounds for immediate divorce, should his wife wish to pursue the separation. Depriving a woman of sexual pleasure is a sin and making a wife feel undesirable is a condemnable act of embarrassment.

Not a mere aspect of marriage, *sex is its living soul and core essence.*

Thus, sex is not treated as a male privilege or a female duty. It is treated as a mutual right within a sacred bond.

It is so important that Jewish law makes it a matter of justice, not romance.

Let that sink in.

In Judaism, satisfying your spouse is not "extra credit." It is moral responsibility.

And that is precisely what enrages the antisemite: Judaism refuses to turn sexuality into either degradation or despair. It refuses the antisemite's preferred emotional climate, which is misery. Because misery is easier to govern.

Judaism's sexual theology is not "anything goes." It's the opposite: discipline with joy. Boundaries with celebration. Commitment with pleasure. Not a pornographic free-for-all and not a puritan prison.

And the texts are unapologetic.

The *Song of Songs*—the biblical canon's holiest text—is an erotic love poem. It is sensuous, intimate, and frank. That's not a modern reinterpretation; it's basic literary reality, widely recognized even in mainstream biblical scholarship.

Judaism also contains the radical moral claim that a woman's sexual needs matter—not as male charity, but as male obligation. The tradition of *onah* (conjugal responsibility) is explicitly discussed as a duty, a recognition that intimacy is part of justice, not a male privilege.

That vision—holy eros, mutual obligation, disciplined pleasure—is a direct threat to every ideology that relies on control through shame.

Because once a man and woman learn to love each other with tenderness and excitement, they become harder to manipulate. They stop needing the mob. They stop needing the strongman. They stop needing the movement. They have a private kingdom: marriage, family, laughter, the weekly holiness of Shabbat, the ordinary ecstasy of being alive.

And tyrants hate private kingdoms.

A joyful marriage is political resistance—because it creates citizens who can't be easily owned.

Maimonides: The Philosopher of Balanced Desire

Moses Maimonides—the Rambam—was the greatest Jewish thinker of the medieval world: rabbi, philosopher, physician, legal codifier, and counselor and doctor to sultans.

His *Guide for the Perplexed* shaped Western philosophy. His *Mishneh Torah* remains the most systematic codification of Jewish law ever written.

The Rambam was *the* master of integration—of reason and revelation, of philosophy and faith, of the Greek inheritance and the Torah.

Moreover, Rabbi Maimonides wrote about sex with a frankness that would make most medieval theologians blush—and many puritans redden today, too.

Generally speaking, the Rambam taught that the ideal human life is one of moderation—the golden mean between excess and deficiency.

He applied this principle to every domain, including sexuality. Promiscuity degrades the soul. But so does celibacy. Appetite enslaves the person who indulges without limit.

However, the person who suppresses desire entirely grows bitter, rigid, and cruel—precisely the authoritarian personality Adorno would describe seven centuries later.

In the *Mishneh Torah*, Maimonides codified the laws of marital intimacy with stunning precision. A husband is obligated to provide his wife with sexual satisfaction—not as an optional kindness, but as a legal duty with specified minimum frequencies depending on his occupation. And sex must be carried out as a pleasurable act of intimate love.

A laborer, for example, must be intimate with his wife at least twice a week. A scholar, once a week—on Friday night, the eve of the Sabbath. A camel-driver, once every thirty days (so maybe swipe left when you see the camel driver). A sailor, once every six months (swipe right, most sailors are super sexy).

These are not suggestions. They are law.

The Rambam also prescribed specific behaviors: A husband must not force intimacy upon his wife and should not approach her while he's drunk. Sex is not an animalistic act driven by intoxication. He should not be thinking of another woman during the act and he should speak tenderly with her beforehand to ensure mutual desire.

Eight hundred years before the modern discourse on consent, Maimonides had already codified it—as Jewish law.

As a physician, the Rambam understood what the Church could not—that the body is not the soul's prison.

It is the soul's instrument.

Health of body and health of mind, the Rambam knew, are inseparable. Thus, sexual health is not a luxury—it is a prerequisite for a life of wisdom, worship, and moral clarity.

The contrast with medieval Christianity could not be starker.

While Christian theologians agonized over whether sexual pleasure within marriage was sinful, Maimonides was codifying a woman's legal right to it. While monks flagellated themselves to suppress desire, the Rambam prescribed Friday night intimacy as a religious obligation.

In the dark, painful recess of the antisemite's imagination, Judaism is sexually depraved.

But, in the truest sense, Rabbi Moses Maimonides reveals Judaism as sexually disciplined.

Neither repression nor indulgence, Judaism is integration: desire guided by law, directed by love, sanctified by covenant.

By no means did the greatest Jewish philosopher of the Middle Ages fear the body. He prescribed for it. And his prescriptions, eight centuries old, remain more humane than anything the modern world has managed to produce.

Rabbi Nachman of Breslov: The Holiness of Sexual Struggle

Most religious leaders avoid the subject of sexual struggle.

They preach purity from a distance—as if desire were a problem that afflicts lesser souls.

As if holiness meant the absence of temptation—rather than its transformation.

But Rabbi Nachman of Breslov—the great-grandson of the Baal Shem Tov, the founder of Hasidism—did something much different. He walked directly into the fire.

More than any other Hasidic master, Rabbi Nachman engaged with the reality of sexual struggle. Treating it not as an abstraction, or some triviality, or a sinful skeleton to hide in the closet, he approached sexuality as a universal human experience.

He spoke about it openly, taught about it constantly, and placed it at the center of his theology of spiritual repair.

Rabbi Nachman formulated perhaps his most famous teaching on the subject in a devastatingly simple way: *"If you believe you can damage, believe you can repair."*

He applied this principle explicitly to sexual transgression.

Where other teachers might have preached despair—*you have sinned, you are fallen, you are beyond redemption*—Rabbi Nachman preached the opposite.

The capacity to damage is itself proof of the capacity to repair. The force that drives a man toward transgression translates to the same force that, redirected, drives him toward the sacred.

Desire is not the enemy. Despair is.

This is a profoundly humane teaching—and a profoundly anti-authoritarian one, too.

Because authoritarianism *needs* despair. It requires people to believe they are irredeemable, that their desires *ruined them*. That only submission to external authority can save them from themselves.

Rabbi Nachman rejected all of that.

He taught that every human being carries within himself the capacity for *teshuvah*—return, repair, transformation—no matter how far he may feel he has fallen.

Rabbi Nachman also emphasized something modern psychology only recently began to understand—*the universality of sexual struggle*.

He did not pretend that holy people are exempt from temptation. He didn't advance a hierarchy where rabbis float above desire and ordinary men wallow in it. He insisted that *everyone struggles*.

The righteous man is not the man stripped entirely of sexual temptation. The righteous man is the man who feels desire—*and chooses holiness anyway.*

Compare this with the sexual theology of antisemitic movements.

The puritanical fascists scream: desire is evil; you are evil for feeling it.

The authoritarian cleric insists: desire must be extinguished, and punish those who cannot extinguish it.

The incel laments: desire has been weaponized against me.

But Rabbi Nachman corrects all this:

Desire is powerful, and you are powerful enough to sanctify it.

That teaching has sustained generations of Breslov Hasidim through every imaginable hardship.

It sustains them still.

And it stands as a living rebuke to every ideology profiting from sexual shame. Because Rabbi Nachman understood, two centuries before Wilhelm Reich, that *a man at war with his own desire will eventually go to war with the world.*

The Antisemite's Two Fantasies

Here is one of the strangest features of antisemitism: it often contains two diametrically opposed fantasies at once.

Fantasy one: The Jew is sexually deviant and corrupting.

Fantasy two: The Jew is sexually disciplined and therefore threatening. The Nazis represented Jewish men as empty husks of human manhood, going to extremes to cut off the *peiot* (sidecurls) and beards of Hasidic rabbis to demonstrate their impotence. They weren't real men. They were cowards. Little did they realize that those "weak" men would outlast them and flourish in their millions while the Nazis were obliterated by Allied bombs and Russian artillery.

Because deep down, the antisemite recognizes something: Jewish continuity is not an accident. Jewish survival is not luck. It comes from family structure, communal loyalty, moral boundaries, and an insistence on life.

A people that sanctifies family is hard to erase. So, the antisemite hates us for our alleged sexual "perversion" while also hating us for our actual marital strength.

He sees Jewish homes, Jewish children, Jewish laughter around the Shabbat table, Jewish couples building a life—and he feels judged.

Not by our words.

By our existence.

So he tries to reduce that existence to a punchline.

This is why the smear is so predictable: take anything Jewish and sexualize it; take anything Jewish and make it obscene; take anything Jewish and turn it into "perversion."

It is not humor. It is warfare.

When they can't defeat Jewish values, they try to make Jewish values look dirty.

The Sexualization of Jews Is a Prelude to Violence

This is where the subject stops being merely psychological and becomes historically lethal.

When a group is eroticized and smeared as sexually corrupt, it becomes easier to brutalize.

History overflows with examples of this trajectory:

Turn the minority into a sexual threat.

Call them "perverse," "predatory," "degenerate."

Claim you are "protecting women" or "protecting children." Then, unleash social persecution and physical violence under the banner of "purity."

Hence, countries around the world and especially in Europe, including, perversely, Germany, regularly speak about banning circumcision. You'll forgive me if I don't count Germany as a particularly reliable partner in safeguarding the security and health of Jewish babies—but I digress.

Over the past few years, as America becomes a sewer for conspiracy theories fueled by illiterates like Candace Owens and Nick Fuentes, some have suggested that circumcision causes, or is in any way linked, to autism.

The ignoble lie rested on a single study, from Scandinavia, that places the blame not on circumcision per se but on the Tylenol often given to the baby to minimize pain. It's worth noting that Tylenol is rarely ever used by Mohels, ritual circumcisers, who prefer to give the baby a tiny drop of wine instead. If you've attended a bris, you will have borne personal witness to how after a minute or two those few drops of wine soothe the baby and the crying subsides.

But that didn't stop the immediate bandwagon of Jew-haters from assailing Judaism's oldest and holiest ritual, practiced by approximately 98 percent of all Jews worldwide (despite only some 20 percent being actually observant).

Circumcision is not a cultural quirk or an elective choice.

It is the oldest continuously practiced religious ritual in the world. For Jews, it is the divine covenant given by God to Abraham:

"This shall be My covenant in your flesh for all generations."

For over three thousand years, through exile, pogrom, and persecution, Jews have circumcised their sons. It is the unbroken chain that has bound us to God and to each other.

Throughout history, from the ancient Greeks to the Romans to the Nazis, our enemies have tried to outlaw circumcision precisely because they knew it safeguarded Jewish continuity and it served as the perfect, targeted attack against Jewish sexuality.

Linking it now to autism is not simply bad science; it echoes an old campaign to delegitimize Jewish existence itself.

The idea that circumcision causes autism traces almost entirely to a 2015 Danish study that suggested a modest association.

But the problems with that paper are glaring:

- It was observational, not causal.
- It suffered from detection bias (circumcised boys had more contact with doctors, skewing diagnosis rates).
- It lumped together diverse populations with different health practices.
- Its results were weak and inconsistent, significant only in small subgroups.
- The supposed mechanism—early pain disrupting brain development—is highly speculative and unsupported.

In the decade since that study, *not a single credible researcher has replicated its claims.* Autism science has moved forward. Circumcision has vanished from serious discussion of autism's causes.

Genetics dominate autism risk, alongside prenatal factors like maternal health, infections, or environmental exposures. Hundreds of genes are implicated. But circumcision?

Not once, in any rigorous study.

In fact, a 2024 study in European Urology Open Science found that circumcised autistic boys showed improvements in behavioral symptoms compared to controls.

The exact opposite of the claim.

What circumcision does provide, however, confirmed by decades of evidence, is substantial health protection:

- HIV/AIDS prevention: Randomized trials in Africa showed male circumcision reduces heterosexual HIV transmission by ~60 percent. The WHO and UNAIDS endorse it as prevention.
- Reduced risk of STDs: Circumcision lowers the risk of herpes, syphilis, chancroid, and HPV infection.
- Urinary tract infections: Uncircumcised boys have a ten to twelve times higher risk of UTIs in infancy, which can cause kidney damage.
- Cancer prevention: Circumcision virtually eliminates penile cancer risk and reduces cervical cancer risk for female partners by up to 28 percent.
- Better hygiene and fewer complications: Conditions like balanitis, phimosis, and foreskin infections are drastically reduced.
- Large scale studies have shown no negative impact on sexual relations.

Science confirms what faith has always taught: *brit milah* brings life, blessing, and health.

To link autism to circumcision is to ignore decades of genetics and neuroscience and to *mislead desperate parents searching for answers.*

What troubles me most is how this claim mirrors Europe's ongoing efforts to outlaw circumcision.

- In Finland, Muslim and Jewish parents have been fined for circumcising their sons.

- In Sweden, strict laws criminalize traditional *brit milah* without medical supervision.
- In Cologne, a 2012 court briefly outlawed circumcision until the Bundestag reversed it. Just imagine that: *Germans teaching Jews how to take care of their sons.* I think I'll pass.
- In San Francisco, activists tried to put circumcision bans on the ballot.

Every time, the justification is the same: circumcision is harmful, barbaric, traumatic. *The autism claim is simply the latest mask on an ancient hostility.*

This is not science. It is secular hostility toward religion, costumed in medical language.

Brit milah is older than science, but it does not fear science. Honest science affirms its benefits and exposes the autism link as a mirage.

For Jews, circumcision is not optional. It is survival, covenant, and identity. To attack it with false claims is to repeat the old mistakes of history.

Indeed, while circumcision might not be a cause of autism, it *is* a cause of Jewish survival. And it will endure, as it always has.

The rhetoric against ancient Jewish rituals like circumcisions always pretends to be moral. But it is always fueled by an unhinged, and actually sick, pornographic imagination. That imagination is not an accident. It is a preparation.

If you can make Jews seem like contaminators of innocence, you can justify *anything against them*. You can make cruelty feel righteous and turn violence into "cleansing."

This is why Jews must refuse shame.

Shame is the first step toward vulnerability. Not vulnerability as in tenderness—vulnerability as in being prey.

Dignity, by contrast, is armor. *And joy—joy that refuses to be extinguished—is a form of defiance that has kept us alive for millennia.*

So when antisemites obsess about Jewish intimacy, we should not giggle it off as mere crude talk.

We should understand it as a diagnostic symptom of a deeper sickness—one that, left untreated, has always led to blood.

Which means the response must be more than defensive. It must be a counter-vision.

A civilization of covenant. A culture of life. *A people who will not trade their holiness for acceptance.*

The Hidden Reason Antisemites Hate Israel

People think antisemites hate Israel because of "politics."

No.

Politics is the pretext.

The deeper reason is that Israel is the global billboard of Jewish vitality. Israel is Jews back in history, back in sovereignty, back in agency, back in family life, back in land, back in language, back in laughter. It is Jews refusing to be the world's fragile punching bag. It is Jews building, innovating, arguing, dancing, making babies, making music, making jokes, making love—under rocket fire and condemnation. That kind of defiant vitality is unbearable to ideologies built on grievance and death.

So, antisemites don't merely oppose Israel's policies. They oppose Israel's existence, because Israel represents the one thing they cannot stand: Jews not broken. And when they can't break Jews, they sexualize Jews. They try to humiliate what they cannot defeat.

The Emotional Algebra of Jew-Hatred

Here is the emotional math antisemites run, whether they admit it or not: If Jews are joyful, then my misery is not inevitable. If my misery is not inevitable, then I'm responsible for my life. If I'm responsible for my life, I can't blame Jews. If I can't blame Jews, I have to face myself. I refuse.

So, they choose hatred.

But hatred is not stable. Hatred needs constant fuel. That's why antisemitism is never satisfied with simple prejudice. It becomes a worldview. It becomes a hobby. It becomes an identity.

And because it is fueled by envy, it will always drift toward the place envy burns hottest: intimacy.

The antisemite does not merely want Jews to die. He wants Jews to be degraded first. Because degradation is how he justifies their death.

Antisemitism Is a War on Life

Start with something most people miss: Antisemitism isn't just a hatred of Jews. It's a hatred of what Jews represent.

Jews represent continuity.

Lineage. Covenant. Family. Text. Memory. Home. Argument. Humor. Ritual. Children. The stubborn insistence that life matters even when life hurts.

And sex—real sex, covenantal sex, husband-and-wife sex—is the engine of all of that. It's the source of generations. It's the glue of intimacy. It's the celebration of existence.

So if you are an ideology built on grievance, death, nihilism, and rage—if you need human beings to be miserable in order to control them—then Jewish joy is intolerable. And Jewish sexual joy, sanctified and disciplined and confident, is an offense you cannot forgive.

That is why antisemites are so often joy-haters. They don't just want Jews to lose. They want Jews to be ashamed—ashamed of our bodies, ashamed of our marriages, ashamed of our desire, ashamed of our delight in life.

Because shame is a leash. Shame is how you domesticate people. And the Jew is the one creature who keeps breaking the leash.

Porn and Puritanism: Two Wings of the Same Demon

One of the biggest lies of our time is that porn is freedom and modesty is repression.

Porn is not freedom. *Porn is captivity.* It hijacks the brain's reward circuitry. It trains men to desire novelty over loyalty, turns women into a slideshow, rewires expectation away from real intimacy and toward fantasy.

It makes actual human connection feel "boring" compared to infinite stimulation.

Indeed, I have long argued, as I did passionately in my book coauthored with Pamela Anderson, that pornography is not sexual at all. Its purpose is to circumvent sexual connection entirely by going straight to orgasm, liberating the body from any sexual desire or lust.

Porn is not designed to enhance lust but *to purge the body of it entirely.* After all, many men use porn quite literally as a sleeping aid rather than an aphrodisiac.

Pornography Conspiracy Theories

The oldest accusation against Jews is that we corrupt.

We corrupt money, politics, blood—whenever, whatever, wherever—and above all, we corrupt sex.

A particularly virulent version of this ancient libel claims Jews founded, control, and weaponize the pornography industry.

Jews, the conspiracy theory holds, created pornography to weaken white and Christian men.

They furthermore promote interracial pornographic content to encourage "race-mixing," profiting from addiction to this (gasp) interracial porn to deliberately destroy the family structure. Most of all, the theory propounds that the entire modern porn industry amounts to a weapon of war—one aimed at the psyches and bedrooms of the gentile world.

The theorists behind this libel love to point out a few prominent early figures in the adult entertainment industry happened to be Jewish—just as a few prominent early figures in Hollywood, in comedy, in publishing, and in a dozen other industries happened to be Jewish.

This is what happens when an immigrant community, barred from established professions, enters emerging industries. It is not a conspiracy. It is sociology—and mundane, banal sociology at that.

But the antisemite does not want sociology. He wants a scapegoat.

And here the erotic engine operates crudely, nakedly, apparently. The man who consumes pornography and feels shame does not examine himself. He does not ask why he watches, why he cannot stop, why real intimacy feels hollow by comparison. Nor does he consider how his own choices might have produced his own misery.

Instead, he blames Jews.

In its transparency, the projection is breathtaking: *I watch porn; I feel disgusted with myself, therefore Jews made me do it.* Thus, the most potent antisemitic move in existence—externalizing internal chaos, pinning it to the nearest Jew—is applied to the most private domain of human life.

And it connects directly to the most ancient accusations: Jews as sexual corruptors, as pimps, as degraders of Christian women. Just as the medieval blood libel imagined Jews defiling Christian innocence through ritual violence, the modern porn conspiracy imagines Jews defiling Christian manhood through ritual seduction.

Different century, same engine.

The truth, of course, is that Judaism's actual sexual ethic—monogamy, intimacy, covenant, mutual pleasure within marriage—*is the antithesis of pornography.*

Porn strips sex of meaning; Judaism insists on it.

Pornography isolates. Judaism connects.

Pornography commodifies the body. Judaism sanctifies it.

But the conspiracy theorist has never read a word of Jewish teaching on sexuality. *He only knows his shame—and a story that makes his shame someone else's fault.*

The Deep Irony

There is a bitter irony here.

The same culture that mocks *Kosher Sex* drowns in pornography. The same commentators who sneer at marital devices are often complicit in a marketplace that sells women's bodies as disposable entertainment. As nothing but the means to the grotesque end of libidinous, toxic masculinity.

The same ideologues who call Judaism "backward" have created a sexual economy so brutal and so corrosive that millions of men cannot function in real intimacy.

They are not offended by sex. They are offended by *meaningful sex.*

Because meaningful sex requires responsibility. It requires vows and self-control. It demands a willingness to serve another human being—rather than consume them.

And consumption is the religion of the age.

Judaism is a revolt against consumption—of food, bodies, relationships, people. That revolt enrages the antisemite because it exposes him.

Not as "ignorant," but as enslaved.

Sexual Repression as Political Technology

If you want to control a population, you do two things: you keep them frightened and you keep them sexually miserable.

Frightened people cling to leaders.

Sexually miserable people seek scapegoats.

It's not complicated; it's ancient.

You see this in totalitarian regimes that regulate bodies, police women, and turn sex into propaganda—the most notable example being the extreme evil of the mullah regime in Tehran.

You see it in extremist movements that obsess over modesty codes, segregation, "purity," "degeneracy," "grooming," "corruption," "traditional values"—all preached by men privately addicted to pornography.

But Judaism, at its best, is an *anti-totalitarian religion.* It declares: You are responsible, not owned.

You answer to God, not to tyrants.

Your home is sacred; your marriage is sacred; your intimacy is sacred.

Which means it can't be easily weaponized by the state. And tyrants hate what they can't weaponize.

Sexual repression is never "just personal." It's a weapon.

Look at authoritarian movements, see the pattern: control sex, control society.

Now you'll understand why criminalizing homosexuality is an essential part of Vladimir Putin's platform. After all, why should he care? Nonetheless, Freedom House describes how strongmen like Putin attack men's and women's sexual rights as part of broader democratic erosion and scapegoating narratives.

And modern research on authoritarianism and sexuality continues to underline that regimes often treat sexual regulation as a *tool of social engineering and control.*

This matters for our purposes because antisemitism thrives in cultures of sexual misery. When people are ashamed of their bodies, frustrated in their relationships, and terrified of desire, they need someone to blame.

The human mind looks for a scapegoat to shoulder its internal chaos. Social science even shows how groups can shift punishment onto innocent minorities—meaning scapegoating is not merely a metaphor; it is a *measurable behavior.*

Antisemites are not "too sexual."

They are usually sexually terrified—then they project that terror onto Jews.

The Jewish Counter-Revolution: Sanctify Desire, Don't Weaponize It

If earlier I established that the opposite of antisemitism is joy, then here I must establish something equally provocative: the opposite of repression is not promiscuity. *It is sanctification.*

Promiscuity is not liberation. It's dispersal, fragmenting the soul and turning the body into currency. It leaves people numb and lonely, then shocked and depressed that they are numb and lonely.

Judaism refuses both traps.

It insists on taking desire seriously enough to give it a home. In this light, marriage, at its best, is not a contract. It's a sanctuary for the wildness of eros to become tenderness—rather than chaos.

And that is precisely why this tome exists.

Because antisemites have always tried to poison Jewish life at its roots: family, covenant, intimacy, joy. And because now, in an age drowning in pornography and starved of commitment, the Jewish model is not merely relevant. It is urgently needed—by Jews and non-Jews alike, which explains why, when I first penned *Kosher Sex* as a book mostly for my Oxford students, where I served as Rabbi at the time, it miraculously and unexpectedly became an international bestseller.

Clearly, the world is not suffering from too much holiness.

It is suffering from *holiness without joy and joy without holiness.*

Judaism insists on both. That insistence is our gift to humanity—and the haters can't stand it.

Sexual Repression Is Not Virtue—It's Fuel

Repression weaponizes desire instead of eliminating it.

Unintegrated sexuality sours into honor cultures, purity panics, and ideological policing. It breeds mobs screaming at strangers, regimes regulating wombs, and movements eroticizing violence.

This energy feeds antisemitism like rot feeds fungus. Jew-hatred supplies an outlet for passions lacking expression in healthy intimacy. It allows rage to masquerade as righteousness. It transforms personal frustration into cosmic grievance.

Hence antisemites sound hysterical rather than confident. They are not defending something they love. They are attacking something they envy.

Jewish marriages—imperfect, noisy, argumentative, affectionate—expose the lie at the heart of repression: that denying desire makes you holy. Instead, it makes you brittle.

And brittle ideologies shatter upon confronting joy.

"Rabbi Buttplug," with which Tucker Carlson disgraced himself yet again, was not an insult crafted by a clever mind. It was the involuntary spasm of a repressed one. It revealed more about its speaker than its target.

Because nothing terrifies the sexually repressed like the idea that intimacy might actually heal people.

That marriages might be saved.

That addictions might be broken.

That eros might be disciplined without being destroyed.

That joy might be moral.

This explains the real scandal of Jewish sexuality—and why antisemites will keep returning to it, circling it, sneering at it, and trying—unsuccessfully—to shame it.

They sense, correctly, that if Jews are right about sex, then their entire worldview collapses.

This book will make sure it does.

CHAPTER FIVE

JOY IS THE MOST SUBVERSIVE FORCE ON EARTH

A Warning and a Promise

Here is the warning: Antisemitism is metastasizing because sexual misery is metastasizing.

Loneliness is up.

Porn use is up.

Marriage is down.

Birthrates are collapsing across the West.

Men are confused, angry, isolated.

Women are exhausted, objectified, disillusioned.

Children are anxious and unmoored.

Into that vacuum marches every demagogue selling an enemy. And the oldest enemy is always available: the Jew.

But here is the promise: the cure is not merely political. It is civilizational.

We fight antisemitism by fighting the despair that feeds it. We fight antisemitism by rebuilding homes where love is strong enough to hold desire without shame. We fight antisemitism by teaching what Judaism has always taught at its best:

That sex is not an animal function. It is a human art.

That desire is not a dirty secret. It is a sacred energy.

That marriage is not a prison.

It is a sanctuary.

And that joy—moral, embodied, covenantal joy—is not weakness.

It is power.

It is the most threatening power in the world to those who rule by misery. Which is exactly why the antisemites keep coming for it. And exactly why we will keep defending it.

The Most Dangerous Lie: That Pleasure Is the Enemy of God

There are religious people who are genuinely humble, decent, and loving.

And then there are religious people who are addicted to the sensation of being "pure" because it gives them moral superiority without requiring moral courage. They don't love God. They love the feeling of being better than you.

And the easiest way to feel superior is to condemn pleasure.

Because pleasure is democratic. Anyone can feel it. The poor can feel it. The powerless can feel it. The oppressed can feel it. So, the tyrant—political or spiritual—must control it.

He must convince you that joy is a vice. And once he convinces you of that, he has you by the throat. Because a person who believes joy is sinful will eventually come to believe cruelty is righteous.

That is how you get mobs chanting for death in the name of "holiness." That is how you get hatred marketed as virtue.

When people cannot access joy, they settle for righteousness—and righteousness becomes a costume for cruelty.

Judaism does not let you do that. Judaism demands moral discipline, yes. But it does not demand emotional starvation.

It insists you bless food before eating it, not to demonize appetite, but to elevate it.

It insists you sanctify Shabbat, not to escape life, but to delight in it.

It insists marriage is a covenant, not a cage.

And it dares to say that erotic love—within commitment—is part of the holiness of life.

The world hates us for it.

Not because it is "provocative." But because it is liberating.

A Key Distinction: Pleasure vs. Joy

The opposite of antisemitism is not tolerance.

Tolerance is cold. Tolerance is distant. Tolerance is what you offer someone you don't actually want near you.

The opposite of antisemitism is joy. And here's where the conversation has to get precise.

Antisemites often accuse Jews of hedonism. They say Jews worship pleasure. They say Jews are materially decadent. They say Jews corrupt societies. They say Jews undermine purity. They say Jews are "dirty."

But that accusation is the antisemite projecting his own confusion. Because Judaism does not worship pleasure. Judaism worships God. And God sanctifies joy.

Those are not the same.

Pleasure is a sensation. Joy is a state of being. Pleasure can be bought, stolen, faked, performed, consumed. Joy cannot.

Joy requires integrity. Joy requires gratitude. Joy requires courage. Joy requires love. Joy requires covenant. Joy requires fidelity to something beyond appetite.

And Jewish joy, in particular, is scandalous—because it is not naïve. It is not denial. It is not cheap optimism. Jewish joy is forged in suffering. We know tragedy. We know loss. We know expulsion and humiliation and murder. And yet we still say L'Chaim.

That is not a slogan. That is a worldview.

So, when I say the opposite of antisemitism is joy, I am not talking about Jews partying while the world burns. I am talking about Jews refusing to let hate define the terms of our humanity. Jews refusing to accept the antisemite's worldview that life is fundamentally shameful. Jews refusing to surrender the body to humiliation or the bedroom to despair.

Because the bedroom is where you either surrender to cynicism or recommit to hope. A couple that keeps loving—really loving—keeps believing in life. That belief is the enemy of every ideology built on hate.

The antisemite cannot understand any of this because he confuses restraint with repression and license with freedom. Judaism does not worship pleasure.

It sanctifies joy—and joy terrifies those who need misery to justify their ideology.

A Hard Truth: Some Jews Have Forgotten Our Own Power

I'm going to say something that will make some people uncomfortable, and good. Discomfort is sometimes the beginning of truth. Too many Jews have internalized the antisemite's framing. We have become skittish about our own joy. We think dignity means being bland. We think seriousness means being grim. We think holiness means being humorless. We think morality means being sexless. And that is a tragedy—because it is not Judaism.

Judaism is wine at Kiddush, not water.

Judaism is a wedding dance, not a funeral march.

Judaism is Shabbat intimacy, not weekday exhaustion.

Judaism is L'Chaim—to life—not "please don't notice us."

Antisemitism thrives when Jews are apologetic about being alive.

So the purpose of this book is not merely to expose the erotic pathology of antisemitism. It is to reawaken Jewish confidence in the sanctity of joy.

Not crude joy. Not empty pleasure. But moral, embodied joy—the kind that builds homes, heals marriages, raises children, stabilizes society, and strengthens the human spirit.

The Bedroom as a Battlefield

Here's the hammer: The war against Jews is a war against life, and the war against life is always fought, sooner or later, in the bedroom.

If you can shame a people's intimacy, you can weaken their bonds.

If you can weaken their bonds, you can fracture their families.

If you can fracture their families, you can break their future.

This is why the Jew-hater obsesses over Jewish sexuality. Because he understands—instinctively, even if not intellectually—that Jewish erotic confidence is not just pleasure.

It is continuity.

It is covenant.

It is defiance.

So yes, I am writing *Kosher Sex for Antisemites.*

Not to provoke.

But to expose.

To pull the mask off the oldest hatred and reveal the pathetic fear beneath it: fear of love, fear of women, fear of tenderness, fear of joy, fear of a people who refuse to die—and refuse to live ashamed.

Why This Matters Now: October 7 and the Pornography of Martyrdom

Since October 7, I have watched something sickening on screens across the world: the glamorization of death.

Not grief. Not mourning.

Glamorization.

People chanting for *intifada* as if it's a music festival.

People praising murderers as "resistance," while families bury children.

People calling rape and kidnapping "context."

This is not politics.

This is a cult of death. And death cults always entail erotic distortion.

Because death cults cannot create life. They cannot build love. Nor can they sustain families. They can only recruit through adrenaline, grievance, and the seduction of violence. Which is why they hate Jews with a religious intensity.

Jews stand for life. Not just survival. Life.

Family. Children. Laughter. Arguments at the Sabbath table.

Music.

A home.

And yes—sex, as covenant.

So they must demonize us. They *must* portray Jewish life as obscene.

Because if Jewish life is beautiful, their cult is exposed as the fraud it is.

A death cult must make life look like a crime.

The Porn Trap and the Puritan Trap: Two Ways to Kill a Marriage

I have spent decades in rooms with couples—straight, religious, secular, Jewish, Christian, Muslim, Jews married to Muslims, atheists married to partners of faith—who are in pain.

And I can tell you the truth that no algorithm will teach you:

Most marriages don't die because people stop loving each other. *They die because people stop touching each other with tenderness.*

They stop flirting.

They stop pursuing.

They cease desiring.

They stop trying.

They get swallowed by exhaustion, resentment, and a culture that teaches men to consume and women to perform.

Porn is not "just visual." Porn is training. It trains men to dissociate desire from affection. It trains women to feel replaced by a fantasy they never agreed to compete with. It turns sex from connection into escape.

And then puritanism swoops in and offers the opposite poison: fear of desire itself.

So couples are trapped between two lies:

"Desire means you are crude."

And:

"Desire means you should consume endlessly."

Judaism says, instead: "desire means you are human."

Now discipline it so it becomes love.

Because porn destroys intimacy by making sex easy. Puritanism destroys intimacy by making sex shameful. Judaism destroys neither—it sanctifies both desire and restraint.

This is not a niche point.

This is civilizational.

A society that cannot sustain marriages becomes a society of lonely people, fatherless children, unstable homes, and angry men *ripe for radicalization.*

And guess who those angry men blame?

The Psychology of the Mob

When a person is happy in his marriage, he is harder to radicalize. When a person has a home filled with affection, he is less susceptible to cults. When a person has real intimacy, he is less desperate for tribal identity. A good marriage immunizes against extremism.

Which is why extremist movements always attack marriage—either by corrupting it through pornography and promiscuity, or by suffocating it through fear and shame.

Then they offer a substitute family: the movement. The movement becomes your "brothers." The ideology becomes your "truth." The leader becomes your "father." The Duce. The Führer.

And the enemy—always—becomes the Jew.

Because the Jew symbolizes the thing the movement cannot provide: stable, enduring covenantal life.

A mob is just a crowd of lonely people pretending rage is community.

The Antidote to Antisemitism is Not Tolerance. It is Muscular Joy.

People keep saying we need "tolerance."

No.

Tolerance is what you offer someone you secretly dislike. Tolerance means stomaching another's differences. Tolerance is to put up with difference rather than be enriched by it.

Tolerance is thin. It breaks under pressure.

Joy constitutes the antithesis of antisemitism. Joy that is disciplined. Joy that is moral. Joy that is embodied. Joy refusing shame, building, and defending itself.

Because if Jews are only allowed to exist as victims—quiet, trembling, apologetic—then the antisemites have already won.

But if Jews thrive as joyful builders of life, as proud celebrants of covenant, as defenders of their families, then antisemitism is exposed for what it really is: *a tantrum against existence.*

A Challenge to the Reader—and a Warning to the Antisemites

If you are reading this and you are a decent person who has been infected by some online poison, let me give you a way back.

Stop staring at Jews. Start staring at your own life.

Are you in love?

Are you faithful?

Are you building a home?

Or are you using politics to avoid the private work of becoming a man or woman of integrity?

Because hatred is the easiest drug in the world. It gives you a high without demanding growth.

But it will rot your soul.

And if you are one of the proud antisemites—the ones who can't stop fixating on Jewish sex, Jewish bodies, Jewish marriages, Jewish families—then hear me clearly: Your obsession is not proof of our corruption.

It is proof of your captivity.

You are trapped in a prison of shame. And you want us to live in that prison with you.

We won't.

The Promise of This Book

In this book, I'm not going to beg antisemites to be nicer. To the contrary. I have spent my life fighting antisemitism rather than ever trying to change it.

My goal, rather, is to expose and annihilate their lies.

This book names the sickness: sexual repression turned into political hatred.

My goal is never to serve as an apologist but rather a promoter of the Jewish erotic tradition—not as a novelty, not as a gimmick, not as provocation, but as moral sanity.

And I make an unapologetic claim: A civilization that cannot integrate sex and dignity will eventually integrate sex and violence.

Judaism offers a different integration: sex and sanctity.

That difference is not academic. It is the dividing line between a society of families and a society of predators. Between tenderness and domination. Between covenant and chaos.

If this chapter sounds like a hammer, good. Because the truth is not here to soothe us. It is here to wake us up.

When sex loses sanctity, it doesn't become "free." It becomes cruel.

The pornography economy—which I will examine later in this book—functions not merely as private temptation but as public destabilization. It weakens men, isolates women, fractures families, and creates the exact psychological conditions in which antisemitic conspiracy theories spread like fire.

Indeed, I wrote an entire book, co-authored with Pamela Anderson, called *Lust for Love*, persuasively making the case that porn is the ultimate enemy of eroticism and intimacy. Porn is not only non-sexual. It is utterly banal, even boring. The proof of which is that, to remain effective in leading men to orgasm, it must be consumed in ever larger quantities. Porn is like a drug slowly wearing off, until it becomes an addiction.

For now, understand this:

They mocked my book *Kosher Sex* and Chana's company Kosher.Sex because they fear it.

Not because it is dirty.

Because it is clean. Because it takes something that can be debased and elevates it to holiness.

Not clean in the sense of prudish. Clean in the sense of life-giving.

And life-giving joy is the one thing the oldest hatred cannot endure.

CHAPTER SIX

FRAGMENTATION AS AN IDEOLOGY

Hate is not merely an emotion.

It is an architecture.

It redesigns the human heart so it can no longer house other people. It turns compassion into weakness, humility into humiliation, love into naiveté, marriage into prison. It mutates family into burden, children into inconvenience, and community into a threat.

And then, once it has hollowed the soul out, it hands the person a single substitute for meaning:

An enemy.

This is why antisemitism always grows in the cracks of social fragmentation. When people no longer know how to live with each other, they start *looking for someone to live against.*

The Business Model of Division

Modern antisemitism is amplified by machines that reward the worst human impulses, valorizing:

- outrage over understanding
- suspicion over trust

- humiliation over persuasion
- mockery over moral seriousness

Every platform built on engagement profits from polarization.

Polarization is fragmentation. Fragmentation is loneliness. Loneliness is grievance. Grievance demands an enemy.

And the Jew arrives right on schedule—mysterious, successful, resilient, hard to categorize, impossible to erase.

Antisemitism isn't only ancient hatred—it's also a modern business model.

When *The Daily Wire* fired Candace Owens, it seemed like curtains for her career. Then she turned to the most grotesque antisemitism and rose to be one of the foremost podcasters in the world. It worked for Hitler, who was a flea-infested vagabond living on the streets in Vienna. Until he turned to Jew-hatred. And it worked for Candace Owens.

If you want to understand why antisemitism spreads even among people who have never met a Jew, here's your answer: the Jew is not their neighbor.

The Jewish people are less than two percent of the global population; statistically, it's unlikely the average person has even met one. The Jew is instead a symbol in their story—a symbol explaining their failure without requiring their repentance.

Why the Antisemites Can't Build

Watch what hate movements create.

They don't build hospitals. They don't strengthen marriages or rescue addicts. They don't comfort the grieving, raise moral children, or create durable communities.

They produce mobs. Scapegoats. They are the world's destroyers. Just look at the condition in which Hitler left not just Europe but his own Germany. A giant pile of putrid rubble.

Often, they gain a sizable following, accrue political power, amass financial fortunes, execute internal purges, generate paranoia. But they build absolutely nothing.

Then they implode.

They can't build because building requires trust, and trust requires vulnerability, and vulnerability requires love.

Hatred refuses vulnerability. It chooses to never be wounded again—which means to never truly love again.

So, the antisemites become experts at deconstruction. Because destruction is easier than intimacy, they dismantle everything—reputation, relationships, institutions, nations, innocence, and human dignity.

A strong marriage, however, takes courage. A strong family requires sacrifice. A strong community demands patience.

Whereas hate takes, requires, and demands almost nothing.

Except hate.

Fragmentation as "Freedom"

The modern world sells fragmentation as liberation:

- "You don't need commitment."
- "You don't need vows."
- "You don't need family."
- "You don't need faith."
- "You don't need children. They're too expensive. Maybe one, two maximum. Three? You've lost your mind."
- "You don't need boundaries."

But it doesn't produce freedom. It produces isolation. And isolation, as Hitler showed with the war-weary, broken veterans of the German army who returned to no jobs, no families, and no nation, makes people easy to control.

A lonely person will join any tribe that promises significance. Even if that tribe is built on cruelty, lies, and bigoted hatred.

The more isolated people become, the more they crave an enemy who makes them feel important.

Judaism as Anti-fragmentation

Stubbornly communal, Judaism is infuriating to ideologues. It insists that you do not get to live as a detached atom floating in a meaningless universe.

- You have obligations.

- You have responsibilities.
- You have a people.
- You have offspring.
- You have family.
- You have a community.
- You have a nation.
- You have a covenant.
- You have a land.
- You have a home.
- You have a God who cares what you do with your body.

The modern world calls that oppression; the antisemites call it conspiracy.

I call it *sanity*.

Because the body is not a toy.

The body is a temple. And when you treat the body as sacred, you are less likely to treat other people as profane, and thus less likely to treat them as disposable.

Which is precisely what hate ideologies require: disposable humans.

Sex as the Ultimate Divider, or the Ultimate Bond

If you want to fragment society, one of the fastest ways is to corrupt sexuality.

Pornography teaches disconnection: bodies without souls, pleasure without responsibility, fantasy without covenant, orgasm without connection.

Promiscuity teaches disconnection: intimacy without commitment, union without loyalty, pleasure without protection.

Repression teaches disconnection too: shame without healing, desire without language, longing without dignity.

In every case, sexuality becomes either an addiction or a wound—never a bond.

Judaism refuses all three distortions.

Judaism teaches that sex is not a battlefield between men and women, but a bridge. Not a commodity, but a covenant.

Not shame, but holiness.

That is why Judaism is a threat to those who feed on fragmentation.

A society that can't sanctify sex will eventually weaponize it—and weaponized sex breeds hatred.

Antisemitism as Anti-love

Here is the core argument of this chapter:

Antisemitism is not simply hatred of Jews. It is hatred of the human capacity to connect without being controlled.

Because connection creates loyalty that is not bought. It creates families that are not manipulated and communities that do not need tyrants.

So, the antisemites do what they always do: target Jewish connection as a scandal, turn Jewish love into something dirty, sexualize Jews as predators or perverts.

They do it because, if they can corrupt the symbol of Jewish intimacy, they can corrupt the idea of intimacy itself.

And once intimacy is corrupted, fragmentation would appear destined.

But Judaism refuses that false fate.

Judaism chooses covenant, joy, and love as resistance.

CHAPTER SEVEN

THE SCAPEGOAT ECONOMY

A fragmented society has a predictable problem: Nobody knows whom to trust.

In that vacuum, scapegoating becomes a currency. It's emotional counterfeiting. It lets people purchase moral certainty without paying the price of self-examination.

And the "best" scapegoat—the most profitable scapegoat—is the Jew.

Not because Jews are weak, but because Jews are symbolically useful. We are the world's mirror. People look at us and see their own anxieties reflected back at them: money, power, intellect, sexuality, success, survival.

So they blame us for what they can't tolerate in themselves.

That is the scapegoat economy.

Old psychology, new delivery system.

Scapegoat theory describes the human tendency to blame others for one's own problems, and it's closely tied to prejudice. The mechanism is simple:

1. I feel pain.
2. I cannot bear my own responsibility.
3. I locate an "other."
4. I blame the "other."

5. I feel relief.
6. I become addicted to the relief.

That's why hatred is so hard to cure. It works.

It numbs the conscience, provides a hit of certainty, and turns complexity into a villain.

And once a society starts paying people in scapegoats, it becomes very hard to return to honest currency: humility, compassion, and truth.

Scapegoating—the drug that turns shame into rage, and rage into ideology.

Why the Scapegoat Is So Often Sexual

Now we return—again—to the erotic pathology at the center of antisemitism.

When a person is deeply lonely, their sexuality often becomes either frozen (repression) or frantic (compulsion). Either way, it becomes a source of shame, and shame is unbearable without transformation.

So shame becomes projection.

And projection often becomes sexual accusation.

That is why antisemitism across history is drenched in sexual imagery: Jews as seducers, corrupters, pornographers, defilers, predators. These accusations tell you far more about the accuser than the accused.

It is the sexual self-hatred of the antisemite looking for a place to land.

And Jews, as ever, are the nearest target.

The Loneliness-to-Scapegoat Route

Let's connect the dots spanning the last few chapters:

- Loneliness creates emptiness.
- Emptiness creates grievance.
- Grievance creates a hunger for meaning.
- Meaning is purchased through scapegoating.
- Scapegoating requires an "other."
- Antisemitism provides the "other" with prepackaged mythology.

Antisemitism becomes a ready-made identity for people who have no stable identity of their own.

They become "someone" by hating Jews.

That's why their hatred is so *theatrical*. Why it's so obsessive. And why they can't stop talking about Jews.

Anyone who listens to the daily podcasts of antisemites Tucker Carlson, Nick Fuentes, or Candace Owens will be gobsmacked at the downright demonic obsession—fueled by demonic possession—they have for Jews. There is no longer any discussion about the economy, immigration, or the national debt. It's all Jews, all the time.

It supplies them confidence. It feeds their misery. It nourishes their grievance.

It's also something they're dependent upon.

The antisemite needs the Jew the way the addict needs the needle. Without a target, he has no identity.

The Lie at Hate's Center

Every scapegoat economy rests on one lie:

"If we destroy them, we will be whole."

But destruction never makes anyone whole. It only makes them emptier. Even when hate "wins," it loses—because it can't create what it claims to want: peace, dignity, belonging, joy.

It creates only more fragmentation, more paranoia, more internal purges, more loneliness.

Hate is a self-consuming fire. That is why every hate movement eventually turns on itself, as was most evidenced in Hitler's "Night of the Long Knives"—and abundantly clear in numerous other examples.

Jewish Joy: The Ultimate Refusal

Here's what I want you to understand, and I want it to land like a hammer:

Jewish joy is not naiveté. It is rebellion.

To build a family in a world addicted to death: rebellion.

To stay married in a world that celebrates betrayal: rebellion.

To sanctify sex in a world that weaponizes it: rebellion.

To insist on covenant in a world that profits from fragmentation: rebellion.

And that is why the antisemites hate not only Jews—but Jewish intimacy. Because intimacy is proof that fragmentation is not inevitable. It's living evidence that love can survive.

We are the scandal of joy.

The audacity of life.

Jewish joy is not a mood. It is a moral stance against a world that profits from despair.

Where We Go Next

How do we build anti-fragmentation communities strong enough to resist the scapegoat economy? How do we create families, synagogues, schools, marriages, and friendships that make antisemitism psychologically unnecessary and socially unacceptable?

Because you don't beat a hate movement by merely condemning it.

You defeat it by building something so warm, connected, joyous, and morally serious that people would rather live within it than within hate.

Now, let's aim straight at the modern mechanisms powering the hate engine: porn culture, humiliation media, conspiracy-as-identity, and the way Jew-hatred is being repackaged as "anti-Zionism" to recruit a new generation.

CHAPTER EIGHT

THE CONSPIRACY MIND

Why Antisemitism Can't Stop Inventing Secret Jews

Antisemitism is not merely hatred. It is a *story engine*—a factory that never stops producing plots.

It needs to be, because antisemitism is fundamentally unstable. It cannot survive daylight or evidence. Nor the plain fact that Jews are human beings—messy, varied, contradictory, sometimes noble, occasionally foolish.

Trying to live our lives, raise our children, love our spouses, and build something better than what we inherited.

So, the antisemite does what every failing ideology does when reality refuses to cooperate: he retreats into the fog.

Antisemitism doesn't argue. It insinuates.

It doesn't prove. It whispers.

And whispering requires veils.

The Antisemite Needs Curtains

The world is complicated. History is tragic.

People get sick. Economies crash. Leaders lie. Institutions fail. Wars break out. Children die.

The human heart is capable of breathtaking cruelty—breathtaking beauty, too—and sometimes in the same hour.

For people who cannot tolerate uncertainty, who cannot bear the humble truth that life is a tangle of causes, accidents, tradeoffs, character flaws, and unintended consequences, that level of complexity is unbearable.

Coping, they create a substitute for truth—the conspiracy.

It offers a seductive structure:

- It turns chaos into a plan.
- It turns tragedy into intention.
- It turns randomness into design.
- It turns discomfort into certainty.
- And above all, it turns personal failure into *righteous victimhood.*

This isn't my opinion—it's a well-studied psychological pattern.

Conspiracy thinking often functions to satisfy motives like hunger for certainty (epistemic), control and safety (existential), and a sense of superiority or belonging (social).

Conspiracy theories are emotional narcotics: They don't cure pain, they numb it—before demanding a higher dose.

But conspiracies require a villain: the hidden hand, the shadow, the puppet master.

And the oldest puppet master in Western history is the Jew.

The Protocols—The Pornography of Antisemitic Fantasy

If you want to understand antisemitic conspiracy culture, begin with the *Protocols of the Elders of Zion*—a fabricated text by the secret police of Russia's Czar—"Bloody Nicholas"—that pretends to reveal a Jewish plan for world domination, first published in Imperial Russia, then spreading across continents like an infectious disease.

Even when exposed as fraudulent, it kept circulating.

Why?

Because it wasn't meant to be true. It was meant to be useful.

The *Protocols* did not persuade the antisemite. *It confirmed him.* It gave his hatred a costume—"research." It let him pretend his prejudice was analysis and disguise envy as empiricism.

The US Holocaust Memorial Museum documents a particularly chilling fact: Nazi leaders knew it was not factual—and used it anyway, because for antisemites, truth is optional.

The antisemite doesn't need evidence: he needs permission.

Blood Libel: The Conspiracy That Drinks Human Blood

Long before social media turned idiocy into a career path, there was the medieval blood libel—the accusation that Jews murder Christian children to use their blood for rituals.

It is one of history's most grotesque lies, and it has been studied and documented in detail by Holocaust historians and scholars of antisemitism.

The point of blood libel was never merely to smear Jews. It was to invert the moral universe. To turn the Jew—who brought to the world the Ten Commandments, the sanctity of life, the dignity of the vulnerable—into a demonic figure feeding on innocence.

Antisemitism survives by reversing reality: it makes the victim the villain; the murderer, "moral."

And notice once more the hallmark pattern: secrecy, ritual, hidden cabals, dark ceremonies; "they" control everything.

Antisemitism is conspiracism pinning a yarmulke onto the villain.

Why Conspiracies Are the Exact Opposite of Kosher Sex

Now we get to the beating heart of this chapter.

Kosher Sex, at its essence, is not a product, a slogan, or provocation: It is a theology of intimacy.

It is the courage to be seen.

Not by strangers—but by the one person you have pledged your life to. Seen without masks or costumes. Without the externalities of clothing. Without manipulation.

It's nakedness, yes—but more than nakedness of the body: nakedness of the soul, of the heart, and of the mind.

Kosher sex is:

- radical honesty,
- mutual vulnerability,

- fidelity as focus,
- trust as foreplay,
- and joy as the fruit of commitment.

The reverse of all of that?

Conspiracy culture.

Conspiracy culture is:

- endless concealment,
- endless suspicion,
- endless insinuation,
- endless, "I'm just asking questions,"
- endless doublespeak,
- and the permanent inability to trust anyone—especially not a spouse, neighbor, community, or society.

Kosher sex is the courage to be fully known.

Antisemitism is the compulsion to believe nothing is ever knowable.

If Kosher Sex is intimacy, conspiracism is paranoia. If kosher sex is candor, conspiracism is the addiction to secrecy. If kosher sex is mutual surrender, conspiracism is total control.

And if Kosher Sex is love, conspiracism is the inability to love—because love requires trust, *and conspiracists train themselves to distrust everything.*

The Antisemite's Favorite Word: "They"

Every antisemite eventually collapses into one word: they.

"They control the banks."

"They control the media."

"They control the government."

"They control Hollywood."

"They control the universities."

"They control the vaccines."

"They control the wars."

"They control your children's minds."

The antisemite does not want to name individuals, because individuals have faces. And faces produce empathy. Faces complicate hatred.

He wants a foggy collective villain, because it keeps the hatred clean, convenient.

The antisemite doesn't fear Jews.

He fears complexity. Jews are the scapegoat he uses to simplify the world.

Modern Variations: Same Old Poison, New Packaging

Today's antisemitic conspiracies are medieval lies wearing modern clothes. Sometimes it's "Rothschilds." Sometimes it's "globalists." Sometimes it's "Zionists." Or it's "Israel controls America," "Jews staged ___," "Mossad did ___."

And yes, some high-profile personalities amplify this nonsense because it's lucrative and invites clickbait in the millions. Outrage sells. So-called "reveals" sell. "Forbidden truth" sells. And Jews, as always, are a reliable target because antisemitism is the one bigotry that keeps getting invited back into polite society with a fresh suit.

For example:

Candace Owens repeatedly accuses "Zionists" of having killed JFK—an explicitly conspiratorial framing that plugs directly into the *Protocols* worldview. This accusation has been amplified by millions of her followers the world over.

I'm not interested in their motives. I'm interested in the mechanism behind them.

It's this: Conspiracy is the erotic substitute for intimacy.

That sounds shocking until you think about it.

Intimacy gives you connection, warmth, belonging, softness, forgiveness, the ability to exhale.

Conspiracy gives you something else: stimulation.

Adrenaline. A hit of secret knowledge. A thrill of superiority. A counterfeit version of meaning.

It is psychological pornography: arousal, without relationship.

Conspiracy is emotional pornography: excitement without intimacy, certainty without truth, power without love.

And just like porn, conspiracy culture escalates. What used to satisfy no longer satisfies. So you need a bigger lie, a darker plot, a more demonic enemy.

And eventually, it circles back to the Jew—because antisemitism is the grand unified theory of conspiracy thinking.

Why Jews Become the "Hidden Hand" in Every Story

Here's the brutal truth: Jews are cast as the secret controllers because Jews represent the opposite of what conspiracists feel inside.

Judaism is public argument. It's questions. Disputation, text, law.

Accountability, a God who demands you don't just feel—you do.

Covenant. Community. Marriage as a moral project. Children as a future.

It's "choose life." It's joy with responsibility.

Conspiracists hate that. It undermines their core identity: the aggrieved hero who refuses responsibility.

So they fantasize that Jews have a master plan—because the conspiracist himself has no plan, beyond resentment. They imagine Jewish unity—because their own lives are fractured. They imagine Jewish control—because they feel powerless. They imagine Jewish cunning—because they feel intellectually humiliated.

They imagine Jewish "impurity"—because they are at war with their own appetites and shame.

And that's why our enemies are so obsessed with Jewish sex, Jewish marriage, Jewish joy, Jewish continuity. It isn't incidental.

It is diagnostic.

The Antisemitic Mind Cannot Tolerate Openness

I want to drive this nail all the way in:

Kosher Sex is openness disciplined by commitment.

Antisemitism is secrecy weaponized by hate.

That is why antisemitism loves:

- anonymous accounts,
- coded language,

- vague insinuations,
- "Many people are saying,"
- "I heard,"
- "They don't want you to know,"
- and "do your own research" (meaning: consume my propaganda).

Judaism counters: Argue in the open, in the *Beit Midrash*—with sources, laws, accountability.

The antisemite insists: Meet me in the alley, where nobody can check my claims.

What Intimacy Does to a Conspiracy Addict

Now we come to perhaps the most important part: how to defeat it.

You do not defeat conspiracism only by debunking it. Debunking is necessary, but it's not sufficient, because conspiracies are not merely wrong ideas—they're emotional shelters.

You defeat conspiracism by rebuilding the human capacity for:

- trust
- intimacy
- community
- marriage
- family
- the innocence of children
- and the kind of joy that doesn't need an enemy.

That is why the message of *Kosher Sex*—properly understood—is not just marital advice.

It is civilizational resistance.

Because a society full of strong marriages, stable families, deep friendships, resilient communities, and embodied joy is harder to radicalize.

Conspiracy theorists recruit among the isolated, the humiliated, the lonely, the sexually angry, the socially untethered, and the spiritually empty.

And yes, this overlaps with what the psychology literature describes: people often turn to conspiracies under uncertainty and perceived powerlessness, because it offers a sense of meaning and control—even if false.

The most dangerous person in politics is not the poor man, but the lonely man with a grievance and a smartphone.

The Covenant of Openness: The Jewish Answer to *Protocols*

The Jewish response to the culture of veils?

A culture of covenant.

We answer insinuation with intimacy.

We answer paranoia with family.

We answer "they" with names, faces, relationships.

And we answer the oldest conspiracy in the world with the oldest Jewish toast in the world:

L'Chaim. To life.

Not as a slogan, but as a strategy.

Because antisemitism is a death cult masquerading as "truth-seeking." And Judaism is life—bold, embodied, joyful, committed, open.

Antisemitism survives in darkness. Jewish joy is the light switch.

CHAPTER NINE

INTIMACY VS. ISOLATION: WHY THE LONELIEST VOICES PREACH FRAGMENTATION

There is a simple truth modern culture refuses to confront: People who are deeply connected do not try to tear the world apart.

They don't need to.

They have someone to come home to. They have a body that is not at war with itself. A life that contains meaning without requiring enemies.

Hatred, by contrast, is almost always broadcast by people who are profoundly alone—emotionally, relationally, erotically, spiritually.

They may be famous, wealthy, and constantly surrounded by noise. But noise is not intimacy. An audience is not a family. Applause is not love.

And loneliness—especially unacknowledged loneliness—is one of the most destabilizing forces in human psychology.

Ultimately, isolation does not stay quiet. It becomes ideology.

Loneliness Is Not Neutral

Loneliness surpasses mere sadness. It becomes pressure.

When the human need for connection is unmet, the psyche looks for substitutes. If it cannot find intimacy, it seeks intensity. Unable to find love, it seeks power. Without belonging, it seeks enemies.

This is why the loneliest public figures often speak in absolutes. Nuance requires patience. Patience requires security. And security—real security—requires relationship.

So lonely people crave certainty because certainty feels like control. And control feels like safety.

They divide the world into:

- good and evil
- pure and corrupt
- us and them

When you are alone, complexity is terrifying.

Loneliness turns complexity into threat.

Why the Most Divisive Figures Are Almost Always Isolated

Note the following:

The figures who specialize in ripping society apart almost always burn through colleagues, alienate allies, and cycle through inner circles. They reduce every disagreement into betrayal. They twist criticism into persecution.

This is not coincidence. It's what happens when someone replaces relationship with grievance.

Because people who can sustain intimacy can also sustain disagreement. But those who cannot sustain intimacy experience disagreement as annihilation.

So every debate becomes a war.

Every critic, an enemy; every difference, a conspiracy.

When intimacy disappears, disagreement becomes existential.

Fragmentation as a Worldview

Antisemites and conspiracy theorists are not trying to bring people together. That is not their project.

Fragmentation is.

They create camps instead of building communities. They cultivate suspicion instead of fostering trust. They eroticize conflict instead of encouraging love.

Why?

Because fragmentation keeps people dependent.

A fragmented society produces:

- isolated individuals
- weak families
- anxious citizens
- brittle identities

And brittle identities are the easiest to manipulate.

Fragmentation: the preferred environment of demagogues.

Love Is Gravity—Hatred Is Anti-Matter

Here is the metaphor explaining everything:

Love is gravity and hatred is anti-matter.

Gravity pulls things together. Anti-matter repels, explodes, and annihilates.

Love binds spouses, parents, and children; neighbors, communities, and generations.

Hatred separates man from woman, parent from child, citizen from citizen, and human from human.

Antisemites are not trying to create a better society. They are trying to blow society apart—so they can stand in the rubble, feeling powerful.

Because rubble has no standards. It does not demand accountability and it does not expose loneliness.

Hatred wants to reduce a city to ruins rather than rule it.

Why Intimacy Is the Enemy of Extremism

Intimacy does something hatred cannot tolerate:

It humanizes.

A man who is deeply loved cannot easily dehumanize others. A woman who feels secure does not need ideological rage to feel strong. A family bound by affection does not need enemies to feel meaningful.

Intimacy softens absolutism. It introduces empathy, complicates narratives, and makes cruelty uncomfortable.

This is why extremist movements attack:

- marriage
- family
- sexuality
- loyalty
- covenant

Because intimacy creates moral friction.

Intimacy makes cruelty harder, so extremism hates it.

The Erotics of Fragmentation

Here is the uncomfortable truth: fragmentation is stimulating. Outrage produces adrenaline, division produces identity, and conflict produces attention.

For lonely people, this stimulation becomes addictive. Rage transforms into a substitute for touch, contempt supplants closeness, and power fantasies trade places with love.

This is why the loudest voices of hate often sound emotionally clenched, physically rigid, humorless, and compulsive.

Their bodies mirror their worldview: *void of softness, surrender, and trust.*

Why Antisemitism Needs a Fragmented World

Antisemitism cannot thrive in a connected society.

It requires mistrust, suspicion, and fear; it revels in rumor and secrecy.

It thrives when people no longer talk to each other, no longer marry, no longer build families, and no longer belong to real communities.

That is why antisemitism takes off during periods of social breakdown—economic collapse, cultural upheaval, sexual confusion, family disintegration.

Fragmentation creates the vacuum that antisemitism fills.

Jewish Intimacy as a Direct Threat

Judaism insists on things fragmentation cannot tolerate:

- marriage as covenant
- sex as mutual responsibility
- family as sacred obligation
- community as destiny

This is not nostalgic. *It's strategic.*

Judaism refuses the modern lie that freedom equates to isolation. It insists that freedom comes from belonging chosen with responsibility.

That insistence makes Jews intolerable to ideologies built on atomization.

Because it teaches people how to belong without being owned, Judaism is antisemitism's enemy.

Why the Loneliest Voices Grow the Loudest

Silence forces self-confrontation: thus, the loneliest people shout the most.

They need constant output—posts, videos, tirades, accusations—to avoid sitting alone with their emptiness. They confuse attention with connection, outrage with intimacy, notoriety with love.

But attention cannot hold you at night. Outrage never forgives you.

And so the aggression escalates. Enemies abound, conspiracies flourish, and division proliferates.

The louder the hate, the deeper the loneliness.

The Jewish Countermove

Judaism does not answer fragmentation with fragmentation.

It answers with covenant.

Instead of tearing down, it binds. Instead of isolating, it gathers. Instead of eroticizing rage, it sanctifies intimacy.

This is not softness. It's strength—durable, because connection is harder than contempt.

After all, marriage is harder than abandonment. Family is harder to form and sustain than a mob.

And only the former—family—builds a future.

The Hammer

I'll say it plainly:

Antisemites are not trying to save society.

They are trying to dismantle it, because dismantlement hides their loneliness.

They demand separation rather than intimacy.

Suspicion, rather than trust.

Leverage. Not love.

Judaism stands in their way—not because Jews are powerful, but because Jews are connected.

Connection is the one thing hatred cannot fake.

CHAPTER TEN

HOW TO BUILD ANTI-FRAGMENTATION COMMUNITIES IN A WORLD ADDICTED TO DIVISION

You do not defeat antisemitism by arguing with it online. So much of those who fight the Jew-haters are simply wasting their time and lives fighting these miscreants in social media posts that last for a few minutes. Posts that are then forgotten by the readers and discarded to the dustbin of history.

Indeed, I buy into the brilliant argument made by one of my favorite columnists, Peggy Noonan in the *Wall Street Journal*, that in a country where men don't make things with their hands any longer, they waste their time thinking up clever yet utterly ephemeral phrases for X and Instagram posts online. Those posts last for a few seconds. And yet their creators, who put hours into thinking of a turn of phrase, actually feel like they accomplished something important. But rebutting their drivel is ultimately not how we defeat hatred.

Rather, you defeat antisemitism and racism by *making it unnecessary.*

Hatred grows where people are isolated, unmoored, sexually frustrated, emotionally starved, and socially anonymous. When real connection returns—when people belong to something concrete and demanding—antisemitism loses its recruiting base.

You don't starve hatred by condemning it. You starve it by rebuilding connection.

Step One: Rebuild Marriage as a Public Good

Marriage is not a private hobby. It is social infrastructure.

When I ran for Congress in 2012, winning the Republican nomination by a landslide but then losing the general election in November (and yes, losing sucks), one of the planks on my platform was for the GOP to stop demonizing gay marriage as the destruction of heterosexual marriage.

Gays and lesbians account, at most, for about 7 percent of the American population. Heterosexual divorce, by contrast, hovers at somewhere around 60 percent. So, which is a bigger threat to marriage? Straight people who first marry and within a few years fall out of love at best, or hate each other's guts at worst—or gay marriage?

When marriages weaken, everything downstream collapses:

- children lose stability
- men lose accountability and love
- women lose security and love
- men and women become lonely
- institutions are eroded
- communities lose continuity

A culture that treats marriage as optional is a culture that quietly prepares itself for scapegoating.

Anti-fragmentation communities do the opposite. They:

- teach marriage before crisis, not after catastrophe
- normalize repair instead of replacement
- speak openly about intimacy, boredom, resentment, and healing
- treat sexual discipline as strength, not repression

This is not "traditionalism." It is realism.

A society that repairs marriages doesn't need enemies to feel alive.

Step Two: Teach Intimacy Without Shame—and Without Chaos

Two lies are crushing children and adults alike.

One: everything sexual is dangerous.

Two: everything sexual is permitted.

Both produce damage, both create shame, and both generate resentment.

Anti-fragmentation communities teach a third way:

- Desire is real
- Desire is powerful
- Desire must be educated, not indulged or demonized

This requires courage. It means talking about sex as a moral force—not a joke, not a commodity, not a taboo.

Silence leaves a vacuum. Porn and conspiracies rush in to fill it.

When communities refuse to teach intimacy, algorithms teach addiction.

Step Three: Make Community Physical Again

Online "communities" are not communities. They are networks without bodies.

Real community requires substantive rituals like shared meals. That's why, in 2001, Michael Jackson and I started a national program called "Turn Friday Night into Family Night," inviting non-Jewish families throughout America to share in the Jewish bounty of the weekly Sabbath dinner. The idea was simple: Families breaking bread together only twice a year—Thanksgiving and Christmas—don't build the ritual rhythm that sustains connection.

Families that come together every week do.

They benefit from:

- shared rituals

- shared responsibilities
- shared presence

Anti-fragmentation communities that gather regularly, physically, and predictably also pray together, argue in person, celebrate birth, and mourn death.

They mark time with ritual.

This embodied rhythm does something critical: it restores trust.

And trust is kryptonite to conspiracy thinking.

Conspiracies thrive online. *Communities thrive at tables.*

Step Four: Replace Ideology with Obligation

Ideologies promise meaning without responsibility. Obligations demand responsibility without spectacle.

Because ideology flatters the ego, hatred movements thrive on it: you get to feel righteous without having to show up for anyone.

Anti-fragmentation communities, though, are obligation-heavy:

- You check on the sick.
- You help the struggling.
- You comfort the bereaved.
- You show up even when it's inconvenient.
- You carry people who can't carry themselves.

This daily burden builds humility—and humility dissolves the need for scapegoats:

People busy fulfilling obligations have no bandwidth for mob ideology.

Step Five: Restore Male Responsibility and Female Security

Fragmented societies produce unaccountable and toxic men (don't believe the MAGA antisemites—toxic masculinity is a real thing, just ask the hundreds of millions of women who have experienced it and served as its victims). They furthermore churn out overburdened and degraded women.

That imbalance breeds resentment, grievance, and rage—*fertile soil for antisemitism.*

Anti-fragmentation communities, however, insist on:

- men who are responsible, not performative
- women who are protected, not exploited
- women who are productive and not sexualized
- mutual sexual responsibility, not power games
- covenant, not conquest

This is not about nostalgia. It is about preventing social breakdowns.

Accountable men and secure women suffocate hate movements.

Step Six: Teach Children Belonging Before Identity Politics

Children do not need slogans. They need roots.

Before asking children to "find themselves," anti-fragmentation communities give them:

- family stories
- communal memory
- shared rituals
- moral language
- a sense of being wanted
- a belief system in something grand, mystical, and magical

A child who belongs does not need to invent enemies to feel significant.

Belonging is the antidote to radicalization.

Step Seven: Practice Radical Openness Inside Covenant

Here is the paradox that breaks hatred. Kosher intimacy teaches:

- radical honesty
- total candor
- emotional nakedness
- trust earned over time

But always inside covenant.

This is the exact opposite of conspiratorial thinking, which depends on endless veils, secret motives, hidden hands, and unseen enemies.

When people learn to be known—truly known—by a spouse, a family, a community, the thrill of "secret knowledge" and endless conspiracy loses its power.

Known people do not need hidden enemies.

Step Eight: Make Joy Visible—and Defend It

Joy is not decorative. It is strategic.

Hatred wants the world gray, humorless, clenched, and fearful. Joy disrupts that ecosystem.

Anti-fragmentation communities:

- celebrate loudly
- laugh unapologetically
- dance at weddings
- sing at tables
- shamelessly mark life's goodness

Joy conveys a dangerous message to antisemitism: *life works*. And if life works, hatred is unnecessary.

Visible joy is antisemitism's worst rival.

Step Nine: Confront Lies Without Becoming a Mob

Anti-fragmentation communities do not appease lies—but they also refuse mob behavior.

They:

- correct falsehoods calmly
- name antisemitism without hysteria
- refuse to dehumanize

Why? Because mobs are the mirror image of hate movements. They feel powerful—but they also fragment.

Whereas strength without cruelty, clarity without chaos, and defense without dehumanization prevail.

The goal is not to defeat enemies. *It is to refuse to become them.*

Step Ten: Choose Covenant Over Crowd—Every Time

Crowds intoxicate. Covenants demand. Crowds supply instant belonging. Covenant requires loyalty. Crowds dissolve responsibility. Covenant multiplies it.

Antisemitism recruits mobs. Judaism constructs covenants.

Every anti-fragmentation community must choose—daily—between these two.

Crowds *seem* powerful.

Covenants *are.*

The Hammer

Let's dispense with euphemisms: Antisemitism thrives where intimacy vacates. Conspiracies thrive where trust evaporates.

Hatred thrives where people are lonely, shamed, and disconnected.

The Jewish answer has never been abstraction.

It is:

- marriage
- family
- community
- covenant
- joy
- responsibility

Build those, and antisemitism starves.

Ignore them, and hatred feasts.

The strongest response to antisemitism is a life that works and is suffused with moral purpose.

CHAPTER ELEVEN

WHY JEWISH JOY IS PUBLIC ENEMY NUMBER ONE

Hatred does not primarily fear power.

It fears happiness.

Power can be negotiated with, contained, defeated, or stolen. Joy cannot. Joy is contagious. It spreads without permission and undermines the central promise of every grievance ideology—that life is fundamentally rigged, hostile, and only survivable through rage.

This is why antisemitism has always fixated not just on Jewish influence, but on Jewish joy: weddings, children, laughter, music, ritual, erotic confidence, family warmth, stubborn optimism.

On the Jewish capacity to do more than survive: *on the Jewish capacity to flourish.*

Joy Is Evidence the Grievance Narrative Is False

Every hate ideology begins with a story: you are oppressed, you are robbed, you are humiliated; someone else—nearly always Jews—has stolen your destiny.

That story can only survive if it monopolizes emotional reality. If people begin to experience genuine connection, belonging, pleasure, and purpose, the story deflates.

Grievance requires despair to feel true.

Jewish joy is the walking contradiction. It says: Life is not a zero-sum theft. It says: Meaning can be built, not seized. It says: Love is effective, not naïve.

And that is unforgivable to ideologies that require misery to justify themselves.

To seem honest, hatred necessitates despair.

Why Antisemites Obsess Over Jewish Celebrations

Watch what antisemitic movements attack first. Not Jewish tragedy, Jewish trauma, or Jewish mourning.

Rather, they attack:

- weddings
- festivals
- birthrates
- dancing
- singing
- family life
- intimacy
- and especially, *circumcision celebrations*

Because these are the places where Jewish life looks most normal—and most successful.

A Jewish wedding is not just a party: it's declaration—amid our suffering, both today and eternally, we believe in tomorrow.

Now and always.

A Jewish child is likewise not just a baby: it is a verdict on history—"You did not win."

Joy announces continuity.

Continuity is the one thing antisemitism cannot tolerate.

The Smear of "Obscene Happiness"

When antisemites cannot deny Jewish joy, they reframe it as obscene. They say Jews are:

- laughing while others suffer
- dancing while the world burns
- enjoying pleasure irresponsibly
- celebrating at the expense of others

It was not a coincidence that the Hamas terrorists focused so much of their bloodthirsty energy on the Nova music festival on October 7. Indeed, Hamas abandoned its original plan of trying to murderously conquer most of the Israeli southern communities to focus on the Nova festival, where they butchered more than 350 victims in cold blood.

This smear of Jewish joy is moral blackmail.

It demands that Jews earn the right to be happy by first surrendering their humanity. It says: "Your joy is only acceptable if it is muted, enslaved, hidden, and apologetic."

No such demand is made of anyone else.

Why?

Because the issue is not empathy. It is envy.

When joy is called immoral, envy is pretending to be ethics.

Why Joy Cannot Be Controlled

Anger can be directed. Fear can be manipulated. Guilt can be exploited.

Joy cannot.

Joy is decentralized. It arises in kitchens, bedrooms, synagogues, schools, playgrounds, musical celebrations, dinner tables. It does not require leaders, slogans, or permission. It spreads through laughter, affection, ritual, and love.

This makes joy a threat to movements that rely on centralized outrage. Antisemitism wants crowds chanting in unison. Jewish joy, on the other hand, wants families singing in harmony. Crowds are controllable. Celebratory families and communities are not.

Joy cannot be mobilized, and that terrifies demagogues.

The Erotics of Joy vs. the Erotics of Rage

There is an erotic dimension to this conflict that most people are afraid to name.

Rage is stimulating. Outrage produces adrenaline. Hatred gives people a sense of power without intimacy. But it is a sterile erotic—a high without warmth, intensity without connection, arousal without tenderness.

Jewish joy offers a different erotic logic:

- pleasure without humiliation
- intimacy without domination
- desire without exploitation
- laughter without cruelty

This kind of joy threatens those who have replaced intimacy with aggression. *Because it reminds them what they gave up.*

Hatred is arousal without love. Jewish joy is love personified and embodied.

Why Joy Is Treated as Provocation

When Jews are joyful, antisemitism reframes it as provocation.

Why are they celebrating now?

How dare they be happy?

This is not a moral question. *It is a demand for submission.* It communicates: "Your happiness makes us uncomfortable. Stop."

I just read a fascinating book, *King of Kings*, about the bloodthirsty radical Ayatollah Ruhollah Khomeini—the father of modern radical, murderous Islamism who came to power in Iran in 1979 and immediately began to murder tens of thousands of Iranians. The author makes an interesting note: Khomeini never smiled.

Never told a humorous anecdote. Always projected severity.

Indeed, on the chartered 747 Air France jet which flew him from Paris to Tehran, only a single Western journalist managed to crawl from the economy section where Western journalists had paid to accompany the tyrant to the home from which he had been exiled for thirteen years.

The reporter asked him how he felt to be returning to his native homeland. Khomeini's infamous response: "Nothing."

Khomeini was not just a tyrant. He was a *miserable* tyrant.

But Jewish history has taught a brutal lesson: Waiting for permission to live fully is waiting to disappear.

So Jews learned to bless life anyway.

Jewish joy is not ignorance of suffering. It is defiance of erasure.

The Joy–Intimacy–Continuity Triangle

Jewish joy is not random. It is structured. It flows from:

- intimacy (marriage, family, covenant)
- continuity (children, tradition, memory)
- meaning (law, ritual, responsibility)

This triangle is lethal to antisemitism.

Break intimacy, and joy weakens. Break continuity and hope collapses. Break meaning, and pleasure numbs.

That is why antisemitism attacks all three.

It mocks marriage. It demonizes fertility. It condemns the birth of male Jewish children and their circumcision celebrations. It ridicules ritual.

Because if any of them survive, *joy survives, too.*

The Politics of Grayness

Antisemitic movements always aestheticize grayness.

No humor. No warmth. No playfulness.

Neither erotic confidence nor celebration unburdened by guilt.

Grayness keeps people compliant. It keeps them tired and suspicious.

Enveloped by grayness, they remain dependent on ideology for emotional stimulation.

Jewish joy explodes grayness. Jewish joy is colorful, loud, and argumentative. Musical. Erotic. Familial.

Alive.

And life is disruptive. Hatred wants a colorless world. *But Jews refuse.*

Why Joy Is Braver Than Rage

Rage is easy. Rage does not require vulnerability. Rage does not risk heartbreak. Rage does not require forgiveness.

Joy does.

To love in a dangerous world is *courageous*. To build families after trauma is courageous, too, as is to laugh after loss.

Jewish joy is not naiveté. It is nerve. Rage hides from pain.

Joy risks it.

The Antisemite's Ultimate Fear

The antisemite's deepest fear is not Jewish power. It is Jewish normalcy. A Jew who is:

- married
- raising children
- reveling in intimacy
- having great sex
- kissing passionately
- exploring their husband's or wife's body as an odyssey of wonder
- feeling embedded in community
- laughing at the Shabbat dinner table
- dancing at a Jewish wedding
- celebrating the major festivals

This is no caricature. Nor is it a symbol or conspiracy.

Just human beings. And, up close, human beings are hard to hate.

The Hammer

Let this be said clearly and without apology:

Jewish joy is public enemy number one to antisemitism because it proves hatred unnecessary.

It proves life can be built.

It proves intimacy can survive.

It proves continuity can persist.

It proves meaning can outlast rage.

First and foremost, before dead Jews, *antisemitism wants joyless Jews*.

But Jews have refused that demand for thousands of years. Not defiance by shouting. *Defiance by living.*

CHAPTER TWELVE

WHY PORN IS THE MOST ANTISEMITIC INDUSTRY ON EARTH

Let's drop the euphemisms.

Pornography is not "adult entertainment." It is not "sexual liberation." Nor is it "free expression." Pornography is a multi-billion-dollar engine of emotional destruction—and it has done more to create the psychological conditions for antisemitism than almost any ideology of the last fifty years.

That may sound provocative. It isn't.

It is observable fact.

Porn does not merely distort sexuality. It destroys the conditions required for love, and when love collapses, resentment rushes in.

When resentment rushes in, scapegoats are needed. And history tells us—mercilessly—who the preferred scapegoat always is.

Porn doesn't just destroy marriages.

It manufactures the emotional rage that antisemitism feeds on.

Porn Creates the Antisemite's Ideal Subject

Every antisemitic movement requires a specific psychological profile in its followers:

- Lonely
- Sexually frustrated
- Ashamed
- Addicted to stimulation
- Deprived of meaning
- Furious at women
- Furious at successful men
- Furious at families
- Furious at the future

Porn produces this profile at scale.

It trains men to:

- desire women they will never know
- climax without intimacy
- equate arousal with domination
- view novelty as entitlement
- associate sex with isolation

Porn trains women to:

- feel replaceable
- feel inadequate
- perform rather than connect
- compete with fantasies
- internalize male detachment
- hate their inadequate bodies

Porn then does something far worse:

It removes the single most stabilizing force in male psychology—bonded erotic purpose.

A bonded man is dangerous to tyrants. An unbonded man becomes, in the words of Vladimir Lenin, a useful idiot.

Porn turns men into consumers of women, *then sells them rage when love collapses.*

Porn and the Collapse of Meaning

On my daily social media feed, amid the hundreds of explicit death threats I receive from all over the world—"I hope you're gassed," "Hitler is alive and coming for you," "Beware us arriving at your home to decapitate you"—is another common refrain.

The antisemites accuse us Jews of having invented and sustaining global pornography.

It's an interesting accusation, especially against me, since I have been arguably the loudest voice condemning the pernicious effects of pornography, for decades, in the English-speaking world.

Indeed, I persuaded Pamela Anderson—who holds the record for most *Playboy* covers in the magazine's history (seventeen)—to co-author our book *Lust for Love.* Our world-famous collaboration, which was launched before an audience of a thousand students at Oxford University, was a convincing argument against pornography and how it utterly destroys not just feminine self-respect but any chance that a relationship will have cohesive intimacy.

Just before the coronavirus began to ravage the world, *Politico* magazine published a major feature on then-Senator and later Vice President Kamala Harris's crusade against revenge porn. As *Politico* reported, in February 2015, Harris, then the California attorney general, summoned Silicon Valley leaders to discuss the devastating effects of "revenge porn"—the distribution of sexually graphic images of individuals without their consent.

At that meeting, Harris made the point that this had nothing to do with love affairs gone wrong, and it wasn't online mischief. It wasn't even about sex, really. It was a crime, the way domestic abuse was a crime.

According to *Politico,* the meeting was demonstrably effective and netted immediate results. The next month, Twitter banned nonconsensual intimate photos and videos from its service. That summer, Google began stripping explicit photos from its search results at victims' request. Next, Microsoft said it would block links to intimate content on its Xbox Live gaming service.

Kamala was right to focus on the catastrophic effects of revenge pornography on women, a point echoed by *New York Times* columnist Nicholas Kristof's unforgettable takedown of a website that featured revenge porn.

But even the everyday, garden variety of porn consumed by millions of mostly men is incredibly destructive.

Yes, I'm aware of the arguments pointing out that porn is watched by women and can help increase erotic interest between them. But these arguments in favor belie the fact that the overwhelming consumers of pornography are indeed men. And proponents ignore that the positive effects of watching porn are undermined by couples' growing dependence on strangers to remain erotically interested in each other.

Those who constantly feed their minds with porn will find themselves hard-pressed not to lose respect for women. Much of pornography falsely depicts women not only as sleazy and vulgar but as greedy, parasitical, and unremittingly slutty. The man watching porn never forgets that some of the women stripping for him are doing so exclusively for financial reward. The not-so-subtle message is that there is little women aren't prepared to do for money.

This is a message that television and social media need to be mindful of as well. The female "gold digger" trope has deep roots in modern American media.

Indeed, the birth of reality TV started with a show called *Who Wants to Marry a Multi-Millionaire* and was premised on the claim that most women would trade their hearts for a man's wallet in a jiffy. That show was followed by *Joe Millionaire*, *For Love or Money*, and other reality TV shows dedicated to the same misogynistic ilk.

The problem is widespread. Some estimates claim that about 30 percent of the internet is dedicated to porn. And with the "gold digger" idea becoming so widespread with so little outrage from women, it should not come as a surprise that in 2000, the *New York Times* reported an increase of 1500 percent in husbands making their wives sign prenuptial agreements over the previous decade because men were becoming consumed by suspicion of female avarice.

Our culture ought to wake up to how this consumption is affecting our assessment of women.

Because pornography portrays women as existing to serve men's lascivious needs, it causes men to have contempt for women. It invites them not merely to sexualize women but to view them as a means rather than an end.

Porn's Real Harm

The harms of porn are not abstract phenomena.

I have seen this degradation of women myself, in the marriage counseling sessions I host.

For married men, excessive exposure to a variety of naked female bodies contributes to their penchant for feeling perennially dissatisfied with their wives. When husbands are constantly barraged with pornographic images—which predominantly feature airbrushed images of the "perfect" female body—their own wives become utterly ordinary by comparison. *When a man sees his wife's naked body, his eye will be immediately drawn to her flaws rather than to her beauty.*

Not only does this lead to the degradation of his wife, but it also hinders his ability to find sexual satisfaction.

Indeed, with the single standard of beauty generally cultivated by porn—large, fake breasts, dyed blonde hair, buxom beauties or, the inverse, women who look like they haven't had a meal since the Middle Ages—it is nearly impossible to be satisfied with the variety of body types that exist in the real world.

Unable to find true contentment with their wives, many men look elsewhere, becoming increasingly addicted to porn. Moreover, men who are used to looking at pornography are rarely contented with a single image of perfection. Notice how *Playboy* rarely repeated playmates in multiple centerfolds. Even "Miss June's" seemingly flawless form is not good enough to win her the "Miss July" or "Miss August" centerfold.

Once she has been seen and digested, she is no longer captivating enough to be seen again.

Variety for men becomes necessary and essential.

More than simply providing the "ideal" measure by which to judge women, pornography hinders a man's attachment to a single woman because it impairs his ability to build deep relationships.

Sexual intimacy should bring a couple together on emotional and mental planes. Once a man feels removed enough to judge his wife by external comparisons, he loses some of his excitement for her and mistakenly believes that a more perfectly formed woman would provide him with the physical titillation he craves.

After a while, pornography becomes an uncontrollable addiction, in which the viewer needs more stimulation to achieve the same level of arousal. Like a drug that slowly wears off and must be consumed in ever larger quantity for the same high, this effect is perfectly illustrated by studies showing the range of pornographic viewing on the internet.

While most men will start looking at adult websites for an average of fifteen minutes, within months, they are online for hours. In the beginning, it only takes a short hit to achieve the desired effect, but with time, these quick glances are no longer enough.

Porn's Degradation of Women

Once pornography enters into a relationship, women become subordinate because they have been objectified and commoditized. In the world of pornography, women are generally portrayed in four ways: as the mindless, brainless, empty-headed playmate; the insatiable nymphomaniac; the cheating spouse seduced by her own stepson (it's fascinating to watch how much porn today is geared toward incest); or as one who craves pain.

And once women are degraded and lose their equal footing, men find themselves looking for validation in bragging rights by being able to boast to their friends about their conquests of multiple women.

King Solomon declared in Proverbs that "He who has found a woman has found goodness."

But in the age of the fraudulently depicted vulgar women of the pornographic universe, we might modify the aphorism to read, "*He who has found only fantasy woman has compromised his ability to* appreciate *goodness.*"

And the emptiness cultivated by porn, especially on the part of men, leads to misery, loneliness, depression, and rage.

When Pamela and I first published our joint condemnation of pornography, first in the *Wall Street Journal* as a joint op-ed, the global reverberations hit like an earthquake.

Was Pamela Anderson, who had made her career as a buxom blonde on *Baywatch*, really now condemning how far the male exploitation of female nudity had gone?

Yes, she was.

And, as a marriage counselor for decades, so was I.

She has since gone much further and now refuses to even put on makeup. And oddly enough, this remake of radical authenticity has made her new career soar through the stratosphere.

I've spent much of my career warning about pornography's corrosive effects on a man's soul and on his ability to function as husband and, by extension, as father. This is a public hazard of unprecedented seriousness given how freely available, anonymously accessible, and easily disseminated pornography is nowadays.

We jointly emphasized the following:

We are a guinea-pig generation for an experiment in mass debasement that few of us would have ever consented to, and whose full nefarious impact may not be known for years. How many families will suffer? How many marriages will implode? How many talented men will scrap their most important relationships and careers for a brief onanistic thrill? How many children will propel, warp-speed, into the dark side of adult sexuality by forced exposure to their fathers' profanations?

Porn's Carnage at Scale

The statistics already available are terrifying.

According to data provided by the American Psychological Association, porn consumption rates are between 50 percent and 99 percent among men and 30 percent to 86 percent among women, with the former group often reporting less satisfactory intimate lives with their wives or girlfriends as a result of the consumption. And this was back in 2016!

In the decade since, it has no doubt only grown far worse.

Nine percent of porn users said they had tried unsuccessfully to stop—an indication of addiction that is all the more startling when you consider that the dependency rate among people who try marijuana is the same (9 percent) and not much higher among those who try cocaine (15 percent), according to the National Center for Biotechnology Information.

But it is a fair guess that whereas drug-dependency data are mostly stable, the incidence of porn addiction will only spiral as the children now being raised in an environment of wall-to-wall, digitized sexual images become adults inured to intimacy, in need of even greater graphic stimulation.

They are the crack babies of porn.

All people are unique individuals, and porn consumption is also, no doubt, a reflection of personal psychopathologies. Yet all too many men, especially in the U.S. or other Western countries that enjoy liberal values and material prosperity, are becoming porn addicts.

These are men who, by any objective measure, have succeeded yet regard themselves as failures. Men who feel marooned in lassitude because they enjoy physical security, who feel bereft and bored even if they are blessed to have the committed love of a wife or girlfriend. Men who believe that cruising the internet for explicit footage of other women, or sharing such images of themselves over the remote communication offered by smartphones, are risqué but risk-free distractions from the tedium.

Yes, the march of technology is irreversible, and we aren't so naïve as to believe that any kind of imposed regulation could ever reseal the Pandora's box of pornography. What is required is an honest dialogue about what we are witnessing—the true nature and danger of porn—and an honor code to tamp it down in the collective interests of our well-being as individuals, as families, and as communities.

The ubiquity of porn is an outgrowth of the sexual revolution that began a half-century ago and which, with gender rights and freedoms now having been established, has arguably run its course. Now is the time for an epochal shift in our private and public lives. Call it a "sensual revolution."

The sensual revolution would replace pornography with eroticism—the alloying of sex with love, of physicality with personality, of the body's mechanics with imagination, of orgasmic release with binding relationships. In an age where public disapproval is no longer an obstacle to personal disgrace, we must turn instead to the appeal of self-interest.

Simply put, we must educate ourselves and our children to understand that *porn is for losers*—a boring, wasteful, and dead-end outlet for people too lazy to reap the ample rewards of healthy sexuality.

And loser is the term that best describes those who descend into the pit of antisemitism.

Antisemitism does not thrive in happy civilizations. It thrives in civilizations where:

- men feel humiliated
- women feel discarded
- children feel unwanted
- marriage feels pointless
- sex feels empty
- *life feels rigged*

Porn accelerates all of this.

When sex no longer points toward love, commitment, family, or future, it becomes pure appetite. Appetite without purpose never satisfies—it only intensifies craving. And craving without satisfaction becomes bitterness.

Bitter men do not ask, "How do I improve my life?"

They ask, "Who stole it from me?"

And this is where antisemitism enters.

Porn weaponizes desire.

Why Antisemites Always Blame Jews for Sexual Chaos

Here is the perverse irony. Pornography destroys intimacy. Then antisemitism blames Jews for moral collapse. This is not accidental.

Throughout history, Jews have been accused of:

- corrupting morals
- degrading culture
- poisoning youth
- undermining family
- spreading decadence

Porn provides the chaos. Antisemitism provides the narrative.

When men cannot form lasting bonds, they look for conspiracies. When families fracture, people look for saboteurs. When sex becomes empty, rage looks for targets. And the Jew—always portrayed as manipulative, controlling, "behind the scenes"—fits the fantasy perfectly.

Porn creates the wound. Antisemitism offers the lie that explains it.

Porn and the Hatred of Jewish Marriage

Now we reach the core reason porn culture collides violently with Judaism.

Judaism insists on:

- marriage with passion
- exclusivity with pleasure
- discipline with delight
- family as sacred
- children as blessing

Porn insists on:

- novelty over loyalty
- fantasy over presence
- consumption over covenant
- isolation over intimacy

These two worldviews cannot coexist.

A pornified culture must mock marriage. It must trivialize fidelity and ridicule sanctity.

So, when Jews defend erotic marriage—not timidly, not apologetically, but confidently—it enrages porn culture and its ideological defenders. They call it "prudish." They call it "repressive," or "backward."

But what they are really saying is: *Stop reminding us that sex was meant to mean something.*

Porn hates Judaism because Judaism proves desire can be disciplined without being destroyed.

Porn Is the Training Ground for Dehumanization

Antisemitism requires one thing above all: dehumanization.

Porn trains dehumanization perfectly.

- Bodies become objects

- Faces become irrelevant
- Consent becomes performative
- Pain becomes entertainment
- Empathy becomes optional

Once you learn to detach arousal from humanity, you can detach outrage from morality. This is why pornified cultures produce mobs that:

- cheer rape as "resistance"
- justify kidnapping as "context"
- excuse murder as "liberation"

The moral reflex is already dead. *Porn killed it.*

Why Jews Are the First Target When Porn Culture Implodes

Porn promises freedom. It delivers emptiness.

When the emptiness becomes unbearable, someone must be blamed. History supplies the scapegoat.

The Jew is blamed because:

- Jews defend family
- Jews defend fertility
- Jews defend children
- Jews defend covenant
- Jews defend meaning

A culture that has lost meaning cannot forgive those who retain it.

So, the hatred sharpens. And suddenly:

- Jewish birthrates are "provocations"
- Jewish marriage is "oppression"
- Jewish intimacy is "perversion"
- Jewish joy is "obscene"

They don't hate Jews for failing civilization.

They hate Jews for surviving it.

Porn vs. Kosher Sex: The Real War

Make no mistake. This book is not fighting antisemites alone. *It is fighting the pornified moral collapse that manufactures antisemites.*

Kosher Sex says:

- choose one person
- deepen desire
- sanctify touch
- protect mystery
- build a future
- find happiness

Porn says:

- choose endlessly
- flatten desire
- erase mystery
- avoid responsibility
- consume and discard
- indulge grievance

One produces families.

The other produces mobs.

One produces children.

The other produces resentment.

One produces life. The other produces death.

One produces empty and numbing orgasm, "the little death."

The other produces the electrifying eroticism of intimate togetherness.

Pornography is antisemitism's most efficient recruitment tool.

The Hammer

Here it is, without cushioning:

Antisemitism is exploding not because Jews are more visible, but because meaning has vanished. Porn helped it disappear.

When sex is stripped of sanctity, life loses gravity.

When life loses gravity, hatred ascends.

Judaism anchors sex in covenant. It anchors pleasure in responsibility and joy in holiness.

Judaism anchors life in God.

And that anchoring provokes a world addicted to drift.

CHAPTER THIRTEEN

THE COLLAPSE OF MASCULINITY AND THE RISE OF JEW-HATRED

Antisemitism does not rise in societies full of confident men. It ascends in societies full of humiliated men—men who feel unnecessary, sexually invisible, economically irrelevant, mocked by culture and abandoned by institutions.

Men who no longer believe women, children, or the future need them.

This is not sociology-lite.

It is the engine room of modern hatred.

When masculinity collapses, it does not disappear.

It curdles.

And curdled masculinity hunts for enemies.

Historically, when men lost land, craft, honor, family authority, and sexual purpose, they did not turn inward with humility. They turned outward with rage. They searched for a rival who seemed to possess what they had lost: confidence, continuity, competence, cohesion.

Over and over again, they found the same figure. The Jew.

The Lie That Men Are No Longer Necessary

Modern culture tells men four corrosive lies:

1. Your strength is dangerous.
2. Your desire is predatory.
3. Your leadership is oppressive.
4. You no longer matter, as you've been replaced by robots and AI.

It offers, however, no replacement identity.

Men are told to feel shame—but not given purpose. They are told to dismantle—but not told what to build. They are told to "listen"—but not trusted to lead.

They are told to suppress—but not taught to sanctify.

This is not moral formation. It is psychological disarmament. And disarmed men do not become peaceful. They become resentful. They either implode into passivity—or explode into extremism. The first produces apathy. The second produces mobs.

Antisemitism recruits from both.

When masculinity is shamed but not transformed, it mutates into hatred.

Porn: The Great Masculinity Saboteur

Pornography is not only a sexual toxin. It is a masculinity-destroying technology. Porn teaches men to:

- seek stimulation without effort
- expect intimacy without risk
- climax without responsibility or connection
- consume without committing
- dominate without protecting

It strips men of the two things that historically anchored masculinity: *competence and covenant.*

A man who must pursue, court, build, protect, and provide grows disciplined.

A man who clicks, scrolls, climaxes, and disappears grows brittle. Porn creates men who are aroused but directionless, stimulated but unformed, entitled but empty.

These men feel something deeply unsettling: they are replaceable.

They are not *chosen*. They are not needed. They are not depended on. And rather than face the internal reckoning—*what kind of man do I need to become*?—they look outward. They look for someone to blame.

Porn doesn't make men dangerous. It makes them weak—and weak men look for someone to hate.

Why Jews Become the Masculine Rival

Hatred always seeks a symbolic rival. The Jew has historically filled this role because Jews represent exactly what humiliated masculinity lacks:

- stable family structures
- intellectual mastery
- generational continuity
- sexual discipline
- communal loyalty
- resilience under pressure

To the insecure man, the Jewish male becomes unbearable. Not because Jews dominate him—but because Jews expose him.

The Jewish husband, committed to his wife. The Jewish father, invested in his children. The Jewish scholar, mastering text. The Jewish soldier, defending land. The Jewish businessman, building something durable—and being charitable.

These images ignite envy in men who have been told they are disposable.

So, hatred forms. The Jew becomes:

- the emasculator
- the manipulator
- the hidden controller
- the unfair competitor

Not because these accusations are true—but because they soothe humiliation.

The antisemite hates Jews the way an insecure man hates a mirror.

The Jewish Male as an Existential Insult

For centuries, antisemitism portrayed Jewish men as effeminate, weak, cowardly.

Now, when Jewish men are visible as soldiers, fathers, innovators, fighters, defenders—antisemitism flips the script.

Suddenly Jews are "too powerful." Suddenly Jewish men are "dangerous." Suddenly Jewish masculinity is "toxic." *Suddenly Jewish warriors are genocidaires.*

The accusation changes, but the resentment stays the same. Because antisemitism does not care about consistency. It cares about relief—the relief of not having to confront personal failure.

Antisemitism doesn't accuse Jews of what they are—it accuses Jews of what the accuser fears he is not.

Israel and the Masculine Reckoning

This is why Israel is such a psychological detonator. Israel does not fit the preferred image of the Jew as weak victim or clever manipulator. *Israel is unapologetically physical*:

- soldiers
- borders
- land
- defense
- risk
- sacrifice

Israel represents masculine responsibility at the national level. And that enrages men who have been taught that masculinity itself is suspect.

It enrages them because Israel proves something dangerous: Masculinity can be disciplined without being cruel. An army can be lethal, but only against terrorists committed to destroying innocent life. Strength can be moral without apologizing. Force can be used to protect life rather than dominate it.

So, Israel must be demonized. Not debated. Not criticized. *Demonized.*

Because Israel is not merely a state. *It is a refutation.*

The Radicalization Pipeline: From Humiliation to Hatred

Here is the pipeline modern culture pretends not to see:

1. Men are shamed for desiring purpose.
2. Men are isolated through porn and digital life.
3. Men lose real-world competence and intimacy.

Then, resentment builds, rage seeks a story, and ideologues supply one: Jews took it from you.

This pipeline in turn produces:

- incels
- extremists
- conspiracy theorists
- grievance addicts
- ideological foot soldiers

The final product? *Antisemitism.*

It is masculinity's revenge fantasy when discipline has been removed.

Why Jewish Masculinity Is the Target

Judaism does not abolish masculinity. It elevates it, refines it, and disciplines it.

It teaches men to:

- master desire
- honor women
- commit sexually
- lead families
- carry responsibility
- answer to God

That is threatening to ideologies that profit from male disintegration. Because disciplined men are hard to manipulate. They don't need mobs. They don't need outrage, either.

They don't need scapegoats.

They need one thing above all—covenant.

So Jewish masculinity must be mocked, slandered, sexualized, and degraded. That is why antisemitism always returns to sex. Because sexuality is where masculinity either finds purpose or collapses into resentment.

The antisemite cannot forgive Jewish masculinity; *it proves manhood requires discipline, not dominance.*

The Feminization Trap

There is another dimension that must be named without flinching.

Modern antisemitism increasingly weaponizes the language of "care," "sensitivity," and "safety" while harboring profound contempt for men—especially Jewish men.

Jewish male confidence is recoded as aggression. Jewish self-defense is recoded as brutality. Assertiveness is recoded as domination.

This is not feminism.

It is emasculation disguised as morality. And emasculation produces backlash—not against the ideology, but against the symbolic target.

Again: Jews.

A culture that demonizes masculinity without offering sanctification breeds rage.

The Return of the Jewish Father

Here is the quiet truth that terrifies antisemitism: Jewish masculinity is resurging.

Jewish men are marrying, having children, and defending Israel.

They're reclaiming their faith, rejecting porn, and choosing covenant.

This is not regression. It is renewal. *And renewal always provokes those invested in collapse.*

The antisemite senses the shift. And he panics. Because if Jewish men can rebuild masculinity without cruelty, without nihilism, without domination—then his entire grievance implodes.

The Hammer

Here is the truth stripped bare:

Antisemitism is the howl of collapsed masculinity refusing to rebuild.

It is easier to hate Jews than to become a man.

It is easier to blame Israel than to protect a family, to scream about power than to cultivate competence, and to accuse Jews than to discipline desire.

Judaism refuses to offer the antisemite that escape hatch.

We insist on becoming—becoming husbands, fathers, defenders.

Becoming builders.

Becoming responsible.

Antisemitism: Undisciplined masculinity desperate for someone to punish.

CHAPTER FOURTEEN

FEMINISM, PORN, AND THE BETRAYAL OF WOMEN

Antisemitism loves to pretend it is defending women.

That pretense is one of its most effective disguises.

Across history, Jew-hatred has repeatedly wrapped itself in the language of "protecting women," "protecting purity," "protecting daughters," "protecting society."

It did this in medieval Europe. It did it in Nazi Germany, too. And it does it today—on campuses, online, and in activist movements speaking the language of justice while trafficking in rage.

But here is the blunt truth: Antisemitism does not protect women.

It exploits them. It uses women as symbols, as props, as excuses—never as people whose dignity actually matters.

And modern culture, intoxicated by pornography yet calling itself feminist, has become the perfect host for this lie.

The Two Lies Women Are Sold at Once

Women today are being sold two contradictory lies, often by the same cultural voices.

Lie one: Your worth depends on sexual availability and desirability. Lie two: Your worth depends on constant victimhood.

Neither produces dignity.

The first lie turns women into commodities. The second turns women into political instruments.

Porn culture teaches women to perform endlessly—to be visible, consumable, replaceable.

Radical grievance culture teaches women to see themselves as permanently endangered, permanently wronged, permanently defined by oppression.

Both steal agency. Both hollow out intimacy. And both create the emotional environment antisemitism thrives in—because antisemitism needs grievance, humiliation; a story in which desire is dangerous and blame must be assigned.

Women are not liberated by this culture.

They are used by it.

A culture that commodifies women and then calls it empowerment prepares women to be sacrificed.

Porn Is Not Pro-Woman. It Is Anti–Female Intimacy.

Pornography markets itself as sexual freedom for women. *This is among the most cynical lies of the modern era.*

Porn does not free women. It trains men to detach arousal from empathy, and it trains women to compete with fantasy.

It tells women:

- You must look like this.
- You must perform like that.
- You must accept being watched.
- You must tolerate being replaced.
- You must call degradation "choice."

And if you object, it tells you you're prudish, repressed, anti-feminist.

But what porn actually does:

- It erodes female bargaining power.

- It reduces men's motivation to commit.
- It destabilizes long-term pair bonding.
- It makes exclusivity feel unnecessary.

The result is insecurity, not empowerment.

Women are left navigating a sexual economy where men are overstimulated, under-attached, and emotionally unavailable. That is not liberation. It is abandonment.

And abandoned women are then told to direct their anger outward—toward "systems," "structures;" conveniently, toward Jews.

Rather than liberate women, porn liberates men from responsibility—and women pay the price.

Why Antisemitism Poses as Feminism

Here is where the scam gets particularly vile.

Modern antisemitism increasingly cloaks itself in feminist language. It claims to oppose Israel or Jews for "for women's rights." It frames Jewish self-defense as patriarchal violence. It accuses Jews of being uniquely oppressive to women—while aligning with regimes and movements, like Hamas and Iran, that actually, as policy, brutalize women.

This is not accidental. Antisemitism has always tried to launder hatred through moral concern.

Today, feminism is the laundering agent.

The logic goes like this:

- Jews are powerful.
- Power is masculine.
- Masculinity is suspect.
- Therefore, Jews are suspect.

And Israel—Jewish sovereignty expressed through borders, defense, and force—is portrayed as the ultimate patriarchal villain.

This framing allows antisemitism to recruit women who are genuinely angry at injustice—but redirect that anger away from real abusers, toward a symbolic target.

The Hypocrisy No One Is Allowed to Name

Look at the alliances. Movements that claim to champion women's rights routinely:

- excuse rape when committed by "resistance fighters," the most famous and sickening example of which is October 7
- deny sexual violence against Jewish women
- celebrate cultures that legally subordinate women
- silence women who contradict the narrative

October 7 exposed this hypocrisy brutally.

Jewish women were raped, mutilated, paraded, and murdered. Terrorists cut off their breasts and tossed them to each other like footballs. Terrorists shot women in their genitalia and left them to bleed out.

And the response from many "feminist" institutions was silence—or worse, justification.

Why?

Because antisemitism overrides feminism when the two conflict. Women only matter when they are useful to the ideology.

When feminist movements abandon Jewish women, *they reveal they were never about women at all.*

Judaism's Radical Claim About Women

Judaism does not treat women as symbols. It treats women as partners, as equals.

This is not modern spin. *It is ancient law.*

Judaism insists:

- A woman's sexual pleasure matters.
- A woman cannot be coerced into intimacy.
- A marriage without mutual desire is unjust.
- A woman's dignity precedes male appetite.

This is why Jewish law obligates a husband to satisfy his wife.

Not emotionally. *Physically.*

Not as a gift. As a *duty*.

This is not patriarchy. This is erotic justice. And it stands in direct opposition to both porn culture and grievance feminism.

Porn counters that women exist to be consumed. Grievance feminism counters that women exist to be mobilized for political power.

Judaism maintains women exist to be cherished.

That's why Judaism does not need to invent feminism. *It built female dignity into the covenant.*

Why Jewish Marriage Threatens Both Extremes

Jewish marriage represents everything both porn culture and grievance culture reject. It says:

- You are chosen—not interchangeable.
- You are desired—not disposable.
- You are bound—not abandoned.
- You are central—not instrumental.

It threatens porn culture by demanding exclusivity. It threatens grievance culture by producing happiness.

Happy women are hard to radicalize. Loved women are hard to mobilize for hatred. Married women with children and purpose are suboptimal foot soldiers for rage movements.

So Jewish marriage must be attacked.

It must be framed as oppressive, outdated, patriarchal, and regressive. *Because if Jewish women are flourishing, the whole narrative implodes.*

The Weaponization of Sexual Trauma

Here is one of the darkest tactics of modern antisemitism: selective belief.

Sexual trauma is believed—except when Jews are the victims. Then it is denied, minimized, contextualized, or erased.

Why?

Because acknowledging Jewish women's suffering would humanize Jews. And antisemitism cannot afford that. It needs Jews to remain symbols, not people.

So Jewish women are sacrificed to the ideology. The ideology dismisses their pain. It ignores their testimony. It considers their humanity negotiable.

That is not feminism. That is cruelty.

A movement that believes all women except Jewish women is not a women's movement—it is a hate movement.

Porn, Rage, and the Collapse of Female Security

Porn does something else no one wants to admit: *It destabilizes women's sense of sexual security.*

Women intuitively know that desire without commitment is dangerous. That being desired but not chosen is destabilizing.

Porn tells women to override those instincts. It tells them:

- jealousy is insecurity
- exclusivity is control
- commitment is boring
- fidelity is optional

And then, when women feel unsafe, anxious, and angry, grievance movements step in and say: "Good. Now aim that anger."

Not at porn. Nor at men's abdication, nor cultural collapse.

At Jews.

Porn breaks women's trust. Antisemitism harvests the fallout.

Why Jewish Women Terrify the Hate Economy

Jewish women are inconvenient to antisemitism; they do not fit the script. They are:

- educated
- outspoken
- maternal
- sexual
- faithful
- beautiful

- ambitious
- rooted

Jewish women refuse the false choice between desire and dignity.

They do not need to be reduced to pornography to feel powerful. They do not need grievance to feel valued.

They build lives.

And lives that work expose ideologies that don't.

The antisemite loathes Jewish women because they refuse to be either victims or objects.

The Hammer

Here is the truth, unvarnished: Porn culture and grievance feminism are not liberating women.

They are preparing women to be used—by markets on one side and by hate movements on the other.

Antisemitism thrives in that confusion.

But Judaism stands in the way.

Judaism insists that women deserve:

- love without exploitation
- desire without humiliation
- intimacy without disposability
- justice without rage

And that insistence must be crushed if antisemitism is to thrive.

Which is why Jewish women are attacked, erased, and mocked.

Which is why Jewish men are demonized.

Which is why Jewish families are slandered.

Antisemitism cannot survive a culture producing women who are loved, sanctified, and centered.

CHAPTER FIFTEEN

WHY MARRIAGE IS THE ULTIMATE ANTISEMITIC TARGET

Antisemitism does not begin with synagogues. It begins with homes.

Before the mob burns the books, it mocks the family.

Before it vandalizes cemeteries, it destabilizes marriages.

Before it shouts "death," it whispers that commitment is naïve, fidelity is oppressive, children are a burden. That permanence is a lie.

Think of the most infamous image and spectacle in the long, sordid history of antisemitism and genocide against Jews. It is the selection process at Auschwitz and other factories of death. A Jewish family would arrive together after barely surviving a hellish journey from Amsterdam, Budapest, or Oslo. They are shouted at by SS holding dogs trying to rip them limb from limb. And then—and here is the crucial point—they are *separated.* The families are immediately torn asunder. Men in one column, women in another. And then, they face the Angel of Death, Josef Mengele himself, wearing a white glove over his demonic hand. Pointing to the right, he sends young mothers and their children to an immediate death by gassing that occurs within thirty minutes. And then, the father, from whom he might get some three months of labor before he dies of starvation or tuberculosis, is sent to the left, his young son pulled away from him and sent to the left as well to be gassed.

The very first thing that Nazis did was separate, destroy, and murder the Jewish family.

Hatred understands something that polite intellectuals prefer to ignore: strong marriages are kryptonite to extremism. They produce people who are anchored, people who are accountable, people who have something to lose.

People who wake up in the morning not looking for enemies—but tending to obligations.

That is anathema to antisemitism. Because antisemitism does not recruit from rooted people.

It recruits from the uprooted.

The Family Is the First Line of Defense Against Hatred

Hatred needs isolation. A man who comes home to a wife who knows him—really knows him—cannot easily be radicalized by strangers online. A woman who is cherished and secure is less susceptible to movements that promise belonging through grievance.

Children raised in intact families with moral language, ritual rhythm, and loving authority are far harder to weaponize.

This is not ideology. It is observable reality. Extremist movements know this, which is why they attack the family relentlessly—sometimes explicitly, sometimes through "liberation," sometimes through mockery.

The end goal is always the same: *sever the bonds that compete with the movement.*

Marriage is the strongest of those bonds.

So, marriage must be degraded. *Hatred cannot compete with a strong family—so it tries to dissolve it.*

Why Antisemitism Targets Jewish Marriage First

Because it is not merely romantic, Jewish marriage is especially threatening.

It is covenantal.

It carries memory, ritual, law, obligation, continuity, and transcendence. Community sturdily reinforces it. It is sanctified weekly and oriented toward both children and future generations.

Jewish marriage is not just two people liking each other.

It is a civilization replicating itself.

That is why antisemitism fixates on Jewish families. It is not coincidental that antisemitic movements obsess over:

- Jewish fertility
- Jewish birthrates
- Jewish education
- Jewish domestic life
- Jewish "clannishness"

These are not neutral observations.

They are admissions of fear. Because every Jewish wedding is a quiet declaration: *We are not going anywhere.*

The War on Marriage Is the War on the Future

Marriage does something radical in a nihilistic age: It binds desire to time.

It says:

- I choose you tomorrow, not just tonight.
- I bind my future to yours.
- I accept limitation in exchange for depth.
- I forgo infinite options for one infinite person.

That act is incomprehensible to ideologies built on immediacy, appetite, and rage. Because rage lives in the present. Marriage lives in the future.

Antisemitism hates the future. It hates the idea that people can build something enduring rather than burn something spectacular. So, marriage must be reframed as:

- oppressive
- outdated

- unrealistic
- boring
- unsafe
- patriarchal

Once marriage is delegitimized, families fracture.

Once families fracture, children drift.

Once children drift, movements recruit.

This is not accidental. It is strategy.

Providing people a future worth protecting, marriage blocks radicalization.

Porn, Promiscuity, and the Mockery of Commitment

Porn culture does not merely undermine marriage. It ridicules it. Porn culture presents fidelity as naiveté, exclusivity as insecurity, permanence as failure, and sacrifice as weakness.

And mocking marriage renders it optional. Once optional, it turns fragile. Fragile, it collapses.

Antisemitism flourishes in the wreckage.

Because broken homes produce:

- unbonded men
- overburdened women
- anxious children
- identity confusion
- resentment

And resentment is antisemitism's raw material. Porn culture mocks marriage because hatred needs broken homes.

Why Jewish Marriage Is Singled Out as "Oppressive"

You will notice something telling in modern discourse. Marriage itself is attacked—but Jewish marriage is attacked with special venom. It is slanderously described as:

- tribal
- regressive

- controlling
- fertility-obsessed
- anti-modern

Why?

Because Jewish marriage refuses to dissolve under pressure. It continues to produce children in a collapsing demographic world. It continues to insist on obligation in an age of entitlement. It continues to sanctify sex in an age of commodification and to prioritize family over ideology.

Since that stubbornness is unacceptable to bigotry, it rebrands Jewish marriage as a problem.

Jewish marriage is called "oppressive" because it still works.

Antisemitism Needs Broken Men and Isolated Women

Hatred movements need recruits who are:

- lonely
- angry
- sexually frustrated
- unmoored
- searching for meaning

Marriage cures all five.

Which is why antisemitism hates it.

A married man with children does not dream of destroying the world. A woman with a devoted partner needs no mob.

So, antisemitism must mock marriage, delegitimize commitment, demonize fidelity.

And when Jews refuse to comply, they become targets.

The Jewish Home as a Moral Fortress

The Jewish home is not a retreat from the world. It is a counterculture. It teaches:

- delayed gratification
- mutual responsibility

- reverence for life
- gratitude
- sexual discipline
- joy within limits

These virtues are poison to ideologies built on outrage.

Outrage demands constant stimulation; marriage demands patience. Outrage thrives on enemies; marriage thrives on repair. Outrage is theatrical; marriage is private.

Antisemitism cannot compete with that quiet power.

So it tries to discredit it.

The Jewish home is antisemitism's most dangerous adversary.

Why Marriage Makes Jews Uncontrollable

Antisemitism wants Jews fragmented. Divided Jews are manageable. Assimilated Jews, silent Jews, and shamed Jews, obedient.

Marriage resists all three. It binds Jews to each other, anchoring them to tradition, tying them to children and grandchildren.

It gives Jews something to defend.

Which is why antisemitism has always attacked Jewish family life first.

The Lie That Marriage Is "Outdated"

Marriage is not outdated.

Hatred is.

Because it aligns with human nature, marriage has survived empires, revolutions, and ideologies. Because marriage keeps outliving antisemitism, it keeps trying to kill it.

The Jew who marries is making a statement:

- I believe in tomorrow.
- I believe in continuity.
- I believe in obligation.
- I believe in joy with responsibility.

Hatred cannot forgive that belief—that ultimate rebuke to nihilism.

The Hammer

Let's say it plainly.

Antisemitism hates marriage because marriage produces:

- stability instead of chaos
- future instead of grievance
- responsibility instead of rage
- joy instead of despair

Tying love to eternity, Jewish marriage intensifies that threat.

Every Jewish wedding is thus an act of defiance. Every Jewish home, a refusal to disappear.

Every Jewish child, a victory.

This is why they come for marriage. This is why they mock it. This is why they lie about it.

This is why they call it oppressive.

This is why they want it gone.

And this is why we must defend it—without apology.

Antisemitism cannot survive a civilization that still believes in marriage.

CHAPTER SIXTEEN

THE CHASAM SOFER WAS RIGHT—AND WE ARE STILL ARGUING WITH HIS GHOST

Judaism did not survive by making itself palatable. It survived by refusing permission.

Rabbi Moshe Sofer, the towering rabbinic authority known to history as the Chasam Sofer, did not merely oppose Reform Judaism. He exposed it.

Living at the precise moment when European Jews were promised emancipation in exchange for self-erasure, he understood something his contemporaries either missed or denied: that modern antisemitism would not be defeated by accommodation, and that Judaism hollowed of obligation would not earn respect, only ridicule.

His most famous dictum—"*Chadash asur min haTorah*" (*that which is new is forbidden by the Torah*)—is routinely caricatured as reactionary obscurantism. This is lazy scholarship and worse history. The Chasam Sofer was not railing against trains, universities, or medicine. He was fighting something far more corrosive: the idea that Judaism must rebrand itself to remain acceptable.

He knew that once Judaism begins negotiating its essence, the negotiation never ends. That once Judaism becomes "reasonable," it becomes optional.

Reform Judaism: Assimilation Dressed as Enlightenment

The Chasam Sofer's principal ideological adversary was the early Reform movement, whose intellectual architect was Abraham Geiger.

Geiger and his colleagues believed they were rescuing Judaism from irrelevance.

In practice, they were dismantling it. Ritual law was reframed as historical artifact. Hebrew was replaced with German. Sexual laws—among the most embodied and demanding mitzvot—were quietly sidelined. Judaism was recast as a set of ethical sentiments, conveniently aligned with Protestant bourgeois values.

The Chasam Sofer saw the fatal flaw immediately:

Judaism, he knew, is not an idea.

It is a way of living in the body.

Strip away embodied practice—kashrut, Shabbat, family purity, covenantal sex—and Judaism becomes a philosophy club with a memory problem.

Reform promised dignity through sameness. The Chasam Sofer knew sameness breeds disappearance.

A Judaism demanding nothing ultimately defends nothing.

Pressburg: Building a Fortress Against Erasure

As Chief Rabbi of Pressburg (Bratislava)—a city very near to my heart, as my wife Debbie's entire family was from Slovakia and more than half were annihilated in the Holocaust—the Chasam Sofer transformed his yeshiva into the most formidable center of Orthodox resistance in Europe.

This was not narrow-mindedness. It was triage.

He trained rabbis to withstand:

- State pressure to modernize Jewish education
- Communal elites desperate for acceptance
- Intellectual fashions masquerading as moral progress

Not because he feared change, but because he understood *sequence*—he rejected mixed seating, vernacular prayer, and cosmetic reforms. Change is never isolated, he knew. It is cumulative.

History vindicated him brutally. German Reform communities that flourished in the nineteenth century all but vanished within two generations through intermarriage and assimilation. While communities shaped by the Chasam Sofer's model endured.

The Chasam Sofer did not freeze Judaism. He preserved it long enough for the future to exist.

The Unintended Inheritance: Charedi vs. Modern Orthodoxy

The Chasam Sofer's legacy fractured into two powerful but divergent heirs.

The first, Charedi Judaism, inherited his resistance and amplified it into near-total insulation. Change itself became suspect. Secular culture was treated as contamination. The walls grew higher than the Chasam Sofer himself might have imagined.

This approach preserved continuity—often heroically—but at the cost of engagement and, at times, moral confidence in the public square.

By contrast, Modern Orthodoxy and Samson Raphael Hirsch sought synthesis. Torah *with* culture, not Torah *against* culture. Hirsch accepted the Chasam Sofer's rejection of Reform theology but insisted that Judaism could confront modernity without surrendering to it.

Both camps invoke the Chasam Sofer. Both inherit fragments of his truth. Neither fully embodies his central insight: *that Judaism must be unapologetic, not insulated or diluted.*

Insulation without confidence breeds fear. Engagement without conviction breeds shame.

Antisemitism's Sexual Core (That Everyone Looks Away From)

Here is where the Chasam Sofer's worldview collides directly with the thesis of this book—and where polite historians grow uncomfortable.

Antisemitism is not primarily political.

It is not primarily economic.

It is psychosexual.

Across centuries, Jews have been accused of:

- Sexual perversion
- Ritual pedophilia
- Seduction of women
- Corruption of family life
- Hypersexual power hidden behind supposed modesty

These accusations are not random. They are projections.

Societies that repress sexuality or commodify it without meaning cannot tolerate a people who insist on *sanctified intimacy*.

Judaism regulates sex not to shame it, but to dignify it. Kosher sexuality is disciplined, covenantal, joyful, and purposeful. It insists that desire be bound to responsibility and love.

This terrifies cultures built on:

- Repression disguised as morality
- Pornography disguised as liberation
- Power disguised as pleasure

The Jew becomes the screen onto which to project sexual anxiety.

Antisemites obsess over Jewish sex because Judaism refuses both sexual chaos and sexual shame.

Reform's Fatal Miscalculation on Sexuality

Reform Judaism believed that by loosening sexual law—by making Judaism less embodied, less demanding, less intimate—hatred would recede.

It didn't.

Instead, antisemitism intensified.

The pattern persisted until recent times. In 2025, some 30 percent of Progressive New York City Jews voted for Zohran Mamdani, an antisemite and Israel hater, as Mayor. Scores of progressive Jewish students across the country participated in campus rallies falsely accusing Israel of genocide—even as the real genocidal state, Iran, escaped their notice.

Why?

Because when Jews abandon moral confidence around sexuality, they do not become invisible. They become *suspect.* A people without visible boundaries are imagined to have secret ones. A people embarrassed by its own intimacy invites pornographic fantasy.

This is why modern antisemites fixate grotesquely on Jews, Israel, and sex.

It is why accusations of pedophilia, rape, and sexual conspiracy recur endlessly. It is why my work on kosher intimacy—and even my daughter's sacred mission to strengthen Jewish marriages—becomes a magnet for obscene attacks.

The Chasam Sofer understood the psychology centuries ago:

When Jews apologize for holiness, others accuse them of filth.

Weak Jewish identity does not soften antisemitism: it sexualizes it.

The Through-Line: Shame Versus Covenant

The Chasam Sofer's real battle was not against Reform per se, but against *shame.*

Shame: The belief that survival requires self-erasure.

Covenant: The belief that survival requires self-respect.

Kosher sex, like kosher faith, is built on the radical idea that boundaries do not diminish pleasure—they make it possible. That commitment does not suffocate desire—it deepens it.

Because it exposes the hollowness of their own sexual cultures, antisemites hate this.

Reform tried to escape hatred by shedding distinctiveness.

The Chasam Sofer chose the opposite path: *to be hated, if necessary—but never hollowed out.*

The Jew who refuses shame will always provoke rage. But he will also endure.

Why the Chasam Sofer Still Haunts Us

The Chasam Sofer unsettles modern Jews because he forces choices we still avoid:

- Approval or permanence

- Relevance or truth
- Applause or covenant

He was not gentle. He was not modern. He was not interested in being liked.

He was interested in dignified survival.

And he understood—as we must now relearn—that antisemitism does not disappear when Jews become smaller, quieter, or more accommodating.

It grows when Jews lose moral confidence and embodied purpose.

The Chasam Sofer is buried in Bratislava, Slovakia (historically Pressburg, as it was known in the Austro-Hungarian Empire). While the Chasam Sofer Memorial (Mausoleum) remains, the original Jewish cemetery was largely destroyed in the twentieth century.

His grave was miraculously preserved.

During World War II and later communist redevelopment, much of the cemetery was erased. The Chasam Sofer's grave—and those of close family and disciples—were saved by building a protective concrete structure around them. Today, visitors reach the site through an underground passage.

This alone tells you something about his stature: *Even regimes hostile to Jewish memory understood that destroying this grave would be unforgivable.*

Today, the site is an active pilgrimage destination and one of the most important Orthodox Jewish graves in Europe.

Even when the cemetery was destroyed, his presence was not moved.

That, in itself, is history making a moral judgment.

May his memory be a blessing that continues to forever inspire us.

CHAPTER SEVENTEEN

ISRAEL, FERTILITY, AND THE RAGE AGAINST JEWISH CONTINUITY

Antisemitism has always hated Jewish reproduction, even more than it hates Jewish survival.

It is one thing for Jews to persist as ghosts—apologetic, diminished, tolerated at the margins. It is another thing entirely for Jews to multiply—to grow younger, louder, more confident, more rooted in land and future.

That second reality produces rage.

Because fertility is the most unforgiving refutation of hatred. You can argue with ideas. You can smear people. You can distort history. You can vandalize symbols.

But you cannot argue with babies.

As the father of nine children, thank God, I have often experienced what I call *the last acceptable form of discrimination in America: that against parents who have chosen to have many children.*

I cannot recount how many times hotels or motels turned us away when our children were younger, the moment they saw the size of our family—no matter how many rooms we were prepared to book.

This is especially true of Orthodox Jewish families, who are treated as backward, antiquated, and primitive for having large families. When

I tell strangers I am the father of nine children, they rarely react with joy. They nearly always respond with unhappy surprise or barely disguised contempt.

It is disgusting, a denigration of both Jewishness and life.

Few of them think to themselves that, with one third of the entire world Jewish population wiped out by the German Nazis in just four years, *Jewish children are an unmitigated blessing.*

Indeed, the Orthodox Jewish emphasis on large families has not even succeeded in restoring Jewish numbers to what they were before the Holocaust.

Prior to the Second World War, the world Jewish population stood at some 18 million. One third were annihilated, leaving twelve million. And today, in 2026?

The world Jewish community has not even crossed 15 million. That is a shocking tragedy, with Jews accounting for less than one out of every three thousand people on earth.

So now more than ever, babies are the ultimate proof of a people that believe in tomorrow. And antisemitism—at its core—is a rebellion against tomorrow and a joyous future.

The Unforgivable Crime: Jewish Children

Watch the language carefully.

Bigots call Jewish births:

- "demographic threats"
- "settler colonial reproduction"
- "weaponized fertility"
- "replacement"
- "provocation"
- "genocide by womb"

These are not metaphors. They are confessions.

They reveal a worldview in which children are not blessings but dangers, in which continuity is aggression, in which life itself becomes suspect when it belongs to Jews.

Antisemitism can tolerate Jews as abstractions. It can tolerate Jews as victims, as museum exhibits.

What it cannot tolerate is Jews as parents.

Why Fertility Is Political Whether We Like It or Not

Every civilization eventually reveals what it believes about life by how it treats birth. A culture that celebrates fertility believes in future. A culture that mocks fertility believes in extinction.

A culture that fears fertility is already dying.

The modern West is experiencing demographic collapse. Birthrates are plummeting. Families are shrinking or disappearing. Children are framed as burdens, climate crimes, lifestyle threats, or economic inconveniences.

And into that collapse steps the Jew—still marrying, still having children, still singing lullabies, still filling schools.

This is not accidental. Jewish life has always treated fertility as sacred defiance. Not reckless reproduction, but covenantal continuity—children raised inside story, ritual, obligation, love.

That persistence enrages cultures that have lost faith in themselves.

Because it exposes despair as a choice, fertility enrages nihilism.

Israel as the Living Proof

Israel magnifies this rage because it makes Jewish fertility visible. Not hidden in diaspora apartments. Nor abstracted in census data. But embodied—on streets, in schools, on buses; at playgrounds, in hospitals, in wedding halls and maternity wards.

Israel is young, and its population is, thank God, bursting.

In 1948, Israel's population stood at 806,000, with 717,000 Jews.

Today, in 2026, Israel's population is around 10.18 million, having surpassed 10 million for the first time in 2025. The population includes Jewish (around 76.3 percent), Arab (around 21.1 percent), and a growing segment of foreign workers who choose Israel as their home and the place where they choose to build. That is why scores of innocent Thai farm workers were either murdered on October 7 while working on Jewish farms, or taken hostage by Hamas.

That youth terrifies ideologies built on exhaustion. Because a young society asks uncomfortable questions:

- Why did you stop believing in family?
- Why did you stop wanting children?
- Why did you trade continuity for comfort?
- Why did you choose ideology over inheritance?

For cultures flirting with extinction, these questions are unbearable. So, Israel must be demonized—not because it exists, but because it thrives.

Israel's youth is antisemitism's nightmare.

The Sexual Politics of Anti-Zionism

Anti-Zionism pretends to be about borders and policies. It isn't.

It is saturated with sexual anxiety. The obsession with:

- Jewish wombs
- Jewish birthrates
- Jewish families
- Jewish domestic life
- Jewish "settlement"

These reveal the truth. The rage is not against land, but against continuity.

When anti-Zionists chant "from the river to the sea," they are not describing geography. *They are expressing a desire for demographic erasure and annihilation*. They want the Jewish future erased—not just the Jewish present.

And nothing represents the future more clearly than children.

The moment it starts counting Jewish babies, anti-Zionism becomes genocidal.

Why Death Cults Hate Mothers

This is one of the hardest truths to say aloud, but it must be said: Death cults hate mothers.

Not because mothers are weak—but because mothers are creative.

A mother produces life. A death cult produces martyrs. A mother nurtures; a death cult radicalizes. A mother ties love to future; a death cult ties death to meaning.

These worldviews cannot coexist.

Which is why antisemitic movements so often:

- erase Jewish mothers
- mock Jewish maternity
- deny Jewish rape
- justify attacks on families
- celebrate child death "as resistance"

This is not accidental. It is ideological consistency.

A death cult must erase mothers to survive.

The Inversion: When Fertility Is Called Violence

We are living in an age of moral inversion. Jewish women giving birth are accused of "violence." Jewish families are accused of "colonial aggression." Jewish continuity is reframed as oppression. Hence the constant and sustained attacks against *Kosher Sex*.

Meanwhile, movements that glorify suicide bombers, child soldiers, and mass death are praised as "resistance." This is what happens when hatred loses any connection to moral reality. Life becomes the enemy. Death becomes virtue.

And Jews—who stubbornly insist on life—become intolerable.

Why Jewish Fertility Cannot Be Apologized Away

Some Jews feel uncomfortable talking about this.

They worry it sounds triumphalist. They worry it sounds tribal. They worry it feeds stereotypes. This discomfort is understandable—and wrong.

Because apologizing for life is how life dies. Jewish fertility is not propaganda. It is not provocation. It is not aggression. It is obedience to life itself. It is the refusal to let hatred decide who gets a future.

Every Jewish child is a quiet "no" to every pogrom, every gas chamber, every massacre, every threat, every slogan screaming for erasure.

The Demographic Panic Behind the Screams

Listen closely to the panic language.

"Replacement."

"Invasion."

"Overpopulation."

"Demographic threat."

These words reveal fear—not of Jews as individuals, but of Jews as a people that continues.

Antisemitism cannot tolerate a people that:

- remembers
- reproduces
- educates
- binds generations
- refuses to disappear

Because disappearance is what hatred promises its followers: you will not have to confront your own emptiness if the other is gone.

Jewish continuity ruins that promise.

The October 7 Truth Revisited

October 7 was not only an attack on Israel. It was an attack on Jewish family life. The targets were: homes, children, and parents; bedrooms, kitchens, and nurseries—young women shot in their genitalia, often after first being brutally raped.

This was not random. It was symbolic.

And the global reaction—justifying, minimizing, contextualizing—exposed something horrifying: *Many were willing to excuse mass murder if it slowed Jewish continuity. That is antisemitism stripped of pretense.*

Why Fertility Is the Final Red Line

You can debate borders. You can criticize leaders. You can argue policy.

But the moment someone rages at Jewish birth, Jewish children, Jewish families, Jewish continuity—you are no longer talking politics. You are talking genocidal ideology.

That is the line. And it is being crossed openly, shamelessly, globally. Which means Jews must respond with clarity, not apology.

When they attack Jewish fertility, they are attacking Jewish existence.

The War on the Fruitful: Bias Against Large Families

I make the above statements about Jewish fertility as someone drawing from concrete, lived experience—as the proud father of nine.

I know that, in the modern West, few things provoke more immediate, visceral judgment than a large family.

People seem to believe a couple with one or two children is "responsible." A couple with three is "ambitious." Five seems to be pushing it, provoking a response—and not a positive one.

A couple with eight? Suspected of belonging to a cult.

And if the couple is visibly religious—Orthodox Jewish, devoutly Catholic, traditionally Muslim—the suspicion hardens. Contempt seems to surface; they are "backward," "irresponsible," "overpopulating the earth," "burdening the system."

Of course, climate anxiety has turbo-charged this bias. Anti-natalism—the philosophical position that it is morally wrong to bring children into the world—has metastasized from academic abstraction to mainstream sensibility.

Having fewer children, or none at all, is increasingly framed as a moral imperative.

Fertility itself: pathologized.

And who, in the Western imagination, has the most children?

Orthodox and Haredi Jews.

So, they endure targeting from two directions simultaneously.

For the antisemitic right, Jewish fertility triggers "outbreeding" panic—the conspiracy theory that Jews are deliberately multiplying to replace or outnumber white Christians.

For the secular progressive left, Jewish fertility triggers contempt for religious fecundity—the assumption that large families are proof of patriarchal control, intellectual backwardness, or environmental recklessness.

So, a visibly Orthodox family—walking down a Brooklyn sidewalk with six children, or strolling through Jerusalem on Shabbat afternoon with a double stroller and a gaggle of siblings—spikes both anxieties at once for either end of the Jew-hating horseshoe.

The right sees replacement. The left sees regression.

Neither recognizes, of course, what is actually there—a couple taking the sacred, biblical command, *"Be fruitful and multiply,"* seriously. A man and woman freely building a home around covenant, who chose life, in the most literal, powerful sense.

Opposing this family and the very propagation of the human race is reproductive anxiety masquerading as social commentary. It's hardly a jump from vilifying reproduction to vilifying sex, pleasure, the body—all the ingredients that comprise the dish of childbearing and families, big and small.

Because any culture that is uncomfortable with desire will also be uncomfortable with its ultimate consequence—children.

If sex is shameful, then its fruit is shameful.

If the body is suspect, then fertility is suspect.

And if Jewish families insist on being visibly, joyfully, unapologetically fruitful—the "enlightened" elect, who cling to quieter, smaller, more "responsible" choices, will resent them.

So the Jew who dares to have many children is an affront to the ideology of scarcity. How dare he—no matter that it's after the Holocaust, or if he's in Israel—insist the world is worth continuing? Doesn't he know how fashionable despair is? That children equal climate catastrophe?

No, they observe, he doesn't seem to.

Rather, that Jewish insistence—that stubborn, fertile, noisy, Shabbat-table insistence—is one more reason they hate us.

The Hammer

Here is the truth without euphemism: Antisemitism hates Jewish fertility because fertility proves hatred failed.

Every Jewish baby is a declaration:

- We are still here.
- We believe in life.
- We are not afraid of the future.

CHAPTER EIGHTEEN

JEWISH EROTIC TRADITION RECLAIMED

It is time to stop defending Jewish sexuality and start promoting Kosher Sex—especially for the repressed antisemites.

Defense is the language of the accused. It assumes shame and accepts the enemy's framing. Judaism does not need to defend its erotic tradition. Rather, it needs to reclaim it—publicly, unapologetically, and with moral confidence.

Jewish sexuality is not a deviation from holiness. It is one of holiness's highest expressions. And the refusal to say this clearly—especially in an age drowning in porn, poisoned by antisemitism—*has cost us dearly.*

The Lie We Were Pressured to Accept

For centuries, Jews were pressured into a posture of apology.

Be quiet.

Be discreet.

Don't draw attention.

Jews were told don't talk about sex, don't provoke, don't embarrass the community.

When I lived in the U.K., I became, according to *The Jewish Chronicle*—the community's principal media organ and the oldest English-language Jewish publication in the world—the highest profile Rabbi in the country.

- You did not win.
- Sex is holy, creative, and the essence of life.

Israel magnifies that declaration because it makes Jewish life public, louc young, and impossible to ignore.

That is why Israel is not merely opposed—but obsessed over.

It is a living, breathing counter-argument to despair. And despair hates being contradicted.

Jewish fertility is antisemitism's defeat made flesh.

I was roundly criticized for it. The community, following a millennia of antisemitism, believed wholeheartedly in Jewish invisibility. Being too public would incite antisemitism, I was continually warned.

I remember the beautiful spring day when I was visiting England's greatest living intellectual, Sir Isaiah Berlin, at his office at Oxford's prestigious All Souls College. It was my great honor to befriend him in the last years of his storied life. I told the elderly Sir Isaiah that we should leave his musty yet scholarly office and take a stroll in the sun.

He readily agreed, but not before he told me that I should tuck my tzitzit in if I was to walk with him. He had no issue with my kippa, and he was world-renowned as a Zionist and a very proud Jew. But why tuck in my tzitzit, I asked him.

"This is not our country," he told me. "We are guests here, and it's inappropriate for us to impose our religious beliefs on others."

Now, understand that Sir Isaiah, with whom I had become very close, visited regularly, and loved, was the single most respected mind in all of British academia—veritably a living legend. But even he, as a refugee who had emigrated as a boy to Britain from Riga, Latvia—then part of the Soviet Union—could not fully shake the trauma of feeling "other."

This posture was understandable in exile.

It was often necessary for survival. *But what begins as survival strategy can calcify into spiritual paralysis.*

And now—when antisemitism no longer whispers but shouts, when it no longer hides but parades, when it no longer merely excludes but seeks erasure—silence is no longer prudence.

It is surrender.

The Jewish erotic tradition must be spoken aloud again—not to titillate, not to provoke, but to teach. *Because silence allowed others to define us.* And they defined us obscenely.

When Jews stopped teaching our sexual ethics, antisemites filled the vacuum with filth.

Judaism Never Feared Desire

Let's say this plainly: Judaism never feared desire. *Judaism feared undisciplined desire.* That distinction matters.

Judaism does not teach that desire is evil.

It teaches that desire is powerful, and powerful forces must be guided—**or they destroy**. This is the opposite of both porn culture and puritanism. Porn culture says, indulge endlessly. Puritanism says, suppress completely.

Judaism says, sanctify deliberately.

Kabbalah and the Holiness of Sexuality

If antisemites knew what Jewish mystics actually teach about sex, *they would lose their minds.*

Kabbalistic thought—the mystical tradition within Judaism, developed most elaborately in medieval Spain and later in sixteenth-century Safed—describes the very structure of the cosmos.

And it often does so in erotic terms.

To understand why, you need to understand how Kabbalah maps the inner life of God.

The Kabbalistic system describes ten *sefirot*—divine emanations or attributes through which the infinite, unknowable God (*Ein Sof*) manifests and relates to creation. Do not think of these as separate deities, God forbid. Rather, they are dimensions of a single divine reality—sometimes likened to differently colored stained glass through which passes the same light. Dimensions, or "stained glass," like wisdom, understanding, mercy, severity, beauty, and so on, cascading from the most hidden depths of God down to the divine presence touching the created world.

The sefirot are not static, but dynamic, relational, alive with tension and desire. *And at every level, the interplay of masculine and feminine structures them.*

The *Zohar*—the quintessential text of Kabbalah, transmitted orally for millennia before being composed in writing in thirteenth-century Spain—depicts these divine emanations as yearning for union. God Himself, in the Kabbalistic imagination, contains masculine and feminine dimensions. The sefirah of *Tiferet* (beauty, compassion) embodies the masculine aspect, often identified in the Zohar's Aramaic as the Holy One, Blessed Be He. The sefirah of *Shekhinah*, the feminine divine presence—also called *Malkhut* (sovereignty)—is the aspect of God most intimately connected to the created world and to the people of Israel.

The Zohar describes their relationship in frankly erotic and marital language. *They long for each other.* Union draws them. And when they unite, blessing and life flows into the world.

But here is where the theology deepens beyond a simple love story.

The Kabbalistic tradition teaches that this union is not the undisturbed default state. It must be *achieved*—and it can be disrupted, too. Sin, exile, and cosmic rupture create a rift within God Himself. The Shekhinah goes into exile with Israel, separated from Tiferet.

This is an extraordinary claim: that human action affects the inner life of God.

That the divine masculine and feminine can be driven apart.

That God, in some sense, suffers from internal fragmentation.

Thus the cosmos longs for wholeness.

That wholeness is called *yichud*: union.

And here is the part that would scandalize every antisemite who has ever called Judaism sexually corrupt: *human marital intimacy mirrors and facilitates this divine union.* When a husband and wife come together on Shabbat evening—in holiness, in joy, in mutual desire—they do not merely satisfy a physical need.

According to the Kabbalah, they participate in the repair of the cosmos itself.

This is not metaphor in the way modern readers might assume.

Indeed, the Kabbalistic system insists on a deep structural correspondence between the human and the divine. The union of husband and wife *below* actively draws together the masculine and feminine *above.*

Shabbat, in particular, is depicted as the time of sacred union within God. The passionate sexual intimacy of a married couple on Friday night is understood *as the human enactment that makes that cosmic union possible.*

The bedroom becomes the Holy of Holies.

The marriage bed becomes an altar.

Sex, in Jewish mysticism, is not a concession to human weakness. It is a *tikkun*—a mending of the universe.

The Arizal's *Tikkun*

The depth of this claim becomes even more radical when understood through the lens of the great sixteenth-century Kabbalist Rabbi Isaac Luria—the Holy Ari—whose teachings transformed Jewish mysticism.

The Ari taught that the very act of creation involved a *cosmic catastrophe.* God contracted Himself (contraction called *tzimtzum* in Hebrew) to make room for Creation, reality, the universe, the world.

In the process, the vessels meant to contain divine light shattered (*shevirat ha-kelim*). Sparks of holiness scattered into every corner of existence, becoming trapped in *kelipot*—shells or husks of materiality and concealment.

Thus the world as we experience it is, in the Lurianic vision, a landscape of sacred light buried in opacity.

But *Tikkun*, in this framework, is no abstraction.

It is the urgent work of gathering and elevating those scattered sparks, liberating holiness from the husks that imprison it. Every commandment, every prayer, every conscious act of sanctification cracks open a shell, releases light.

And here the sexual dimension takes on staggering weight: The physical body itself, the realm of desire and sensation, *is precisely where some of the deepest sparks are trapped.* To engage the body in holiness is not merely permitted. *It is imperative.* Necessary. Indispensable.

The sparks embedded in physical desire cannot be elevated by those who reject the body. *They can only be elevated by those who sanctify it.*

This is why the thirteenth-century text *Iggeret HaKodesh*—"The Holy Letter," often attributed to Rabbi Joseph ben Abraham Gikatilla, though of contested authorship—states its position with breathtaking clarity. It explicitly rejects the view, common in medieval Christianity, that sexuality is base or animalistic. If God created the body, and if the body contains sparks of divine light, then nothing about the body is shameful. Sexual union within marriage, performed with proper intention, is *kadosh*—holy.

Not despite the body, but through it.

Not by transcending desire, but by sanctifying it.

Indeed, the Kabbalistic ethic emphasizes *mutuality*—both partners' pleasure matters, not as an afterthought, but as a precondition of holiness.

It emphasizes *Kavanah*, too—intention, presence, spiritual awareness during the act itself. And it emphasizes *sanctification*—the elevation of physical desire into something that participates in the divine.

The *Zohar* is explicit: union without mutuality, without the wife's desire and fulfillment, is incomplete. It does not achieve *yichud*. The feminine dimension—both human and divine—must be an active, desiring participant, not a passive recipient.

The Hasidim and *Yichud*

The Hasidic masters of the eighteenth and nineteenth centuries carried this vision further.

Hasidic thought, heir to the Lurianic tradition, taught that God's presence pervades all of reality—even and especially those dimensions that appear most distant from holiness. The task of the righteous person is *avodah be-gashmiyut*—service of God through physicality.

Eating, drinking, sleeping, making love—all of these, when performed with awareness and intention, become potential sites of divine encounter.

Rabbi Levi Yitzchak of Berditchev, the great Hasidic advocate for the Jewish people before God, built an entire theology around the idea that even imperfect human engagement with the physical world testifies to an unbreakable bond between God and Israel. If even our stumbling attempts at holiness reveal a deep, intimate relationship, how much more so the act the tradition itself designates as a mirror of divine union?

The Hasidic framework adds another layer to the theology of sacred sexuality: *the idea that concealment is itself a form of divine intimacy.*

Rabbi Shneur Zalman of Liadi, the founder of Chabad Hasidism—the *Alter* Rebbe—taught that God's apparent absence from the world *is not a genuine withdrawal.* Rather, it is a deliberate veiling—a *tzimtzum*, one seemingly real from our perspective but transparent from God's.

The world appears material, secular, devoid of the sacred.

But this concealment is itself also an act of love: God hides so that human beings can *choose* to find Him, so that the discovery of holiness within the physical becomes an achievement. A gift freely offered rather than an overwhelming revelation that leaves no room for freedom.

In this reading, the physical dimension of sexuality—its sheer embodied, sensory intensity—is not a barrier to holiness, but the very medium through which the concealed divine presence is encountered and revealed. *The most intimate act between human beings becomes the moment when the veil is thinnest.*

Now consider the antisemitic accusation: that Jews are sexually corrupt, degraded, animalistic.

That Jewish sexuality is filth.

Kabbalah inverts this slander completely. Because Jewish mysticism does not merely tolerate sexuality.

It divinizes it.

It teaches that human lovemaking is a *mirror of cosmic love.* That the bedroom is a sanctuary. That desire, properly channeled, touches God.

The body is not a prison from which the soul must escape, *but a vessel containing sparks of divine light—a spark that can only be liberated through sanctification.*

While the antisemite slanders Jews as sexual degenerates, Jewish mysticism teaches that sexuality—sanctified, mutual, intentional—is among the holiest acts a human being can perform.

You don't put that in your most sacred texts if you believe desire is shameful.

You put it there if you believe desire is a doorway to the divine.

And that is precisely what the antisemite cannot forgive: not that Jews are sexual or holy, but that Jews are sexual *and* holy. That we refuse the choice between pleasure and piety. That we insist—at the deepest, most mystical level of our tradition—*that the two are one.*

Because the mystics who spent their lives mapping the hidden structure of God's inner life placed erotic union at its very center. From the *Zohar* in medieval Spain to the Holy Ari in Safed to the Hasidic masters of Eastern Europe, the tradition has returned, again and again, to the same luminous claim:

When two human beings come together in love and holiness, they do not descend into the merely physical.

They ascend into the architecture of the divine.

L'Chaim.

The Erotic Core of Jewish Scripture

The most misunderstood truth in Jewish life is also the most radical. The most sacred book in all of the Hebrew Bible is, after all, as mentioned before, an erotic love poem—the Song of Solomon, upon which my bestselling book *Kosher Lust* is based.

The Song of Solomon does not apologize for the body. It does not whisper desire. It does not hide longing behind allegory alone. It celebrates attraction, pursuit, touch, scent, voice, skin, absence, and reunion. And Jewish tradition refused to exile that poem from holiness.

It canonized it.

That decision was revolutionary.

It said something shocking, then and now: Human erotic love is a legitimate language for divine love. Not metaphorically convenient—*structurally true*. If that makes some people uncomfortable, good. Holiness is not meant to flatter repression.

Instead of exiling it, Judaism canonized desire.

Covenant, Not Consumption

Here is the central difference between Jewish eroticism and everything else on offer today:

Judaism insists that sex belongs inside covenant—not because covenant kills desire, but because covenant deepens it. Consumption flattens desire; covenant intensifies it. Porn promises endless novelty and delivers numbness. Judaism promises exclusivity and delivers depth.

In Jewish thought, the restriction of erotic focus is not deprivation but concentration. A laser cuts deeper than a floodlight. That is why Jewish law does something extraordinary: it does not merely permit sex in marriage, it obligates it. *Halacha* treats marital sex as the soul and essence of marriage, the uniting of two into bone of one bone and flesh of one flesh—not duty without joy, but joy with responsibility.

Erotic Justice: A Dangerous Idea

Judaism contains a concept almost no modern ideology can tolerate: erotic justice. The idea that a spouse—especially a wife—has a right to pleasure.

That intimacy withheld is not neutral—but unjust. That emotional and physical closeness are moral obligations.

This shatters every caricature. It smashes the porn narrative that women exist to serve male appetite. It obliterates the puritan narrative that holiness requires female sacrifice. It decimates the antisemitic fantasy that Jewish sexuality is predatory or oppressive.

Erotic justice is threatening because it demands maturity, self-regulation, attentiveness, presence, and service. Those demands terrify cultures built on appetite or grievance. Demanding sexual responsibility, Judaism frightens both libertines and tyrants.

Why Antisemites Must Desecrate Jewish Sexuality

Now the pieces lock together. Antisemitism cannot tolerate Jewish erotic ethics because those ethics prove something devastating: Human desire need not become violence, and power does not need to become domination.

That proof is intolerable to ideologies built on despair. So, antisemitism must sexualize Jews grotesquely, mock their intimacy, and smear Jewish family life—not because Jewish sexuality is obscene, but because it is coherent. And coherence is dangerous to hate.

Antisemitism mocks Jewish sex because Jewish sex exposes antisemitism as a philosophy of failure.

The Exile of Eros—and Its Cost

In exile, Jews often retreated from public teaching about sexuality, keeping it private, coded, and behind closed doors. The cost was real. Silence allowed pornographers to define "sexual freedom," puritans to define "sexual holiness," and antisemites to define Jewish intimacy.

The results are now visible everywhere: a world flooded with sex and starving for intimacy, obsessed with bodies and terrified of commitment, unable to imagine desire without exploitation.

Judaism has an answer to this crisis.

Reclaiming Erotic Language Without Vulgarity

Reclaiming Jewish erotic tradition does not mean mimicking porn culture. It means recovering dignified erotic language—language that honors mystery rather than erasing it. Judaism understands something porn does not: mystery fuels desire, and exposure kills it.

That is why modesty in Judaism is about more than shame.

It is about protecting erotic power from trivialization and safeguarding mystery against overexposure. Modesty says: you do not get automatic access; desire must be earned; intimacy requires trust. These are moral ideas.

Modesty in Judaism is not repression—it is erotic intelligence.

Why Joy Is the Strategy

We are now at the hinge of the book. Everything up to this point has named the pathology. Now comes the counter-offensive.

The Jewish response to antisemitism is not retreat, appeasement, or silence. It is joy—disciplined, embodied, unapologetic joy in marriage, intimacy, children, continuity, and sanctified desire.

This is not escapism. *It's warfare.*

Because nothing enrages antisemitism more than Jews who are unashamed to be alive.

Joy is antisemitism's most effective enemy.

Reclaiming Without Apology

Reclaiming the Jewish erotic tradition requires courage. It means refusing to let antisemites define our sexuality, or porn define our desire, or puritans define our holiness. It means saying clearly: We believe sex can be sacred, desire can be disciplined, pleasure can be moral, marriage can be passionate, and joy can be holy.

We will not whisper it.

The Hammer

Judaism does not fear eros. Judaism redeems it. That redemption—desire bound to covenant, pleasure bound to responsibility, intimacy bound to eternity—is not a relic of the past.

It is the antidote to an unraveling world.

Antisemitism rages because Jewish sexuality refuses both nihilism and cruelty, offering instead a third way: life with meaning.

Jewish erotic joy is not a scandal. It is a civilizational answer.

CHAPTER NINETEEN

WHY SAVING MARRIAGES IS CIVILIZATIONAL WARFARE

Civilizations do not collapse first in parliaments or stock markets. They collapse in bedrooms—when intimacy dies, when couples become roommates, and sex becomes transactional or disappears entirely. Resentment replaces tenderness and people stop believing that repair is possible.

When repair feels impossible, rage looks for somewhere else to go. That rage does not remain in private places for long. It ventures into the political.

Saving Marriages Is Not "Conservative." It Is Subversive.

People assume marriage repair is reactionary. It isn't.

Rather, it is revolutionary. It commits economic sabotage in a culture that monetizes loneliness. It commits political sabotage in a culture that profits from rage.

In a culture that thrives on fragmentation, repairing marriages is existential anarchy.

Every marriage saved is:

- one less recruit for extremism

- one less child raised in chaos
- one less adult searching for someone to hate

This is why those who mock *Kosher Sex* and marital repair do so with such venom. They sense the threat.

Saving marriages starves the grievance economy.

The Marriage Collapse → Hatred Pipeline

Here is the sequence no one wants to name:

1. Marriages grow cold.
2. People feel unwanted and unseen.
3. Sexual frustration turns into shame.
4. Shame turns into bitterness.
5. Bitterness seeks moral permission.
6. Ideology supplies an enemy.
7. Antisemitism becomes that ideology and the enemy becomes the Jew.

This is not theory. This is pattern.

Every mass movement built on resentment recruits people whose private lives have failed.

People who feel humiliated rarely admit it—they externalize it, looking for villains who "stole" their dignity, their future, their power. And once again, history answers the question of who is most convenient.

A man whose marriage lives, breathes, and thrives does not need a movement to feel powerful.

Why Marriage Repair Threatens Hate Movements

Hate movements depend on people being lonely, sexually frustrated, emotionally unregulated, unbonded, and searching for belonging.

Marriage repair attacks all five. A healed marriage restores dignity, intimacy, purpose, patience, and hope.

And hope is poison to grievance. The kryptonite of resentment and bitterness.

Make no mistake: A man who rediscovers desire for his wife is less interested in rage pornography. A woman who feels cherished is less interested in ideological mobs. And a couple rebuilding trust is less interested in burning the world down.

This is why movements built on outrage quietly root for marital failure. They *need* broken homes.

Hatred relies on unhappy marriages the way fire relies on oxygen.

Porn as Public Weapon

Porn doesn't merely damage individuals. It disarms families.

It teaches people to expect pleasure without effort and novelty without loyalty, draining erotic energy out of marriages and dumping it into fantasy. It primes spouses to compete with pixels—instead of choosing each other.

The result—a silent epidemic:

- sexless marriages,
- dead bedrooms,
- emotional withdrawal,
- quiet despair.

And despair is *never* politically neutral. **Despair radicalizes.** People who feel sexually defeated are easily seduced by ideologies promising power through destruction.

This is why porn culture and antisemitism coexist so comfortably. Porn empties people; hatred gives them a story to explain the emptiness. Porn hollows out marriages; antisemitism fills the void with blame.

The Jewish Insistence

Judaism keeps insisting on marriage because Judaism understands something modern culture refuses to accept: Sex without commitment won't liberate people, and commitment without sex won't sustain.

You need both.

Judaism treats marriage not as a lifestyle option but as a *moral engine*—where eros is trained into generosity, patience, loyalty, and joy. That insistence enrages cultures addicted to exit strategies, because marriage says:

You stay. You work it out.

You repair.

You choose again. You grow.

Grievance cultures hate this.

Repair Over Replacement

Modern culture treats relationships like software: if it glitches, uninstall; if it slows down, replace; if it disappoints, upgrade.

Judaism rejects this model. It teaches *teshuvah*—return, repair, re-choosing. You don't discard sacred things. You restore them.

That ethic teaches people that failure is not final. And people who believe failure is not final do not need scapegoats. Repair is thus the enemy of resentment.

Antisemitism is built on a single psychological refusal: "I refuse to take responsibility."

Repair requires responsibility, humility, effort, and facing one's own shortcomings. Hatred offers an easier alternative: "It's *their* fault." So, when Jews speak openly about repairing marriages—confronting porn addiction, emotional neglect, boredom, resentment, betrayal—we are attacking the core seduction of antisemitism.

We are saying: You don't need an enemy, you need courage; you don't need rage, you need discipline.

You don't need destruction, you need love.

That message terrifies hate movements, which survive by convincing people repair is impossible.

Covenant Versus Consumption

For decades, the culture war was framed incorrectly—"liberation" versus "repression," "progress" versus "tradition." That conceptualization was a lie.

The real conflict: connection versus consumption, repair versus replacement. Covenant versus chaos.

Kosher Sex—and the broader Jewish erotic ethic—sits squarely on the side of connection, repair, and covenant. That is why it is attacked from every direction. Not because it is backward, but because it is effective. The most radical sexual act today is choosing your spouse again and again, on a daily basis.

Porn culture claims to be neutral, liberating, and inevitable. It is none of these. Rather, it is a moral system that repeats one lesson relentlessly: *people exist to be consumed.* Bodies thus become content. Intimacy, spectacle. Desire, appetite.

Porn culture never asks: Who is this person? What do I owe them? What am I building?

It asks only: What can I take?

There is no covenant here, no memory, no obligation, and no future.

Kosher Sex is not about doing more. It is about meaning more. It begins with a statement porn cannot make: *you are irreplaceable.*

Not desirable today and discardable tomorrow. Not exciting until novelty fades. *Chosen.*

Exclusively and endlessly.

Porn, on the other hand, promises infinity and delivers emptiness. *Covenant embraces limits and discovers overabundance.*

The Jewish Erotic Heresy

From the perspective of porn culture, Judaism commits an unforgivable heresy: it insists that erotic pleasure has moral structure. That desire is not sovereign, that arousal must answer to love. That sex without covenant is incomplete. That freedom without responsibility is hollow.

This is heresy to a culture that worships appetite. So Jewish sexuality must be caricatured, labeled: hypocritical, perverse, secretly repressive, secretly exploitative. Because if Jewish erotic ethics were seen clearly, *if people realized they actually work*, the porn empire would be seen clearly, too. As what it is:

An extraction industry that feeds on loneliness.

Judaism threatens porn culture by proving sex can be both moral and ecstatic.

Why Porn Must Mock Marriage

Porn culture cannot tolerate covenant, because covenant exposes porn's fraud. If one person can satisfy another erotically for decades, porn's promise collapses. If depth can outperform novelty, the entire industry is revealed as parasitic.

So porn culture mocks what threatens it. Marriage becomes boring. Fidelity is slandered as naïve. Discipline is mischaracterized as repression. Modesty is mutated into shame. This mocking is not accidental—it is defensive.

Porn culture survives only if people believe commitment kills desire, exclusivity suffocates passion, and permanence equals stagnation. Kosher Sex is living proof that all three are lies.

Porn and the Manufacturing of Rage

Porn does something insidious that rarely gets discussed honestly: *it disconnects arousal from empathy.* Fundamentally, the human nervous system is not built for constant stimulation without attachment. When arousal is severed from relational meaning, the result is not liberation—it is slavery.

People become overstimulated but under-fulfilled; sexually activated but emotionally deadened. Equal parts hungry and numb. This contradiction produces discontent.

Discontent seeks explanation. And explanation is supplied by ideology.

This is why porn culture and antisemitism travel together so often. Porn creates the emotional wound; antisemitism offers a story about who caused it.

Why Antisemites Are Addicted to Porn Culture

Antisemites thrive in porn culture for a simple reason: porn culture destroys the conditions for love. Love is the rival of hatred.

A man who loves one woman deeply does not need fantasies of domination. A woman who is cherished does not need ideological rage to feel powerful. A couple bonded through intimacy does not need mobs to feel significant. Porn culture strips people of these stabilizers, and antisemitism steps in to exploit the vacuum.

This explains why antisemites are frequently obsessed with accusing Jews of sexual degeneracy, blaming Jews for cultural corruption, and framing Jews as pornographers or groomers. It is projection. And it's layered on top of addiction.

Antisemitism blames Jews for the damage porn culture actually causes.

The Death of Mystery

Porn kills mystery, and mystery is not ignorance—it is inexhaustible depth. Desire thrives on mystery. Love deepens through mystery. Intimacy endures on mystery.

A simple maxim: reveal everything, feel nothing.

Judaism understood this thousands of years ago. Modesty is not prudishness—it is erotic strategy. It protects desire from dilution, preserves longing, and sustains pursuit. Porn culture names this repression because mystery terrifies it; mystery cannot be monetized endlessly.

Why Kosher Sex Is a Moral Insurrection

Kosher Sex—covenantal sex—is not a lifestyle choice. It is a refusal—to turn people into content, to treat bodies as disposable, to surrender desire to algorithms.

It refuses to accept numbness as normal.

Kosher sexuality loudly, proudly declares: I will discipline my desire rather than outsource it. I will invest erotically where I have invested my life. I will build intimacy.

This is a radical refusal.

When porn culture accuses *Kosher Sex* of repression, it reveals its deepest insecurity. Repression is denied desire.

Kosher Sex does not deny desire—it channels it.

A river dammed becomes a swamp.

A river channeled becomes power. Judaism channels eros into covenant, and covenant generates an intensity porn cannot replicate. Truthfully, porn culture cannot compete.

Covenant multiplies the desire repression kills.

The Civilizational Stakes

This is not a private morality debate.

This is about what kind of people a civilization produces.

Porn culture produces detached men, anxious women, fractured families, isolated individuals, and resentful mobs.

Covenantal culture produces bonded couples, disciplined desire, stable homes, resilient children, and people with vibrant, exciting futures.

The first feeds antisemitism, then offers it seconds. The second *starves it.*

When families weaken, states grow stronger, mobs grow louder, and ideologues grow richer. Marriage repair threatens all three.

This is why rebuilding intimacy is not merely therapeutic—*it is strategic.* Strong marriages create people who cannot be easily controlled or radicalized.

Porn culture creates the emotional chaos antisemitism feeds on. *Covenant drains the swamp.*

Why Jews Must Stop Apologizing

Here is the final turn of the knife.

Jews are often pressured to apologize for talking about sex with moral clarity. The never-ending attacks are designed to put us on the defensive. My solution—and this book—is to attack, attack, attack.

It's okay to provoke. Likewise to offend. You can sound judgmental. Those who tell you otherwise are dressing cowardice up as sensitivity.

We are not the ones destroying families, after all. We are not the ones flooding children with porn or radicalizing lonely men.

We are the ones offering an alternative. And alternatives terrify collapsing systems.

Jews do not owe porn silence or the culture of sexual repression an apology.

Because *Kosher Sex* and porn culture are not merely two preferences. *They are two moral universes.* One sees people as sacred; the other sees people as consumable. One builds intimacy; the other monetizes loneliness.

One creates families; the other destroys them.

Antisemitism will always side with porn culture because porn culture weakens human bonds—and weakened bonds make hatred easy. Judaism sides with covenant because covenant makes people whole. And whole people do not need enemies.

Saving marriages is civilizational warfare.

The Hammer

When intimacy returns, hatred loses relevance.

When desire is disciplined, rage loses fuel.

When love is repaired, scapegoats lose utility.

Judaism heals the broken bonds antisemitism feeds upon.

And healing is the most dangerous thing you can do—especially to a culture addicted to grievance.

CHAPTER TWENTY

RAISING CHILDREN WITHOUT SHAME IN AN AGE OF HATRED

Hatred begins with shame, not ideology. A child taught to despise his body will eventually despise other bodies, too. A child taught to fear desire will eventually seek control. And a child taught that identity is fragile will eventually look for enemies.

Antisemitism does not need sophisticated arguments. It needs wounded children who grow into adults still carrying humiliation they were never taught how to heal. This is why every culture war eventually turns toward children—not accidentally, but strategically.

Shame: The First Weapon

There are two dominant forces shaping childhood today, and both are catastrophic. The first, porn culture, exposes children too early and tells them they are objects. The second, moral panic culture, frightens children and tells them their instincts are dangerous.

Between them, childhood innocence is destroyed from opposite ends.

Porn culture says:

- Look now.

- Know everything now.
- Feel everything now.

Moral panic says:

- Don't ask.
- Don't feel.
- Don't trust yourself.

Both produce shame. And shame is antisemitism's favorite nutrient. It's easy to radicalize shamed children.

Why Children Are Always the Target

Every antisemitic movement eventually obsesses over children. Who teaches them? What stories do they hear? What bodies do they inhabit? What loyalties do they inherit?

Children represent the future—and hatred cannot survive an unbroken one.

This is why antisemitic ideologies attack Jewish schools, demonize Jewish parents, accuse Jews of indoctrination, obsess over Jewish education, and spread panic about corruption. Ideas don't worry them. Continuity does. It terrifies them, in fact.

Porn Culture and the Theft of Childhood

Porn culture is a system that collapses boundaries.

Algorithms do not respect innocence. Platforms do not protect vulnerability. Markets do not care about childhood.

Children are exposed to porn before they have language and moral scaffolding. The result is predictable: confusion, anxiety, distorted expectations, premature sexualization, and loss of wonder. And wonder is essential.

A child without wonder becomes cynical early. Cynicism becomes contempt and contempt seeks targets.

Porn does not mature children—it brutalizes them. *Sexual repression does not produce moral children, but rather children incapable of sanctifying intimacy.*

Shame-Based Education Is Just as Dangerous

Here is the trap: reacting to porn culture with fear-based repression produces the same damage.

Children taught that:

- their bodies are dangerous
- their questions are dirty
- their curiosity is shameful
- their desire is sinful

Children forced to imbibe these lessons do not grow into moral adults. They grow into rebels or hypocrites—or both. And hypocrites are prime recruits for hatred, because hypocrisy needs someone else to punish.

Judaism rejects both extremes.

The Jewish Parenting Revolution No One Talks About

Judaism does something almost no modern culture manages: It teaches children without shaming them. It acknowledges that bodies exist, that curiosity is natural, that desire is real, and that boundaries matter—without panic, without hysteria, and without humiliation.

Children are not taught "you are disgusting."

They are taught "you are powerful—and power requires guidance."

That distinction is everything.

Judaism educates and focuses desire instead of terrorizing it.

Why Shame Creates Antisemites

Shame fractures the self, and a fractured self seeks enemies to explain its pain. People ashamed of their bodies resent those comfortable in theirs. People ashamed of desire resent those who sanctify it.

People ashamed of their identity resent those who *inherit theirs proudly.*

This is why antisemitism so often manifests as sexual accusation. It is the scream of a psyche that never learned how to integrate body, identity, and meaning. It is shame looking for a target.

Raising Children Who Don't Need Enemies

Children raised without shame but with structure grow differently. They learn:

- restraint without repression
- confidence without arrogance
- pride without superiority
- desire without compulsion

These children don't need scapegoats or toxic ideologies to feel powerful. They already belong.

Belonging is the greatest defense against hatred. Rooted children do not need to rage.

Jewish Ritual as Psychological Armor

Judaism does something extraordinary for children: it embeds identity in ritual rather than ideology. Children don't learn who they are through slogans. They learn through:

- Shabbat dinners
- blessings
- songs
- stories
- family rhythms
- shared memory

This creates security.

A secure child does not need to annihilate others to feel real. This is why antisemitism attacks ritual—it wants children unmoored. Ritual fortifies children against radicalization.

The War on Parental Authority

Modern culture treats parental authority as suspicious, while hatred loves weak parents. Weak parents produce anxious children, and anxious children turn into malleable adults.

Judaism insists parents are not tyrants, but guides; not owners, but stewards; not dictators, but teachers.

This balanced authority creates resilient children who are hard to radicalize.

Hatred recruits best where parents have been disempowered.

Teaching Children About Sex Without Shame

This may be the hardest task of all—and the most important. Children must learn that sex exists, that it matters, that it is powerful, and that it belongs in covenant. But not through exposure. Not through panic, and not through silence.

Judaism teaches timing.

Not everything at once, it says. Not everything too early. Not everything hidden forever.

This wisdom is both ancient and urgently modern. Healthy sexual education prevents both addiction and extremism.

Why Jewish Children Must Not Inherit Fear

There is a temptation—especially now—to raise Jewish children in fear.

Fear of antisemitism, visibility, difference. Fear of joy, life. Fear of self-defense that may lead to the taking of a guilty, terrorist's life.

This would be a tragic mistake.

Fearful children do not become strong Jews. They become meek ghosts. Judaism does not raise ghosts. It raises people—people who know who they are, who carry joy without apology, who defend life without hatred.

A fearful child inherits the enemy's victory.

The Hammer

If you want to destroy a civilization, you do not start with laws.

You start with children.

You shame them.

Confuse them.

Expose them too early.

Terrify them too much.

Rob them of trust, teach them that their nature is inherently corrupt and sinful.

Antisemitism understands this instinctively.

Judaism resists it deliberately—by raising children:

Without shame. With structure. With love. With ritual, identity, and joy.

Children raised this way do not need to hate. And hatred cannot survive a generation that doesn't need it.

Raising children without shame is the most radical act of resistance.

CHAPTER TWENTY-ONE

HOW JEWS MUST FIGHT BACK: WITHOUT APOLOGY

Antisemitism does not retreat when Jews whisper.

It advances.

For two thousand years, Jews learned a survival reflex that made sense in exile: keep your head down, don't provoke, don't be too visible, don't be too proud, don't be too loud, don't be too joyful, don't be too Jewish.

That reflex may have saved lives.

But it will certainly not save us now.

The hatred we face today is not embarrassed, after all. It is not fringe. It does not hide behind polite euphemisms. It marches, chants, and posts. It organizes.

It justifies murder in the language of morality. It mocks Jewish suffering and denies Jewish humanity—without flinching.

This is not a moment for etiquette. This is a moment for clarity.

The First Rule: Stop Asking to Be Liked

Antisemitism is not a misunderstanding. It is not ignorance or lack of education or something that disappears if Jews just explain themselves better.

Antisemitism is resentment toward Jewish existence itself.

The Jew who thinks he can charm antisemites into decency misunderstands the pathology. Hatred wants nothing to do with dialogue. It wants submission or disappearance. So, the first act of resistance is simple and difficult: stop trying to be liked by people who need you to be ashamed.

You do not win against antisemitism by being palatable. You win by being unashamed.

Jews don't need better PR; we need firmer moral spine.

The Second Rule: Refuse the Enemy's Language

Antisemitism always tries to define the terms of the debate. It wants Jews to speak in its vocabulary:

- apologize
- contextualize
- condemn ourselves first
- explain our right to exist
- prove our humanity
- disavow our people

This is a trap.

When Jews accept the enemy's language, they accept the enemy's authority. We must refuse it. We do not "justify" Jewish life. We do not "contextualize" Jewish murder. We do not apologize for Jewish survival.

We do not ask permission to defend ourselves and reject the inversion that turns victims into aggressors.

When Jews argue on antisemitic terms, antisemitism has already won.

The Third Rule: Name the Hatred Without Euphemism

Polite language protects evil. The following words have been used to launder Jew-hatred into respectability:

- "anti-Zionism"
- "controversial rhetoric"
- "heated discourse"

- "strong criticism"
- "moral outrage"

Enough.

When someone calls for the erasure of Israel, that is antisemitism. When someone celebrates Jewish death, that is antisemitism. When someone denies rape because the victims are Jewish, that is antisemitism. When someone singles out Jews for standards applied to no one else, that is antisemitism. When Jews are given impossibly high standards that no nation on earth could ever possibly match, that is antisemitism. When influencers attack a Rabbi who has saved hundreds of thousands of marriages by teaching the joy of *Kosher Sex* as "Rabbi Buttplug," that is antisemitism.

Naming the hatred does not escalate conflict.

It clarifies it. *Euphemism is antisemitism's camouflage.*

The Fourth Rule: Defend Joy as Aggressively as You Defend Safety

Jews have learned to defend themselves physically. That is necessary. But it's not enough.

We must also defend joy—joy in marriage, children, faith, pleasure, and Jewish life.

Antisemitism wants Jews frightened, dour, apologetic, morally contorted, and spiritually shrunken. But joy disrupts that agenda. Joy is defiance. A people that celebrates life in the face of hatred sends an unbearable message to their enemies: You do not get to decide whether life is worth living.

Jewish joy is not escapism. It's resistance.

The Fifth Rule: Stop Dividing Jews to Appease the Mob

Antisemitism always tries to split Jews into "good" and "bad."

Good Jews:

- criticize Israel loudly
- disavow Jewish power
- downplay Jewish suffering
- condemn other Jews

- beg for acceptance
- embrace a quasi-Christian hatred of sex and denial of the legitimate pleasures of the body.

Bad Jews:

- defend Israel
- embrace Jewish identity
- refuse to apologize
- celebrate Jewish continuity
- live visibly Jewish lives
- talk openly about the blessings of passionate sex in marriage and the electricity of a passionate marital sexual connection.

This divide-and-conquer strategy is ancient. And Jews keep falling for it.

Enough.

The antisemite does not care how you voted. He does not care how secular you are or how critical you are of other Jews. He may come for you last—but he will come.

The Sixth Rule: Reject the False Choice Between Strength and Morality

One of the most corrosive lies Jews are told is this: If you are strong, you are immoral; if you are moral, you must be weak. This lie has destroyed entire civilizations. Judaism rejects it. Judaism insists:

- strength can be ethical
- power can be restrained
- defense can be just
- force can serve life

Israel embodies this refusal—and that is why it is so hated. Jews must stop apologizing for strength exercised in defense of life. *Strength is not cruelty. Weakness is not virtue.* Jewish strength is not a betrayal of ethics.

It is their enforcement.

The Seventh Rule: Fight Pornification and Sexual Repression as Seriously as You Fight Hate

Antisemitism today is inseparable from cultural collapse. It thrives in pornified, cynical, nihilistic environments where intimacy is dead, meaning is thin, and shame is rampant.

Jews must fight antisemitism not only by opposing hate speech, but by opposing the cultural forces that manufacture hatred. This means defending marriage, restoring sexual dignity, and resisting porn culture.

This requires teaching covenant and rebuilding families.

All of this is not a distraction from the fight. It is the fight.

A culture that restores intimacy starves antisemitism at its source.

The Eighth Rule: Raise Jews Who Are Not Afraid to Be Jews

The ultimate answer to antisemitism is not argument. It is continuity.

Children who know who they are. Children who are proud, not paranoid; educated, not indoctrinated; who love life, not grievance.

Children who know joy without shame.

A Jew raised to apologize for existence is already half-defeated. A Jew raised to cherish life is undefeated. Antisemitism loses when Jews raise children who refuse to shrink.

The Ninth Rule: Stop Confusing Silence with Wisdom

There are moments when silence is prudent.

This is not one of them.

Silence now is interpreted as consent. Caution is read as weakness.

Antisemitism is loud because it believes Jews fear and shrink.

We must disabuse it of that belief—not with screaming, nor with hysteria, but with *calm, unapologetic presence.*

Silence is only golden when it is chosen, not when it is imposed.

The Tenth Rule: Choose Life Publicly

This is the deepest rule of all.

Judaism's ultimate answer to hatred has always been the same: *L'Chaim.* Not survival. Not endurance.

Life.

Life with laughter.

Life with love.

Life with children.

Life with pleasure, faith, and meaning.

Life with visibility.

Life with passionate marital sex.

Antisemitism cannot defeat that. It can only try to shame it.

The Hammer

Here is the truth that must end all confusion:

Antisemitism does not stop when Jews make themselves smaller.

It stops when Jews refuse to disappear.

It stops when Jews live fully.

Love deeply. Marry passionately. Make love intimately. Raise children proudly. Defend without apology. Speak truth without euphemism. Celebrate joy without fear.

This is not arrogance. It is responsibility.

And it is time.

CHAPTER TWENTY-TWO

FROM KOSHER SEX TO A JOYFUL CIVILIZATION

Civilizations do not rise because they shout the right slogans. They rise because *enough people learn how to belong*—to one another, to time, to responsibility, to life itself.

That is the through-line of this book.

From the bedroom to the dinner table, from marriage to community, from covenant to culture, the same force operates at every scale: intimacy gravitates; fragmentation detonates.

Kosher Sex is not a niche teaching about marital technique.

It is the smallest, most intense laboratory of a truth, scaling outward. What happens between two people who choose each other faithfully becomes the template for how a society treats human beings—at large.

Intimacy Is the Atomic Unit of Civilization

Every civilization has an "atom"—the smallest unit that still contains its moral code. For Judaism, that atom is not the state, the market, or an ideology.

It is the covenantal bond.

Two people who can:

- be fully seen
- tell the truth

- accept limits
- practice repair
- choose loyalty over novelty
- turn desire into devotion

These two people practice the very skills a civilization needs to survive without scapegoats.

Where intimacy works, people learn:

- patience instead of panic
- repair instead of replacement
- humility instead of humiliation
- responsibility instead of rage

Those lessons do not stay private. They radiate outward. A civilization cannot be more intimate than its marriages.

Why Hatred Cannot Scale Love

Hatred is efficient in crowds and useless in families. It scales through:

- abstraction
- distance
- slogans
- anonymity
- moral shortcuts

Love, however, scales through:

- presence
- obligation
- memory
- continuity
- accountability

That is why antisemitism can spread rapidly during moments of collapse—but cannot build anything durable afterward. *It destroys trust faster than it can replace it.*

Love, by contrast, is slow and permanent. It requires practice, demands patience, and asks for courage. And once embedded, it creates resilience hatred cannot penetrate.

Hatred spreads fast. But love lasts.

The Sexual Core of Social Health

Modern society keeps pretending that sex is either a private indulgence with no public consequences, or a dangerous force best silenced.

Both views are wrong. Sex is formative.

How a culture understands sex determines:

- how it treats bodies
- how it handles power
- how it understands consent
- how it values permanence
- how it imagines the future

Pornified cultures turn people into consumables.

Repressive cultures turn desire into pathology.

Judaism rejects both and insists on a third way: sanctified desire.

That insistence—desire disciplined by covenant—creates people who can experience pleasure without cruelty and intensity without destruction. And those people are immunized against hate.

Cultures that can't sanctify sex will eventually weaponize it.

From Marriage to Community

Marriage teaches skills conspiracy theories cannot survive. In a healthy marriage you learn:

- to verify, not fantasize
- to communicate, not insinuate

- to confront directly, not recruit mobs
- to repair after rupture

Those habits translate into public life. Communities built from intact marriages:

- talk to each other
- argue without dehumanizing
- tolerate disagreement
- refuse mythic enemies

This is why movements built on grievance attack marriage so aggressively. Because marriage produces people who don't need conspiracies to feel important.

A person practiced in intimacy has no appetite for scapegoats.

Why Jewish Civilization Is So Threatening

Jewish civilization did not survive by accident. It survived because it embedded intimacy into law, ritual, rhythm, and memory.

Weekly Shabbat meals. Festival celebrations and gatherings. Public blessings. Marriage as obligation.

Children as continuity, argument as sacred practice, and joy as commandment.

This produces a people who are:

- stubbornly alive
- inconveniently connected
- resistant to despair
- difficult to radicalize

Antisemitism rages not because Jews are powerful—*but because Jewish life works.*

It offers meaning without mythic enemies. It offers joy without denial. Discipline without repression. Intimacy without exploitation.

Why Fragmentation Is the Enemy's Strategy

If intimacy is gravity, fragmentation is anti-gravity.

Fragmentation:

- isolates individuals
- dissolves trust
- erodes families
- replaces community with crowds
- turns identity into performance

A fragmented society is easy to manipulate. Lonely people are hungry for meaning; hungry people are vulnerable to lies.

That is why antisemitism always rides waves of social breakdown—when families weaken, when sexuality is confused, when community collapses, when people no longer know who they are.

Fragmentation creates the vacuum. Hatred fills it.

Where fragmentation spreads, antisemitism follows.

Joy as the Only Sustainable Counterforce

You cannot build a humane civilization on rage. Rage exhausts, corrodes, and must be constantly fed. Joy, by contrast, replenishes. It is rooted in covenant.

Joy:

- renews energy
- binds generations
- softens cruelty
- stabilizes desire
- anchors hope

This is why Jewish joy is so subversive.

It refuses the emotional economy of grievance, and says:

- life is worth building
- love is worth risking

- children are blessings
- the future matters

And nothing undermines hatred faster than people who believe those things—and live them publicly. *Joy is the only renewable energy hatred can't hijack.*

What a Joyful Civilization Looks Like

A joyful civilization is not utopian. It is disciplined.

It has:

- strong marriages
- accountable men
- secure women
- protected children
- robust communities
- moral language
- shared rituals
- visible celebration

It does not deny suffering—but it refuses to let suffering define reality. It does not silence disagreement—but it forbids dehumanization. It does not abolish desire—but it educates it.

This is not softness. It's strength.

Because joy without discipline collapses and discipline without joy suffocates, civilization requires both.

The Final Synthesis

Kosher Sex is where the whole argument converges.

It is:

- intimacy without illusion
- pleasure without exploitation
- openness without chaos

- nakedness without fear
- love without lies

What happens in the bedroom determines what happens everywhere. *If two people can build trust at the most vulnerable point of human life, a society can build trust at scale.*

If they cannot, no amount of ideology will save it.

Antisemitism is the civilization-level expression of failed intimacy. *Judaism is the civilization-level expression of repaired intimacy. Fix intimacy, disarm hatred.*

The Hammer

Here is the unvarnished truth: the future will not be decided by those who scream the loudest.

It will be decided by those who build families, repair marriages, raise children without shame; by people who sanctify desire, practice joy, and refuse to live by lies.

That is how civilizations endure. It's how antisemitism dies. It's how life wins.

A joyful civilization is hatred's extinction event.

CHAPTER TWENTY-THREE

THE BARBARISM OF FEMALE GENITAL MUTILATION—AND WHY THE ISLAMIC WORLD NEEDS A "KOSHER SEX" REVOLUTION

In this book I have focused for the most part on the denigration of sex on the sexual abnormality of so many antisemites, both past and present. In this penultimate chapter, I focus briefly on our brothers and sisters in the Islamic world. Though the subject of female genital mutilation is beyond the scope of this book, and I may provide a follow-up that I will write as part of the "Kosher Sex" series, its barbarism has become so acute and so widespread that the book would be incomplete without addressing it, however briefly.

Let's not use soft language.

Removing a woman's clitoris so she cannot experience sexual pleasure is not "tradition." It is not "custom." It is not "culture." It is an act of absolute and unforgivable barbarism.

There is no moral gray zone here. No nuance that redeems it. No context that excuses it.

When I read that roughly 85 percent to 92 percent of Egyptian women—nearly nine in ten—have undergone female genital mutilation, I didn't just feel sorrow. I felt something deeper: a kind of civilizational alarm. Egypt is the largest Arab country on earth. It was once home, for millennia, to the world's most advanced civilization. It is an American ally and it has a peace treaty with Israel, albeit one that is as cold as the Northern polar ice cap. Can those who built the pyramids of Geza really be engaged in such Stone-Aged acts of savagery against women?

According to the United Nations Population Fund, despite legal bans, the practice remains widespread in Egypt, often carried out by medical professionals. Let that reality land. Doctors—people trained to heal—are participating in the systematic destruction of a woman's capacity for pleasure.

We are not dealing with isolated cruelty. We are dealing with a worldview.

A War on Women's Pleasure

The statistics across multiple countries are positively staggering. In many nations—primarily across the Horn of Africa and West Africa—female genital mutilation (FGM) remains nearly universal, with prevalence rates exceeding 80 percent.

The numbers tell a grim story. Somalia leads the world with an estimated 98–99 percent prevalence rate, a figure that has held for over three decades, with most procedures performed on girls between the ages of five and eleven. Guinea follows closely at 94–97 percent, where the practice cuts across all religious groups. In Djibouti, the rate stands at 93–94 percent, with two-thirds of women having undergone infibulation—the most extreme form of the procedure. Mali reports figures near 89–91 percent; Sudan around 87–90 percent, despite a 2020 law outlawing the practice; Sierra Leone between 83–90 percent—reaching 97 percent in the north, where it is tied to traditional secret society initiations; and Eritrea between 83–89 percent, where a disturbing 68 percent of procedures are performed on infants under one year old.

High prevalence rates, however, do not always reflect the full scale of harm. UNICEF reports that Indonesia, though not among the highest by percentage, has the largest raw number of affected girls aged 0–14—over 17 million—followed by Nigeria with nearly 5 million. The youngest victims are concentrated in The Gambia and Mauritania, where more than half of girls aged fourteen and under have already been cut. A further troubling trend is the growing "medicalization" of FGM, in which healthcare workers themselves perform the procedure—most notably in Egypt, Indonesia, and Kenya.

The global scope is vast. Africa accounts for over 144 million cases, Asia for more than 80 million, and the Middle East for roughly 6 million. In 2026 alone, an estimated 4.5 million girls are at risk.

These are not marginal numbers. This is not a fringe practice. This is a widespread, normalized assault on female sexuality.

And the justification is always the same: to preserve purity, to ensure modesty, to control desire, and to make certain that women are not sexually unfaithful to their husbands.

But let's strip away the euphemisms.

This is about erasing a woman's ability to feel sexual pleasure.

It is about the fear of female desire—fear so intense that it manifests as mutilation.

A society that fears a woman's pleasure will inevitably seek to control her body. And a society that controls the body will eventually crush the soul.

The Jewish Counterrevolution

Now here is where the story turns—and where the Jewish experience becomes not incidental, but essential.

For millennia, Jews have been attacked by antisemites for being "too carnal," too focused on the physical, too invested in life's pleasures. The accusation is as old as hatred itself: that Jews are obsessed with the body.

And you know what?

There is a grain of truth in it—and it is something to be proud of.

Judaism does not fear the body. Judaism sanctifies it.

Judaism teaches that sexual intimacy within marriage is not a concession—it is a commandment. A husband is obligated to bring his wife pleasure. Not as a favor. Not as a luxury. But as a *religious duty and spiritual obligation.*

Let that contrast hit you:

- In one worldview, pleasure is so dangerous that it must be cut out of a woman's body.
- In another, pleasure is so sacred that it is elevated to a divine obligation.

That is not a small difference. That is a civilizational divide.

The Solution Found in *Kosher Sex for Antisemites*

This is why I am publishing this book, *Kosher Sex for Antisemites.* Not that my Muslim brothers and sisters are, God forbid, Jew-haters. But Islamists are. And many of those insisting on the mutilation of Muslim women are not God-fearing Muslims but terrorist-inclined, inhumane, and barbaric individuals. Only a sadistic man cuts off a woman's clitoris and labia to extract her essential womanhood.

Because the same people who accuse Jews of being "too physical" often come from cultures that are terrified of physical intimacy—terrified of its power, terrified of its joy, terrified of its equality.

They look at Jewish life—at our emphasis on marriage, on family, on intimacy—and they misunderstand it. They see indulgence where there is actually discipline. They see excess where there is actually sanctity.

What they fail to grasp is this:

Kosher sex is not about indulgence. It is about elevating pleasure into a sacred bond between husband and wife.

And in a world where millions of women are mutilated to prevent them from experiencing that bond, this message is not optional. It is urgent.

A Personal Battle

I don't speak about this in the abstract.

For decades, I have been attacked—often viciously—by antisemites for writing about "kosher sex." They mock it. They distort it. They use it as ammunition in their broader hatred of Jews.

And now my daughter, Chana, faces similar attacks for running the Kosher Sex company—an enterprise dedicated to one simple, radical idea:

Married women deserve sexual pleasure.

Not as a luxury. Not as an afterthought. But as a necessity.

Think about how outrageous it is that this even needs to be said.

In a world where millions of women have had their ability to feel pleasure surgically removed, advocating for their right to intimacy is somehow controversial.

That tells you everything you need to know about the depth of the problem.

The Consequences of Killing Pleasure

When you destroy a woman's capacity for pleasure, you are not just committing a physical act. You are reshaping the entire structure of human relationships.

You are creating marriages where:

- Intimacy is one-sided
- Desire is suppressed
- Connection is weakened

You are creating families where emotional bonds are fragile, where equality is absent, where love struggles to breathe.

And then we act surprised when societies marked by such practices also struggle with broader issues of gender inequality and social instability.

You cannot mutilate intimacy and expect to preserve humanity.

The West Is Not Innocent

Before anyone congratulates themselves, let's be honest: the West has its own dysfunction.

If some societies mutilate sexuality, others trivialize it.

- Pornography has replaced intimacy
- Hookup culture has replaced commitment
- Desire has been detached from meaning

On one side, sex is feared. On the other, it is emptied of purpose.

Both are failures.

What the world needs is not repression or indulgence, but *sanctification.*

The Moral Clarity We've Lost

There was a time when the world could say, without hesitation, that certain practices are simply wrong.

Today, we hesitate. We hedge. We worry about offending.

But there are moments when moral clarity is not just appropriate—it is required.

This is one of them.

Mutilating a girl's body to prevent her from experiencing pleasure is evil.

Not complicated. Not contextual. Evil.

And if we cannot say that plainly, then we have surrendered the very idea of human dignity.

A Call for a Global Intimacy Revolution

So what is the alternative?

What do we offer in place of barbarism and brokenness?

We offer a vision rooted in dignity, equality, and sanctity:

- That the human body is sacred
- That sexual pleasure within marriage is holy
- That intimacy is a bond of mutual fulfillment

This is the essence of "kosher sex."

It is not a Jewish curiosity. It is a universal blueprint for restoring what has been lost.

Imagine a world where:

- Girls grow up knowing their bodies are whole and worthy
- Women enter marriage expecting joy, not sacrifice
- Men are taught that their role is to give, not control

That is not utopian. It is achievable.

But it requires courage.

The Choice Before Us

We are facing a stark choice.

We can continue to excuse practices that mutilate the human spirit in the name of culture.

Or we can stand up and say:

- *Enough.*
- Enough of the silence.
- Enough of the euphemisms.
- Enough of the fear.

When nearly 90 percent of women in one of the world's most famous and populated countries have undergone genital mutilation, we are not looking at a cultural quirk. We are looking at a humanitarian crisis of staggering proportions.

And the response cannot be timid.

It must be bold. It must be clear. It must be relentless.

The Revolution Starts Now

The battle for the sanctity of intimacy is one of the defining struggles of our time.

It is not just about sex. It is about dignity. It is about equality. It is about what it means to be human.

That is why I am writing. That is why my daughter is working. That is why this message matters.

Because until the world learns to honor the sacred bond between husband and wife—until it learns to celebrate, rather than fear, human connection—we will continue to see the kinds of atrocities that should have been left in the darkest chapters of history.

It is time to bring them into the light.

It is time to confront them without apology.

It is time for a *kosher sex revolution.*

CHAPTER TWENTY-FOUR

A PRESCRIPTION FOR THE EROTICALLY BROKEN

Throughout this book, I have prosecuted a case, arguing, with evidence, that the antisemites documented in these pages are not merely wrong about Jews—they are broken in ways that precede and generate their Jew-hatred. Their antisemitism lies downstream of something more fundamental: a fractured relationship with intimacy, the body, desire, and love.

The prosecution rests, and I want to replace it with prescription.

Not because I expect Tucker Carlson to read this book and weep with recognition. Nor do I imagine Andrew Tate will undergo a sudden conversion to covenantal monogamy. I also doubt Mohammed Hijab will call me to apologize for the body-bag posts about my son that followed our televised debate—though the invitation, like any debate invitation, remains permanently open.

I offer this prescription simply because it is true.

The diagnosis demands it.

Because if this book is correct—if antisemitism is indeed the civilization-level expression of failed intimacy—then the cure must be named—and offered. And because, in my experience of decades counseling couples across every faith background and cultural context, I have seen it work. Not as theory. *As life.*

The cure is neither argument nor counterprogramming.

It's Kosher Sex.

It's covenantal intimacy: The disciplined, joyful, mutual, vulnerable, fully embodied practice of choosing one person, telling the truth to that person, and building a life of sanctified desire within that shared choice.

I mean the golden middle path: the one civilization keeps abandoning and that Judaism keeps holding open.

This path diverges from the porn-saturated, commitment-phobic, transactional sexual nihilism of men like Andrew Tate and Dan Bilzerian—those who mistake consumption of women for well-lived life, and who discover, eventually—inevitably—this consumption produces only emptiness.

It also avoids the opposite pole: the clenched, punitive, death-haunted sexual repression of men like Nick Fuentes and Tucker Carlson—those who confuse shame with holiness, who discover, eventually, this repression produces only projection.

Both paths lead to the same destination: loneliness.

And loneliness, as this book has documented at length, is antisemitism's most reliable recruiter.

The middle path of Kosher Sex—sanctified desire within covenant—overflows with something neither side can manufacture: *a person who is known.* Truly known by another human being: *their* human being.

And a person who is known does not need enemies.

So let me speak directly to those who have made themselves my enemies.

Let me speak to each of them directly.

Tucker Carlson: Come Home

Tucker, you have described yourself publicly, on multiple occasions, as a man who finds his greatest peace alone in nature. You have spoken about fly fishing in Maine, about hunting, about the particular solitude of a man and a river or a man and a field. You have made this solitude something close to a brand—the image of the thoughtful, self-sufficient

American man, at peace in the wilderness, unbothered by the chaos of civilization.

I do not doubt the sincerity of it. I think you genuinely find something in those solitary hours.

But I want to ask you something that I ask every man who speaks to me with that particular reverence about solitude: What are you resting from? And more to the point—who are you coming home to?

You have been married to Susan Andrews since 1991. More than thirty years. You have four children. By any external measure, you have the thing that this book argues is civilization's most important unit: a long marriage and a family.

And yet, the portrait you paint of your inner life is not the portrait of a man anchored by intimacy. It is the portrait of a man who escapes to rivers. A man whose public persona is defined by grievance, by darkness, by the relentless cataloguing of everything that is broken and everyone who is to blame—which, in your telling, increasingly means the Jews.

After all, you recycled the blood libel at a memorial service for Charlie Kirk, of blessed memory, attended by eighty thousand people, laughing as you did it—laughing so hard you couldn't stop—which is itself a kind of confession, Tucker. Laughter that uncontrollable is laughter trying to escape something.

Here is what I believe, and what I offer not as an attack but as a genuine observation, having spent decades in this work:

A man who finds more peace in a river than in his own home is a man whose home has not yet become what it could be. A man whose public life is an unbroken stream of fear, contempt, and darkness is a man who has not found, in private life, enough joy to counterbalance it.

Joy is not weakness. Joy is not naivety. Joy is not the absence of seriousness.

It is what a man carries back from a marriage that works—from a bed that is alive, from a table loud with children, from a life built in covenant, rather than solitude.

The leaked recordings from your radio appearances—where you called women primitive, dismissed rape shield laws, defended underage marriage, described Hillary Clinton as someone who "would castrate you if she could"—are not the words of a man at peace with humanity's female half. They are the words of a man afraid of it.

Afraid of women who speak.

Afraid of desire that cannot be controlled or dismissed.

Afraid, perhaps, of the vulnerability that genuine intimacy demands—the laying down of performance, of persona—and the terrifying, necessary exposure of being simply a man who needs another person.

Tucker: The river will still be there. Go home first. Be known by the woman you chose and let her be known by you. That is not a retreat from public life. That is the foundation without which public life becomes a darkness machine.

You were not always this. You can choose otherwise.

Candace Owens: Misery Behind Moralism

Candace, I will not pretend that I approach this section without personal feeling. You called my daughter a hag. You called me "the unholy rabbi." You liked a post on X asking if I was "drunk on Christian blood again"—a medieval blood libel leveled at a man you have met, whose family you know exists. You incited your followers against us.

And yet.

I am a rabbi. And what I see, underneath the performative fury and the unhinged online campaigns and the blood libels and the Holocaust-minimization, is a woman who is profoundly, achingly unhappy.

This is not an insult.

This is a diagnosis.

Your obsession with my family's work—the specific, sustained, almost personal fury you directed at the concept of Kosher Sex—tells me something. It tells me that the concept disturbs you in a way that is not political.

It is personal.

You have written and spoken about sexuality from a framework that is, at its core, medieval Catholic in its anxiety: Sex is for procreation, erotic pleasure within marriage is suspect at best, the body is a source of shame rather than sanctity. There are also persistent rumors in the public conversation about the nature of your marriage—about your husband, about what joy or its absence looks like in your private life.

I will not traffic in rumors, and I do not need to. What I observe publicly is sufficient.

A woman who is sexually joyful, loved, and known and desired within her marriage—who experiences the Kosher Sex framework in lived practice—that woman does not spend her days in a rage about a sex shop in Tel Aviv.

She has better things to do with her time. *She has a life.*

Candace: Whatever is or is not happening in your marriage—whatever joy is present or absent, whatever intimacy exists or has been foreclosed—I say this without mockery: You deserve more.

The medieval framework that shaped your sexual theology was not designed for your flourishing. *It was designed for your control.* It told women that desire was dangerous, the body was fallen, pleasure within marriage was a concession to weakness rather than an expression of holiness.

Judaism disagrees.

It has always disagreed.

The fury with which you attack it suggests you know, somewhere, what you are missing.

The invitation stands, Candace—not just to debate, but to consider: *What if the thing you hate most is the thing you need most?*

Andrew Tate: The Loneliest Man in the Mansion

Yours, Andrew Tate, is an empire built on the performance of masculine invulnerability. The cars, the cigars, the combat training, the "Hustler's University," the iron-jawed proclamations about female nature, the casual celebration of dominance, the women as accessories—all of it is the most elaborate, expensive, and tragic defense mechanism I have encountered in public life.

Because what are you, beneath the performance?

A man who has been charged with rape and sex trafficking. A man who, when the subject of Hamas's October 7 atrocities arose, refused to condemn the murder and rape of Jewish women because he did not wish to condemn "the masculine spirit of resistance."

I know something about real, covenantal masculine strength—and it bears no resemblance to Andrew Tate's performance of it. Real masculine strength is the capacity to be vulnerable with one woman. To tell her the truth when the truth is unflattering. To stay when staying is hard. To choose, day after day, the demanding intimacy of a covenant over the easy, disposable transactions of a man who never has to be known by anyone.

Andrew Tate cannot be known.

That is the secret beneath the performance. A man who treats women as interchangeable instruments of his pleasure does not allow any single woman to see him fully—because being seen fully requires trust, and trust requires the kind of sustained commitment that his entire ideology forbids. He has constructed a philosophy that protects him, perfectly and permanently, from the one experience that could heal him.

And the result? You are one of the loneliest men alive. Surrounded by cameras and followers and women and cars, living in a palace of performance, with no one who knows you. No one to whom you are accountable. No one whose knowledge of you makes you better rather than worse.

I am not naïve enough to think you will accept this from me. But I am hopeful enough—having seen it work, *having seen it transform marriages I thought were beyond saving*—to offer it.

Apologize to the women you have harmed. Not in a press release or online. In private, with sincerity, to specific women whose dignity you violated. Then choose one woman—one—and practice the terrifying, irreplaceable discipline of being known by her. Fully. Not performatively.

That is where your real masculinity begins. *It's more powerful than anything you can imagine.*

Nick Fuentes: The Purity That Poisons

Nick Fuentes is twenty-seven years old and has never been intimate with a woman. He is proud of this. He announces it. He preaches strict sexual traditionalism—sex only within marriage, the evils of pornography and the sexual revolution, the necessity of chastity—and packages this as the last defense of Christian civilization against its Jewish-orchestrated destruction.

And Tucker Carlson, as I mentioned, called him "some gay kid."

I genuinely could not care less about his sexuality, as I also mentioned. But Fuentes's followers care—and they are among the most viciously homophobic people in American public life. And Fuentes knows this. Which means that if Tucker's remark reflects any reality, Fuentes is a man engaged in the most destructive possible relationship with his own desire: preaching against what he may be, despising what he may want, and channeling the resulting self-hatred outward onto Jews.

The men who most loudly police the sexuality of others are, with extraordinary regularity, the men most tormented by their own. Whether or not Fuentes is gay, he describes women as "annoying" and "talking too much," argues they should not vote, and advises his followers to marry them anyway—a necessary evil, for procreation alone. This is a clinical description of a man who has constructed an ideology to justify his own impossibility of intimacy.

Nick: This is not the wholesome sexual traditionalism you claim to be defending. Genuine sexual traditionalism affirms the dignity of women. It requires a man to honor his wife, to be accountable to her, to recognize her as his equal before God. It demands of him not celibacy-as-performance, but the far harder discipline of covenant: choosing one woman, for life, out of love rather than duty, and building with her the kind of home where children are welcomed and desire is sanctified.

That is the tradition you claim to be protecting.

You are not protecting it. You are strangling it.

And the Jews you blame for its decline are, in fact, its oldest living practitioners.

Whatever your sexuality is—and you alone know that—the path forward is the same: Stop performing purity and start practicing honesty. Honesty about what you want. Honesty about who you are. The tradition you claim to revere has a framework for almost any human reality, including yours. But it cannot help you while you hide from it behind antisemitism.

The hatred will not save you.

Covenant will.

Dan Bilzerian: The Emptiness at the Heart of the Harem

Dan: Let's set aside for a moment that the invitation to put an IDF-trained MMA fighter in the ring with you remains outstanding.

Let's move on to a more serious point: A man who has slept with hundreds of women and posts them like trophies is not a man who has found abundance.

Rather, he has found the abundant emptiness left in the wake of abundance's failure to satisfy. The void howling as you chase the same "cure" because admitting the cure is wrong is intolerable.

The Instagram harem does not suffice. It is the insufficient answer to the wrong questions asked over and over: *Am I enough? Does this prove it?* And it never does; the answer to that question cannot be provided by a woman you do not know. Who you do not care about. Who you use.

It can only be provided by a woman who knows you fully—and who chooses you anyway.

Dan: You, too, may achieve solace, peace, and wellness within an ethics of desire. A framework in which a man's sexual energy is directed rather than dissipated—toward one woman, over a lifetime—and in which that direction produces not deprivation but the deepest satisfaction available to a human being. Stop acquiring. Start choosing. The real man in you waits there.

Kanye West: The Man Who Diagnosed Himself

Kanye West, it should be acknowledged, has done something remarkable, separating from the other purveyors of Jew-hatred in this book. He named his own pathology.

"Pornography destroyed my family," he said, then announced a thirty-day cleanse, recognizing that his relationship to sexuality was destroying him.

But then, rather than follow that recognition inward, he turned outward and blamed the Jews.

Sadly, despite identifying the wound correctly, and at the precise moment when that recognition could have led to repair, Kanye deflected it onto us. Because repair requires what addiction does not: accountability. Sitting with what you have done. Turning and returning—not on Twitter, not on Alex Jones, not in a press moment, but in private, as a man—to the person whose trust you broke, and saying: *I did this. I am sorry. Show me what repair looks like.*

Let's learn repair together.

Kanye, you know this. "Pornography destroyed my family."

The Jewish tradition you have chosen to despise has a word for what comes next: *teshuvah*. Return. Not a new religion or a new wife paraded naked.

Return—to the specific person you harmed, with a specific intention to heal, raise yourselves upward, and ascend to a place higher than you ever could have before. It requires courage. But you can be courageous.

We all can.

The Prescription at Scale: What Kosher Sex Offers a Civilization

I have addressed each of above individually because the book's argument is, ultimately, about individuals. Civilization is made of individuals. Antisemitism is committed by individuals. And the cure—the repair—begins with individuals.

But let me close this chapter by saying what the prescription means at large.

Kosher Sex—covenantal, disciplined, joyful, embodied intimacy between two people who have chosen each other and refuse to stop choosing—is no mere marital counsel. It is a civilization model. *It scales.*

It produces, at every scale from the bedroom to the civilization:

People who can be known.

Known people do not need conspiracies. Conspiracies, after all, thrive on anonymity, on the conviction that others are hiding things, the paranoid certainty that the world is shadowy, dreadful web of concealed motives and hidden enemies.

But a person who has been genuinely known by another human being—who has been seen, in the fullness of their desire and their weakness and their fear, and loved anyway: this person has a reference point for trust.

They know, from lived experience, that being seen need not be catastrophic. That vulnerability need not be punished. That another person can hold your reality without weaponizing it.

Thus, a functioning marriage is the greatest school of accountability available to human beings. You cannot live with another person for decades without being wrong, repeatedly, and learning to say so. The habit of repair—of acknowledging harm, making amends, beginning again—is mastered in the marital bedroom long before it is utilized in public life.

Let me tell you what actually happens.

I have been a marriage counselor for four decades. I have sat with couples in crisis so severe that the room felt combustible. With couples who had not touched each other in years, who had become strangers sharing a mortgage.

And I have watched what happens when those people choose to come back. When they choose, against every impulse of a culture telling them replacement is easier than repair, to turn toward each other instead of away.

That is what kosher sex heals. Not primarily the sex—though yes, the sex—but the starvation that precedes it. The profound, unacknowledged, civilization-level hunger to be known by another human being and to find that the knowledge does not destroy you.

This is why it cures antisemitism and hatred. Not metaphorically. Mechanically.

The antisemite requires an enemy because he requires an explanation for his own emptiness. The emptiness is real. The loneliness is real. The fractured desire, the unfulfilled life, the ambient sense that something essential is missing and that someone must be responsible—all of it is real.

What is false is the explanation.

Fill the emptiness with the real thing, and the false explanation becomes unnecessary.

What I prescribe is not complicated. It is the hardest thing in the world, which is also the simplest: one person, chosen freely. The truth told to that person without performance or protection. The body offered not as a trophy or a transaction but as a gift, within a covenant that makes the gift safe. The daily, imperfect, irreplaceable practice of staying, and discovering that the staying is itself the source of the joy that makes hatred pointless.

The prescription is the same for all antisemites, and for every person who has found in Jew-hatred an answer to a question that is actually about themselves. It is the prescription Judaism has offered civilization for four thousand years, through every attempt to destroy us, through every ideology that promised a world without Jews but delivered only rubble:

Choose life.

Choose it in the most intimate, demanding, irreducible way available—in the choice of one other person, in the covenant made with that person, in the joy built within that covenant.

Choose a life so full of genuine connection that the need for enemies simply dies for want of air.

That is what Kosher Sex is. Not a technique. Nor a product.

It is the cure. The only one there is. The one that has always worked, for those with the courage to take it.

L'Chaim.

CONCLUSION

THE CURE THE ANTISEMITE REFUSES

Antisemitism survives by misdiagnosis.

It tells people their pain comes from Jews. That their emptiness is political and their rage is moral.

It never tells them the truth: Their problem is not the Jew. Their problem is a broken relationship with life.

Why Hatred Never Heals

Hatred offers relief without repair. It allows people to:

- avoid intimacy
- avoid responsibility
- avoid vulnerability
- avoid self-examination

But hatred never integrates desire. It only displaces it. That is why antisemitism never satisfies. It escalates. Hatred radicalizes and devours its own adherents. Every antisemitic movement eventually collapses into paranoia, purges, and self-destruction—because repression cannot build anything.

It only burns.

What the Antisemite Cannot Accept

This book has argued one central truth: Jewish erotic life—marital, disciplined, joyful, covenantal—is an existential rebuke to hatred. Not because it is perfect, but because it is integrated.

Integrated people do not need scapegoats. Integrated societies do not need extermination myths. Integrated desire does not need violence.

This is why antisemitism must sexualize Jews grotesquely. It is why modern antisemites obsess over demonizing me and my daughter. They must turn joy into obscenity, fertility into aggression, intimacy into "perversion"—because if Jewish life is allowed to appear normal, healthy, loving, and continuous, the entire antisemitic worldview collapses.

The Final Choice

Because the cure requires courage, antisemites refuse it. The cure:

- intimacy instead of ideology
- covenant instead of conquest
- discipline instead of indulgence
- joy instead of grievance
- life instead of death

Judaism has offered this cure for millennia. Hatred keeps rejecting it.

So, Jews will keep doing what we have always done:

Marrying. Loving. Building.

Arguing, laughing, raising children.

Choosing life.

Not to persuade antisemites. But to outlive them.

L'Chaim

Not defiance through rage. Defiance through life. Because in the end, antisemitism is a rebellion against existence.

And existence always wins.

ACKNOWLEDGMENTS

My wife Debbie is my rock, my balance, my soulmate, my foremost critic, my most staunch defender, and my most fearsome advocate. Life without her is, God forbid, unthinkable.

My nine children—Mushki, Chana, Shterny, Mendy, Shaina, Rochel Leah, Yosef, Dovid Chaim, and Cheftziba—are my joy and my existence.

My grandchildren are my hope, my love, and my future. I remember that every time my father, of blessed memory, was asked, "How many grandchildren do you have?" his response was always the same. "Not enough." Never have truer words been spoken.

To the brave soldiers of the IDF, among whom I count three of my children—Chana, Mendy, and Yosef, as well as my daughter-in-law Dalia—I say, "You are my heroes, my inspiration, and my guiding light."

To my children who serve as emissaries of the Lubavitcher Rebbe spreading the light and joy of Judaism—Mushki, Shterny, Shaina, Rochel Leah, Dovid Chaim, and Cheftziba—you have followed in the footsteps of your mother and me in being the Rebbe's foot soldiers and promoters of the faith.

To my sons-in-law and daughter-in-law—Arik, Yossi, Moshe, and Dalia—thank you for the love you give my children and having added immeasurably to the joy of our family.

To the brave troops of the American military I add, "You are the single greatest force for good on earth."